THE

CIVILIZATIONS OF THE EAST

✣ ✣

Japan

THE

CIVILIZATIONS OF THE EAST

By René Grousset

TRANSLATED FROM THE FRENCH
BY CATHERINE ALISON PHILLIPS

VOLUME I
The Near and Middle East

VOLUME II
India

VOLUME III
China

VOLUME IV
Japan

NEW YORK · ALFRED A KNOPF

THE CIVILIZATIONS OF THE EAST

✣ ✣

Japan

✣ ✣

By René Grousset

TRANSLATED FROM THE FRENCH FOR THE FIRST TIME BY CATHERINE ALISON PHILLIPS

With 211 Illustrations

1941

NEW YORK · ALFRED · A · KNOPF

Published October 8, 1934
Second Printing, April 1941

Originally Published as
TOME IV—LE JAPON
LES CIVILISATIONS DE L'ORIENT

MANUFACTURED IN THE UNITED STATES OF AMERICA

TO

MONSIEUR ULRICH ODIN

THIS VOLUME IS AFFECTIONATELY

AND ADMIRINGLY DEDICATED

TABLE OF CONTENTS

The Civilizations of the East

Volume IV: Japan

INTRODUCTION

CHAPTER I

JAPAN

CHAPTER II

BENGAL, NEPAL, TIBET

INTRODUCTION

The Civilizations of the East

Volume IV: Japan

THE PRESENT VOLUME, LIKE THE PREVIOUS ONES IN THE SAME series, sets out to be no more than an introduction to Eastern ideals and schools of art. As the dedication shows, it has profited very greatly by the advice of M. Ulrich Odin, who has conferred upon me the privilege of his friendship and the freedom of his collections. It owes an equal debt to M. Serge Elisséev, whose lectures on Japanese art at the École du Louvre, supplemented by his personal suggestions, have given me an assistance which I desire to take this opportunity of acknowledging. Nor can I omit to express my gratitude to Monsieur Vever and his " museum," which in this department, as in so many others, is richer than those of the State and has once more been so generously thrown open to me.

In other words, this introduction aspires to be no more than a stepping-stone to M. Elisséev's great work on Japanese archæology, which will shortly be published by Messrs. Auguste Picard, and to the catalogue of the Odin collection, forming Volume XIV of the *Ars Asiatica* series, published by Messrs. Van Oest; as well as a reminder of the great debt which enthusiasts for Oriental art and the ideals which inspire it owe to M. Henri Vever.

I avail myself of this opportunity of once more expressing my thanks to my friend M. Van Oest, the learned publisher of *Ars*

Asiatica and of the *Bibliothèque d'Art du Musée Guimet,* whose generous friendship has made an exception in my favour by removing all difficulties about copyright with which I have been faced in the course of these four volumes.

I also offer my thanks to the Japanese publishers of the *Shimbi Shoin,*[1] who, through the intervention of M. Sylvain Lévi, have kindly given me permission to reproduce some of the plates from their magnificent series of illustrated works: *Japanese Temples and their Treasures,* and *Selected Relics of Japanese Art,* to which great publications, needless to say, every student of Japanese art is bound to refer.

Finally, in this volume, as in the three preceding ones, I must request the reader not to be surprised at the small space devoted to certain types of technique, branches of art, and secondary schools, whose intrinsic importance I none the less recognize. My intention has been to present a general view of the subject as a whole, and to show the continuity and interpenetration of the various æsthetic ideals. Frequently, while pursuing the main path of my theme, I have had cause to deplore the impossibility of lingering over side paths which invited at least a digression. I hope, however, to take up the question again elsewhere and attempt, from the point of view of universal humanity, to establish the comparative values of the ideals of which an account has been given in the course of these four volumes.[2]

[1] The Shimbi Shoin, Ltd., 13 Shinsakana-cho, Kyobashi-ku, Tōkyō, Japan.

[2] Bibliography: See *Bibliography of the Japanese Empire up to the year 1906*, compiled by Fr. von Wenckstern, Tōkyō, 1907; *Bibliography of the Japanese Empire, 1906–1926*, compiled by Oskar Nachod, 2 vols., E. Goldston, 1928. Of the great illustrated Japanese publications I would specially refer the reader to the following: *Tōyei Shukō, Illustrated Catalogue of the Imperial Treasury in the Shōsōin at Nara*, 4 vols. (Shimbi Shoin, Tōkyō); *Kobijutsu Taikan, Illustrated Catalogue of Fine Arts. Museum of Kyōto, Coronation Exhibition*, 1928; the *Kokka* series; and, above all, the splendid publications of the *Shimbi Shoin*, referred to in the Introduction.

THE

CIVILIZATIONS OF THE EAST

✣ ✣

Japan

CHAPTER I

Japan

JAPAN DEFINED: HER NATIONAL ORIGINALITY AND POWER OF ADAPTING FOREIGN INFLUENCES

THE EXPRESSIONS USED BY LAVISSE IN DEFINING THE CHARACTER of Greece might be applied word for word to Japan; for Japan, too, has " reaped the benefit of the experience " acquired by the peoples of the Hoang-ho, the Yang-tze, the Indus, and the Ganges. This country, " with the sea running up into the innumerable indentations of its coast," this mountainous and fragmentary archipelago, is, in spite of its peculiar geological features, the whole of great Asia " reflected and condensed as though in a mirror." In it the ramifications of the Malayan system and of the Chino-Siberian mass known to geologists as Angara meet in a delicately articulated group of volcanic islands. Lying off the coast of the amorphous and compact mass of the continent, it is a part of Asia — but with a difference. The predominating influence of the sea has given rise to historical conditions which are quite peculiar. Japanese insularity has created the individual qualities of the Japanese character: untrammelled activity, a readiness to take the initiative, a happy mixture of tenacity and pliancy, a sense of personality and of honour. In sharp contrast with the passivity of the Asiatic races in general, Japan is aggressive in temperament.

Just as Greece devised fresh modes of expression for the Egyptian, Assyrian, and Phœnician elements which found their way into the nooks and crannies of her coasts, so Japan became the crucible in which Indo-Buddhist, Greco-Buddhist, central Asiatic, and Chinese traditions were blended under the influence of a new discipline. Lying on the fringe of Asia, Japan was an epitome of its history, reflecting in the mirror of its Inland Sea the civilizations of the coasts which faced it: in the first place ancient China with her subtle culture; then, ranged behind her, the Mongol Altai with its military strength, the Malay Archipelago and Farther India with their adventurous maritime powers, and Buddhist India with its dream of moral beauty, its gentleness, and its mystery. The Japanese civilization was a blend of all these, but a blend possessing a character of its own. Though near enough to the continent to receive its influences, Japan was none the less protected by her insular position from being too completely penetrated by them. Again, the territory of Japan, extending in a long line from Kamchatka to Formosa, might be expected to offer violent variations of climate; but these were tempered by the sea, which softened all contrasts and enabled human activity to develop harmoniously without being crushed by the extremes of nature.

The history of Japan, as of Greece, was dominated by this influence of the sea. In Japan, as in Greece, the seaman passes from one to another of a chain of rocky islands without losing sight of the shore. Both countries have the same volcanic structure, with the sea running far up into its deep indentations, both offer the same general aspect of wooded hill-sides, bays, creeks, and inland seas, both are broken up into small valleys, forming a number of separate compartments open to the sea and each living a life of its own; in both the landscape has the same harmonious grace; while in the background there rises against the blue sky, in the one the snowy peak of Olympus, and in the other that of Fuji-san.

In Japan, as in Greece, the smiling character and moderation of nature exert a decisive influence upon the cast of mind of the inhabitants. The lightness and charm of the outer world explain why, in Greece and Japan alike, artists have never taken the universe and

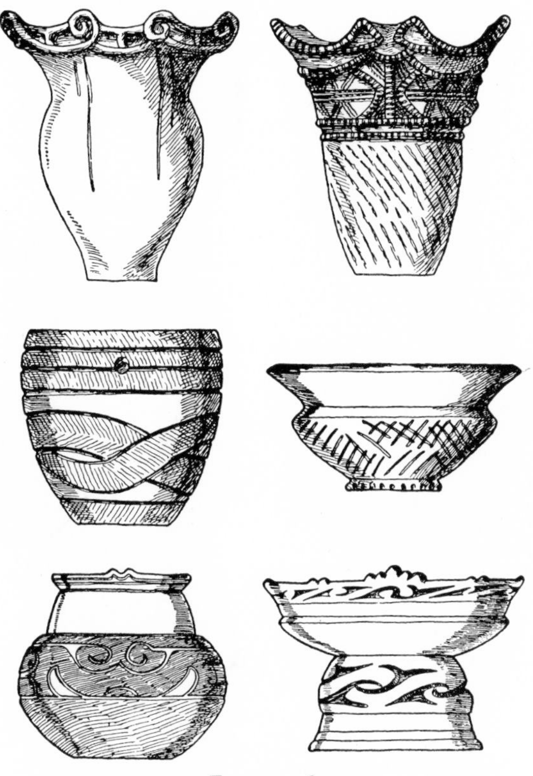

FIGURE 1
The three styles of neolithic pottery in Japan.
— *After Professor Nakaya*

life too tragically. The darkest myths of the antique East failed to affect the serenity of the Greeks: a touch of smiling good humour always accompanies the legends of Olympus. In like fashion the artists and poets of Nippon have never forgotten that the divinities of China and India need not be taken with entire seriousness, so long as the heart is pure. The Japanese have the same spice of sly humour as the characters of Lucian and, like them, refuse to lose their self-possession or abdicate their personality in the presence of nature, which the Japanese and the Hellene alike approach on its most ac-

FIGURE 2
Temples of Hōryūji, Nara.
— *From* Japanese Temples. *By courtesy of the* Shimbi Shoin

cessible side, both harmonizing and humanizing it. Like the Hellene, the Japanese passes lightly over the great problems and brings them within our reach in some fragment of brilliant poetry or delightful conversation. It is true that his well-balanced nature, like that of the Greek or the Frenchman, has its compensating disadvantages. Disciples though they are of the Chinese, we shall not find among the

Japanese either the metaphysical genius of a Chu Hsi or the prodigious romanticism of a Li T'ai-po or a Mu Ch'i. The sphere of the Japanese, as of the Greek, is that of fancy brought within the limits of good taste. A Japanese *netsuke* reveals the same view of life as a Tanagra figure. But this winged fancy in no way prevents a serious

FIGURE 3
The Chūmon, Hōryūji.
— *From* Japanese Temples. *By courtesy of the* Shimbi Shoin

outlook upon life. While nourishing no illusions about the truth of the traditional legends, both Greeks and Japanese take a delicate pleasure in their antique charm and respect them as one of the pillars of their national life. Like the Athenian of the fifth century, the Japanese is at once the most irreverent and the most pious of men.[1]

[1] See M. W. de Visser: "The Fox and Badger in Japanese Folk-lore," in *Transactions of the Asiatic Society of Japan* (Yokohama, 1908), Vol. XXXVII, Pt. 3, pp. 1–159.

And we shall find many other points of resemblance. The Japanese admires cold-blooded heroism, the free sacrifice of the individual to the interests of local or national patriotism, as much as did the Hellenes of the best period. Like them, he has a sense of personal honour and of the unwritten code. Like them, he is capable of

FIGURE 4
The Tōdaiji
— *From* Japanese Temples. *By courtesy of the* Shimbi Shoin

smiling self-sacrifice. The moderation and tact of Socrates in his last moments are shared by none save the Japanese. He is no slave in the sense that the subjects of Xerxes, Suleiman, or Aurungzeb were slaves. His strength is not that of a mass set in motion from without, but is inspired by an indwelling soul — it is the strength of Marathon and Salamis. For the rest, the heroism of Nippon is hidden beneath a veil of glib wiliness and sly humour: a Ulysses lurks in every Japanese.

At the two extremities of the same continent, separated by vast distances in both time and space, inhabiting two happy sea-girt lands, these two peoples favoured by the gods brought light and order into the often confused conceptions of Asiatic thought and coined its heavy wealth into pure metal — and the smile of Athene shone upon the land of Amaterasu.

JAPAN IN PREHISTORIC DAYS

IT MUST BE FRANKLY RECOGNIZED THAT IN JAPAN THE PREHISTORIC period lasted till the introduction of Buddhism as a generally accepted religion in the sixth century of our era. Otherwise, in the present state of our knowledge, the origin and constituent parts of the Japanese race still remain a problem. Philologists have, however, attempted to establish a connexion between the Japanese and neighbouring groups. Monsieur Ramstedt has pointed out the analogies between old Japanese on the one hand and Korean and the Altaic languages on the other. Mr. Matsumoto Nobuhiro has been no less successful in pointing out the affinities between Japanese and the languages of the southern Pacific, such as Malay and the languages of Indo-China, as well as between southern Asiatic folk-lore and Japanese mythology.[1] It is, indeed, fairly likely that, in proportions which we are unable to determine, a Malay and a continental element went to the composition of the Japanese race. But at the moment when its history began, these elements must have been long since fused, the Japanese race already forming a coherent whole, which we next see engaged in winning the island of Hondo from the barbarians of another race, known as the Ainus or Ebisus.

1 N. Matsumoto: *Le Japonais et les langues austroasiatiques, étude de vocabulaire comparé* (Paris: Geuthner, 1928); id., *Recherches sur quelques thèmes de la mythologie japonaise* (Paris: Geuthner, 1928).

Does this mean that it is impossible to distinguish different political centres in the Japan of the earliest historical period? On the contrary, the traditions recorded in the oldest chronicles, the *Kojiki* and the *Nihongi*, enable us to assume at least three such centres.[1] One was in Izumo, a province of the island of Hondo, which worshipped the god Susanoo, the divinity of storm, water, and thunder, and another was in Yamato, which worshipped the sun-goddess Amaterasu, from whom the dynasty of the *tennō* or " sovereigns of the heavens " — that is, the imperial dynasty of Yamato, which founded the unity of Japan — was to claim descent. Other centres had formed themselves among the tribes on the island of Kyūshū — for example, the Kumasos and Hayatos, the latter of whom inhabited the provinces of Satsuma and Hyuga and observed various maritime cults. Japanese mythology, as Mr. Matsumoto observes, was the result of the fusion of these different cults and their subordination to that of Amaterasu when the principality of Yamato imposed its hegemony upon the other Japanese tribes. The work of unification was carried out side by side with the racial war against the Ainu barbarians. Thus legend shows us Prince Yamatotake (81–113?) putting down a revolt of the Kumasos of Kyūshū in the south and then turning northward to wrest from the Ainus the region known as the Kantō — that is, the region of what is now Tōkyō. The expeditions by sea against Korea, too, must already have started, the first of them, according to national tradition, purporting to have taken place under the Empress Jingō-Kōgō (A.D. 201–269, or 363–389?).[2]

[1] See Y. Isobé: *The Story of Ancient Japan, or Tales from the Kojiki* (1928); *Nihongi, Chronicles of Old Japan, from the earliest times to A. D. 697*, translated by Professor W. G. Aston (London, 1896); B. H. Chamberlain: *Kojiki, or Records of Ancient Matters* (1882); K. Florenz: *Japanische Mythologie, Nihongi, Zeitalter der Götter* (1901).

[2] See K. Hara: *An Introduction to the History of Japan* (1920); A. Wedemeyer: *Japanische Frühgeschichte, Untersuchungen zur Chronologie und Territorialverfassung von Altjapan bis zum fünften Jahrhundert nach Christ* (Tōkyō, 1930) (*Asia Major* series), pp. 24–56; O. Nachod: *Geschichte von Japan*, Vol. I., *Die Urzeit* (to A.D. 645) (Leipzig, 1906); M. C. Hagenauer: "Neolithic Japan," in *Bulletin de la Maison Franco-Japonaise de Tōkyō* (Tōkyō, 1931), Vol. III, No. 1–2; *Nihongi*, translated by W. G. Aston (1896).

Recent excavations have brought to light interesting prehistoric and protohistoric pottery of these periods. The neolithic and aeneolithic types of ware known as *jomon shiki* have been found principally in the north. Authorities on the prehistoric age of Japan distinguish various styles among these: the *Atsude* style in the province of Shinano, the *Usude* style in the province of Musashi, and the *Mutsu* style in the province of the same name. The decoration consists either in corded lines, known as the "knotted cord" design, characteristic of the Atsude style, or in undulating lines in the form of waves, characteristic of the Usude style, or else in a combination of these two elements, characteristic of the Mutsu style (Fig. 1).[1] These motives are already remarkable for their force, strength, and elegance, but appear to be totally distinct from those on Chinese neolithic or aeneolithic pottery, of which we spoke in Volumes I and III. Associated with this pottery are found curious little terracotta figures which, like it, are already singularly powerful, balanced, and compact. Authorities on the prehistoric age of Japan are beginning to make a systematic study of these, and classify them under a number of categories: figurines which are realistic in style; grotesque figures (which are particularly numerous in

FIGURE 5
Yumedono-Kannon. Wooden figure, 6 ft. 6 ins. in height. Hōryūji, early seventh century.
— *From* Hōryūji Taikyō

[1] Jiujiro Nakaya: "*L'Age de pierre au Japon*," in *Formes*, April 1930.

the provinces of Shinano and Iwashiro); figures of persons "with triangular faces," represented chiefly in Hitachi and Musashi; the "owl-faced" ones coming from the same places; those in the Mutsu style, which are more architectural and decorative in construction and have something Polynesian or Amerindian about them.[1] Another type of prehistoric pottery, known as *yayoishiki* ware — which is aeneolithic, because bronze objects are already found with it — is far more simple and occurs chiefly in the west and south.[2] According to Mr. J. Nakaya, neolithic culture must have lingered on in the north for a very long time, almost up to the sixth century of our era, when the south and the west had already been acquainted with metal for a long time, for the bronze age certainly reached its culminating point in these regions during the first two centuries of our era.[3]

The use of terracotta figurines was carried on well into the earliest historic age in the form of the funeral *haniwa,* clay statuettes representing armed warriors, women, horses in full trappings, birds, etc., which, in Japan as in China, were substituted for the living victims who had accompanied the dead to the tomb in the interments of ancient days.[4] According to Japanese tradition, this substitution was

[1] Id., "*Figurines néolithiques du Japon,*" *Documents,* 2nd year, No. 1 (March 1930); id., *Nihon sekki jidai teiyo* (*Manual of the Stone Age in Japan*) (Tōkyō, 1929).

[2] *Kaizuka* — shell-mounds or kitchen middens (*Kjoekken moeddings*) — are often associated with the different styles of neolithic pottery. The learned researches of Prince Ōyama have shown that these *kaizuka* can be classified chronologically in three periods: (1) ancient *kaizuka* (e.g., those of Egasaki), associated with Hasuda pottery; (2) intermediate *kaizuka* (e.g., those of Nagasaki), associated with pottery of the *atsude* type; (3) recent *kaizuka* (e.g., those of Shinjiku), associated with pottery of the Ōmori type (see Hagenauer, op. cit., p. 55).

[3] In the south of the archipelago pure neolithic work continues down to the third century B.C. As early as the second century B.C. we see bronzes of Chinese inspiration appearing in Kyūshū. On the contrary, in the north, in the Kantō, the neolithic, according to Professor Elisséev, was to last down to the fourth century of our era. For Han bronzes in Japan, see *Baisen, Kyo-zō, Nihon shutsudo kanshiki-kyō zushū* (*Album of the Mirrors of Han Style Excavated in Japan*), with preface by Professor Umehara.

[4] We should also mention the most curious primitive drawings — e.g., the frescoes of horses — found in the tombs at Jōgashita and Yawata, in the province of Higo. Cf. Professor Kenji Takahashi: "The Primitive Painting of Japan in Ancient Times," Pt. VIII, *Kokka,* No. 431 (October 1926).

decided upon in Yamato in the second year of the Christian era, under the reign of the Emperor Suinin.[1]

The factor which unified the various racial elements of what was afterwards to become Japan and made them into one of the most homogeneous peoples known to history was its insular position. If the old legends are to be believed, it was the gods who presided over this organization. Like the " Sacred Archipelago," Japan is, indeed, the land of the gods. Its very soil is divine, for it formed the race and is the object of worship in Shintoism, the primitive religion of Japan.[2] Shintō is, strictly speaking, the cult of the native land. The *Kamis,* venerated by the Shintoists, include, together with the ancestors of the clans, the nature-divinities: those of the mountains and the plains, the seasons and the hours, those who whisper among the reeds and dance upon the waves. In addition to Amaterasu, the sun-goddess from whom the Japanese imperial dynasty is descended, the great deities of Shintoism are Tsukiyomi no kami, by whose agency the moonlight sheds its silver gleam on the sea of Isé; Izanagi and Izanami, who brought forth the land of the archipelago; and Sengen, the goddess of Fuji-san, the spirit who causes the trees to bloom. Like the Hellenic cults, Shintoism seeks out the most picturesque sites for its sanctuaries. Its religious centre, the Naikū of Yamada in Isé, stands in a sacred wood which breathes a romantic sense of awe. Its sacred porticoes, or *torii,* are to be found in the midst of famous landscapes, on the edge of lakes, at the end of promontories, looking

[1] In this connexion, and in the light of the most recent archæological discoveries, we may note how general these human hecatombs seem to have been in primitive burial rites: for instance, in Egypt during the earliest historic age, as described in M. Moret's lecture at the Musée Guimet in 1929; and in ancient Chaldea — witness Mr. Woolley's excavations at Ur, in 1928, etc.

[2] See Genchi Katō: *Study of Shintō, the Religion of the Japanese Nation* (Tōkyō: Meiji Japan Society, 1926); K. Kanokogi: *Der Geist Japans* (Leipzig, 1930), p. 57, "Shintoism as a National Religion"; Shun Ōsumi: *History of the Religious and Philosophical Ideals of Japan,* ed. Professor T. Haneda (Kyōto, 1929); K. Florenz: *Historische Quellen der Shintō Religion* (Göttingen, 1919).

steeply down upon the sea among the mountains, or at the turn of an ancient path among secular pine-trees.

In this religion of the black Earth, the trees and waters, the liturgy often rises to heights of real grandeur: "Give ear," says the officiat-

FIGURE 6

Kannon, or other Bosatsu, in the Kondō, Hōryūji. Wooden figure, about 6 ft. 10 ins. in height. Early seventh century.
— *From* Japanese Temples

FIGURE 7

Miroku (Maitrēya). Wooden figure, about 4 ft. 6 ins. in height. In the Kōryūji, Kyōto. Early seventh century.
— *From* Japanese Temples

ing priest; "I declare in the presence of the sovereign gods of the harvest that if they cause the late-ripening harvest, produced by the sweat of our arms and the slime of the rice-field, pressed between our thighs, to be lavish in ears of corn, I will offer them as first-fruits a thousand ears of rice and the *saké* contained in the bulging jars drawn up in a row." This might almost be a poem of Hesiod's.

Shintoism lies at the root of the whole of Japanese culture. Japanese drama and lyrical poetry have their origin in the religious dances and liturgical songs in which the Shintoists proclaimed their participation in the universal life and joy. The following is one of the songs: "The Earth is the mother from whom all creatures have received their being and their life; and so all creatures join their voices in the universal hymn. The tall trees and humble herbs, the stones, the sand, the earth we tread, the winds, the waves — all things, all, have a divine soul. The murmur of the breezes among the woods in springtime, the buzz of the insects among the moist autumn plants, are so many verses in the song of the Earth. The sigh of the breeze, the roar of the torrent, are so many hymns of life in which all should rejoice." A religion, as we see, that was at once very simple and most profound, and had affinities in many respects with the Greek cults.[1]

INTRODUCTION OF BUDDHISM

TO THOSE WHO HAVE JUST BEEN STUDYING THE HISTORY OF CHINA Japan constitutes a phenomenon of intense interest. In the preceding volume of the present work we saw what strata of indigenous civilization and what a powerful and age-old originality underlay Buddhist culture in China. After a short period of surprise — which was, moreover, confined to the northern provinces and the foreign Wei dynasty — the national tradition rapidly regained the upper hand. As early as the middle of the T'ang period the Buddhist element had

[1] See H. L. Joly: *Legend in Japanese Art* (London and New York: J. Lane and Co., 1908). For the relation to Shintoism of the rock frescoes in the archaic tombs recently discovered at various places in Japan, see the fine study by Professor Kenji Takahashi: "The Primitive Painting of Japan in Ancient Times," Pt. XII, in *Kokka*, No. 440 (July 1927).

been assimilated, and the internal evolution of the Chinese genius resumed its logical course. When superadded to a people with a very old literary and artistic tradition, Buddhism merely proved an element of enrichment and stimulus — in fact, an episode.[1]

FIGURE 8
East Pagoda of the Yakushiji.
— *From* Japanese Temples

In Japan, on the contrary, the introduction of Buddhism took place among a people which was culturally young, and in consequence infinitely more receptive. Not that this people was passive; on the contrary, the Japanese temperament is distinguished by the spontaneity

[1] See Vol. III of the present work, pp. 283–4.

FIGURE 9

Miroku Bosatsu (Maitrēya) or Nyoirin Kannon (?), in the Chūgūji, Nara. Wooden figure about 5 ft. in height.
— *Date, about 650. Photo, U. Odin*

of its reactions and an assertion of its own personality, the strength of which can be explained only by the insular position of the country. However that may be, the very fact of the absence of all earlier culture, combined with the outstanding quality of the human material, was this time to give Buddhism an importance which ancient China had never been able to concede it, in spite of the passing vogue which it enjoyed at some periods. But what is more important is that, through Buddhism, Chinese civilization was introduced into Japan.

The interest of what we may call the "Japanese experiment" is obvious. In the second volume of the present work we saw how Buddhist thought and sentiment were the product of the very flower of the Indo-Aryan soul. In the third volume we followed Buddhism in its expansion across central Asia and saw it brought into contact with Greek, Iranian, and Indo-Gupta art. It will therefore be of absorbing interest to watch how, enriched with these various accretions, it was to penetrate, not, this time, into a civilization which had long since arrived at a stable form and could not possibly forget its own traditions, but into an untouched people for whom it was to constitute the whole of civilization. The spirituality characterizing the Buddhism of the Mahāyāna — the "Greater Vehicle" — Greek plastic art,[1] something of Iranian elegance [2] and the whole softness of Gupta art — such was the revelation which was to be received all of a sudden and, as it were, overnight by one of the most intelligent peoples in history, on the arrival of the missionaries of the "Greater Vehicle." [3]

[1] See Sei-ichi Taki: "A Statue of Shaka in the Seiryō-ji Temple, Showing Indo-Greek Influence," *Kokka*, No. 236 (January 1910), p. 232. We may note that here the Greek influence shows at times a touch of Roman realism. See *Hōryūji Ōkagami*, No. 21, Pl. 1–3.

[2] See *Tōyei Shukō: Illustrated Catalogue of the . . . Shōsōin*, I, Pl. 46–51; *Tō-sō Seikwa, Selected Relics of T'ang and Sung dynasties from collections in Europe and America*, by Sadadjiro Yamanaka, Ōsaka, Pl. VI B (brocade with deer and fowls, Aurel Stein mission, British Museum); Matsumoto Yeiichi: "Development of the Buddhist Picture in Central Asia, in its Relation to the Far East," in *Kokka*, No. 465 (August 1929) and No. 466 (September 1929).

[3] See Reischauer: *Study in Japanese Buddhism* (New York, 1917) (very important for the origins and constitution of the Mahāyāna); K. Kanokogi: *Der Geist Japans* (Leipzig,

It was in the sixth century of our era, at an age when Buddhist fervour had reached its height in China under the Wei dynasty in the north, and the Liang in the south, that the religion of Śākyamuni was introduced into Japan. The first reference to this subject occurs, according to tradition, in the reign of the Emperor Kimmei, from about 540 to 571. In 552, we are told, the King of Kudara or Pei-chi (Pei-tsi), in the south-west of Korea, sent some Buddhist *sūtras* and a statue of the Buddha as a present to Kimmei. A split took place, however, between the great families who surrounded the throne — those of Nakatomi, Mononobe, and Soga — with regard to the reception to be given to the new religion. The Sogas showed themselves favourable to it, but the Nakatomis and the Mononobes proclaimed themselves hostile, and it was not till forty years later that it was granted official recognition. During the reigns which followed, the minister Soga no Umako — who died in 626 — secured the triumph of Buddhism by armed force. Having defeated the Mononobes at Mount Shigi in 587, he set up a sort of dictatorship for the benefit of his own clan, whose interests were bound up with those of the new ideas. In order to maintain his position, moreover, he did not scruple to bring about the assassination of the Emperor Sujun (or Sushun), who had shown himself impatient of his tutelage, and replace him in 592 by the victim's sister, the Empress Suiko, under whose reign he governed in association with the prince Shōtoku-taishi (cf. Fig. 24 and 28).[1]

1930), p. 119, "Buddhism as a Religion of Beauty"; Masaharu Anesaki: *History of Japanese Religion* (London, 1930), p. 66, "Buddhist Inspiration and its Manifestations, the Culture of Nara," etc. For the various Japanese sects, their history and dogmas, see also Bunyu Nanjio: *History of the Twelve Japanese Buddhist Sects* (Tōkyō, undated); and M. V. de Visser: *Ancient Buddhism in Japan, Sūtras and Ceremonies in Use in the Seventh and Eighth Centuries A. D. and their History in Later Times* (Paris, 1928–30); id., *The Arhats in China and Japan*, with 16 plates, *Ostasiatische Zeitschrift* (Berlin, 1923). Finally, for the influence of Buddhism upon Japanese art, Professor Masaharu Anesaki's important work: *Buddhist Art in its Relation to Buddhist Ideals* (Boston, 1916).

[1] Fig. 24 is taken from the coloured reproduction in *Selected Relics* (ed. S. Tajima, *Shimbi Shoin*), Vol. VI, Fig. 2. See also *Hōryūji Ōkagami*, No. 58, Pl. 1–4; also a charming wooden statue of the Tempyō period, representing Shōtoku-taishi as a young man,

Shōtoku-taishi (574–622), nephew of the Empress Suiko, who recognized him as heir to the throne (*taishi*), and, in effect, as regent, was the real ruler of Japan from 592 to 622. His first act was to proclaim Buddhism as the state religion.[1] To him is due the foundation of some of the most venerable temples in the Nara region — for instance, that of Hōryūji, dating from 607 (Fig. 2 and 3). He caused Buddhist morality to be taught in accordance with his favourite book, *The Lotus of the Good Law,* and at the same time promulgated in 604 a code borrowed from China, for while, in the eyes of the Sogas, the introduction of Buddhism and of the Chinese civilization which it brought in its train was a means of strengthening the prestige of their own clan, Shōtoku-taishi further saw in it a means of reinforcing the imperial authority by assimilating the power of the Japanese *tennō* to that of the Chinese Sons of Heaven. And, as a matter of fact, it was Chinese centralization and etiquette that converted the ancient princes of Yamato, whose authority had constantly been called in question by the clans, into absolute monarchs on the model of the Han and Sui sovereigns. In this sense the embassy sent by Shōtoku-taishi to the Chinese court in 607 was significant of a political as well as of a religious revolution.

So soon as the imperial dynasty itself assumed the leadership of the Chinese and Buddhist movement, there was no further need for the help of the Soga family, who had only favoured this movement in the interests of their own clan. Soga no Iruka having presumed to obtain the assassination of a prince of the imperial house who stood in the way of his ambition, another imperial prince, Naka no Ōe, placed himself at the head of a conspiracy and in 645 caused Iruka to be assassinated and the Soga family disgraced.

---

preserved at Hōryūji, reproduced in *Hōryūji Ōkagami,* No. 22, Pl. 1–5, and the fine painting at Hōryūji representing a delightful young Shōtoku-taishi in *Hōryūji Ōkagami,* No. 13, Pl. 18–19; and, finally, a picture of Shōtoku-taishi as a young prince aged sixteen in the Muroyama collection. See Mr. Matsumoto Yeiichi's study of this fine painting in *Kokka,* No. 467 (October 1929).

[1] See Masaharu Anesaki: *History of Japanese Religion,* p. 57.

FIGURE 10
Detail of Figure 9.

The fall of the Sogas was marked by a fresh progress of Chinese influence. Under the reign of the Emperor Kōtoku (645–54) the court and the provincial administration were reformed on the T'ang model — a process known as the reform of the Taika period.[1] Prince Naka no Ōe, who is known as the Emperor Tenchi-tennō (662–71), continued this reform movement by promulgating the Ōmiryō code in 670; and finally the Emperor Temmu (673–86) completed it by issuing regulations for court ceremonial, costume, family names, provincial boundaries, etc. Thus the ancient federation of Japanese clans, more or less grouped under the patriarchal authority of the princes of Yamato, was replaced by a centralized state copied from that of T'ang China. Up till now Japan had had no fixed capital; the cities of Yamato had vied with one another for precedence, tradition demanding that each emperor should choose a new residence. Following the example of the T'ang Sons of Heaven, the Japanese tennō now decided to have a settled capital worthy to rival Si-ngan-fu or Loyang. In 710 the court accordingly took up its residence at Nara, which remained the imperial capital till 794.

FIGURE 11
Central Bodhisattva of the Yakushiji trinity.
— *Photo*, Shimbi Shoin

[1] See J. Murdoch: *History of Japan*, I, 143–80 ("The Great Reform of 645"); O. Nachod: *Geschichte von Japan*, II ("*Übernahme der chinesischen Kultur*, 645–850") (Leipzig, 1929–30); Shun Ōsumi: *History of the Religious and Philosophical Ideals of Japan*, pp. 87–145.

FIGURE 12

Bonten, lacquer upon clay, in the Sangatsu-dō, Nara.
Middle of the eighth century.
— *By courtesy of Professor Sato*

The establishment of a court and administration on the Chinese type was, none the less, not without its drawbacks even for the imperial dynasty itself. It was not long before the tennō, like their T'ang contemporaries, became the slaves of court life and the official hierarchy. Shut up in their palaces, they began more and more to shift the affairs of state which the new centralization had concentrated in their hands on to the backs of their entourage. Gradually a powerful ministerial family — that of the Fujiwara — came to occupy the position of mayors of the palace. Kamatari, the historic founder of this family, who died in 669, had distinguished himself by helping the imperial princes to get rid of the Soga clan; in reality, however, the Fujiwaras only repeated what the Sogas had attempted to do, but with greater moderation and success. They established what was in effect a ministerial dynasty — which was granted after 882 the title of *kampaku* or mayor of the palace — side by side with the imperial dynasty, with which it pro-

FIGURE 13

Shitennō (Lokapāla, Lord of Heaven). Painted clay figure in the Kaidan-in at the Tōdaiji, Nara, about 5 ft. 6 ins. in height. About the middle of the eighth century.
— *From* Japanese Temples

ceeded to connect itself by a series of marriages, so that in the end it became a traditional custom for the tennō to take wives from among the Fujiwara family. In the course of the eighth century a moment even arrived when Fujiwara Nakamaro (who died in 764) assumed for a time the role of king-maker and dictator. But since this was an administrative and not a military clan, absolutism and a centralized administration went on as in the past.

During this time Buddhism, too, was completing its peaceful conquest of the country. During the reign of Shōmu-tennō (724–48) the famous Korean monk Gyōgi (670–749) came and settled in Japan and, in order to overcome Shintoist opposition, preached the doctrine known as Ryōbu-Shintō, according to which the national gods were merely manifestations of the Buddha. The same principles were developed by the bonze Ryōben (689–773). All these monks actively propagated the arts of the continent, and, by order of Shōmu, Ryōben set up in 746 a great statue of the Buddha (Daibutsu), over fifty feet in height, in the Tōdaiji at Nara (Fig. 4).[1] He was also distinguished as a painter. Another famous monk of this period was the Chinese bonze Kanshin or Ganjin (Ch'ien-ch'en) (687–763), who arrived in Japan in 754.[2]

THE NARA PERIOD

THE NARA PERIOD (710–94) WAS THE GOLDEN AGE OF JAPANESE poetry. "The reader," says W. G. Aston,[3] "who expects to find this

[1] See Professor Seiichi Taki: "The Fine Arts of the Tempyō Era," in *Kokka*, No. 453 (August 1928). According to Professor Taki, the colossal bronze statue represents Vairocana Buddha, the worship of whom was generally in fashion at this time, and forms the subject of the *Kegon-gyo* (*Avataṃsaka sūtra*).

[2] For the ancient Buddhist art of Japan, in addition to the great publications of the *Shimbi Shoin* mentioned in the preface, cf. A. Maybon: *Les Temples du Japon, architecture et sculpture* (1929); Langdon Warner: *Japanese Sculpture of the Suiko Period* (New Haven: Yale University Press, 1923) (a very important and quite indispensable book); and Karl With: *Buddhistische Plastik in Japan bis in den Beginn des VIIIen Jahrhunderts nach Christ* (Vienna, 1919); also Professor Anesaki's admirable study *Buddhist Art in its Relation to Buddhist Ideals*.

[3] W. G. Aston: *A History of Japanese Literature* (New York and London, 1899), p. 34.

poetry of a nation just emerging from the barbaric stage of culture a poetry characterized by a rude, untutored vigour will be surprised to learn that, on the contrary, it is distinguished by polish rather than power. It is delicate in sentiment and refined in language."

FIGURE 14
Head of Figure 13.

This delicacy is explained by the fact that we have here a court poetry. The famous collection of the *Man-yo-shu,* or "*Ten Thousand Pages,*" compiled about 750 and completed at the beginning of the ninth century, contains many echoes of this already almost over-cultured society. The poets contained in this collection, Hitomaro, Akahito, and Prince Aki, surpass even their contemporaries, the great T'ang poets whom we mentioned in Volume III,[1] in quivering sensibility and impressionism:

On the plum blossoms
Thick fell the snow;
I wished to gather some
To show to thee,
But it melted in my hands.

Or:

Among the hills
The snow still lies —
But the willows
Where the torrents rush together
Are in full bud.

Or again:

Fall gently
O thou rain of spring!
And scatter not
The cherry-flowers
Until I have seen them.

Or:

When I went out
Over the moor,
Where the haze was rising,
The nightingale sang;
Spring, it seems, has come.

Or:

To what shall I compare
This life of ours?
It is like a boat
Which at daybreak rows away
And leaves no trace behind it.

Or:

The sky is a sea
Where the cloud-billows rise;
And the moon is a bark;
To the groves of the stars
It is oaring its way.[2]

In the history of art, as in that of political organization, Japan provides an example of a phenomenon intensely interesting to the phi-

[1] Pages 286–98.
[2] Translated by W. G. Aston, op. cit., pp. 44, 45, 47, 48. Cf. also the *Manyōsū*, translated by J. L. Pierson (Leiden, 1929).

losopher: that of a "chosen type of humanity," which, owing to its isolation, had hitherto remained "barbarous," suddenly plunged, almost from one day to another, into contact with the most subtle civilizations of the continent, which it adopted, adapted, and made so much its own as almost to surpass them.

The medium through which this education or, rather, this artistic revelation was imparted was Buddhism. Indeed, Buddhism brought with it into the archipelago not only Indian philosophy, but also Chinese architecture, Indo-Greek, Indo-Gupta, Wei, and T'ang sculpture, and all the pictorial traditions of Indian, Iranian, and T'ang painting, now familiar to us from the discoveries in central Asia and Korea.[1]

The Japanese architecture whose antiquity is best substantiated is that of the temples of Izumo, on the coast opposite Korea, and of Isé, on the gulf of the same name, to the east of Hondo, which are highly primitive Shintoist constructions in which the ancient technique of the native carpenters was beginning to be enriched by the example of what must have been the Chinese architecture of the Six Dynasties. Professor S. Elisséev, who has made a learned study of these various styles, shows how the primitive Shintoist temple was merely an enlarged version of the Japanese house, "the dwelling-place of the ancestors, who," to quote a remark of Dr. Hamada's, "did not require an abode planned in any different fashion from that of ordinary dwellings." The curving lines of the roof-frame, however, already bore witness to Sino-Korean influence. The same influence is responsible for the shifting of the entrance door from the right-hand side — that is, from one of the short sides of the rectangle, as in the Izumo type — to the centre of one of the long sides, as in the Isé type. Yet in spite of the growing complication of the internal arrangement, this type of architecture was to become stereotyped

[1] Yeiichi Matsumoto: "Development of the Characteristics of Buddhist Pictures in Central Asia, in Relation to the Far East," *Kokka*, 1929.

FIGURE 15
Head of a *shitennō*, in the Shinyakushiji, Nara. Middle of the eighth century.
— *By courtesy of Professor Sato*

throughout all the centuries to come, the imperial palaces, in particular, remaining true to the style of the temples of Isé.

The use of ornamental bells (*dōtaku*) was also an importation from the Sino-Korean world, but it may be noted that the decoration of these archaic bells remained specifically Japanese, as is shown by a good specimen in the Musée Guimet.[1]

As early as the Suiko period (which lasted from about 540 to 646) [2] great Buddhist temples were springing up in increasing numbers in various parts of Yamato; among them may be mentioned the Shitennō-ji or temple of the four *lokapālas,* built by Shōtoku-taishi in 587 on the shores of the Inland Sea and moved to Osaka in 593; next the Hōryūji group, built near Nara between 593 and 607 by the same prince, with the aid of Korean workmen, on a definitely Chinese model (Fig. 2–3). The principal temple at Hōryūji, the Kondō, or Golden Temple, raised upon two stone terraces and covered with a double roof in the Chinese fashion, is an example of the symmetrical and majestically classic construction which characterizes all the architecture of Yamato. So experienced an authority as Professor Elisséev distinguishes in the distribution of the buildings the direct influence of the Wei architecture of China.

This influence is still more noticeable in the sculpture of the same age.[3] The advent of Buddhism and its iconography involved the sud-

[1] Cf. Kenji Takahashi: "Primitive Designs in Prehistoric Japan," in *Kokka,* No. 416 (July 1915).

[2] The Empress Suiko reigned from 593 to 628; but Professor Kyōsuke Ōguchi proposes a different chronology for the Suiko period of art: from the fifteenth year of the reign of the Empress Suiko (A.D. 607) to the close of that of the Emperor Tenji (A.D. 671). See *Kokka,* No. 455 (October 1928).

[3] Cf. Langdon Warner: *Japanese Sculpture of the Suiko Period;* and Kyōsuke Ōguchi: "The Buddhist Sculpture of the Suiko Epoch," in *Kokka,* 1928–9, starting in No. 455 (October 1928). Professor Ōguchi points out that "the characteristics of the Suiko period were, firstly, that all the statues in either wood or bronze had limitations imposed upon them by the technique used in incising the smooth surfaces of rock caves, instead of allowing free scope for the attaining of artistic effect within the capacity of the medium used; secondly, that formal beauty was heightened by suppressing sensitiveness in the outward forms of the statues; and, thirdly, that, as the natural consequence of such efforts, the spiritual beauty was consciously sought after. Another characteristic was

FIGURE 16

FIGURE 17

Bodhisattvas from the Hōryūji frescoes.
— From the copy in the Musée Guimet

den importation of the whole Chinese conception of art in the Wei period, including all the Indo-Greek traditions embodied in it, which had already been adapted to quite a new type of religious feeling. In Volume III of this series we have shown how, at the very time when Greco-Buddhist art reached Wei China, it was in course of undergoing a transformation analogous to that affecting late Greco-Roman art six centuries later in the south of France, which was to give rise to the first truly native French work, the *opus francigenum.* Plastic art was by now so far emptied of its content as to have become no more than a soaring aspiration, full of prayerful and mystic ardour, towards the world beyond. The art of the Wei dynasty accentuated these tendencies to such an extent as to produce works which can only be compared to the Romanesque sculpture of western Europe. It was this " Buddhist Romanesque," as it has been called, which was introduced into Japan by way of Korea during the Suiko period.

One of the earliest works of this age is the Buddhist trinity in the Kondō, Hōryūji, a bronze group about two feet in height, attributed to Kuratsukuribe no Tori and consisting of Śākyamuni flanked by two bodhisattvas.[1] It is a group of decidedly Korean workmanship, but the style goes back beyond Korea and has affinities with Wei art — with that of the earliest reliefs at Lung-mēn [2] quite as much as with that of the school of stelæ which flourished in Shen-si at the same period.[3] The scalloped effect of the folds of the garment and draperies is exactly that of Figures 149, 150, and 151 in Volume III of the present work, and, similarly, the enormous nimbuses, with their decoration of flames, which form a background to the statues

most manifest in the marvellous kind of spirituality that was inherent in the unostentatious simplicity and the purity of outward expression."

[1] Cf. *Hōryūji Ōkagami*, No. 49, Pl. 1–10; Otto Kümmel: *Kunst Chinas, Japans und Koreas*, Pl. VII; Langdon Warner, op. cit., Pl. 23; also Pl. 18–22, showing the beautiful Yakushi in the Kondō.

[2] Sirén: *Sculpture chinoise*, I, Pl. 80.

[3] Ibid., Pl. 136–138, 141, etc.

and to the whole group are the same as those which crown the statues in Figures 145, 147, 149, etc.; and, lastly, the garments of the two standing bodhisattvas flanking the Buddha fall in the same angular folds as those on the Wei stele from the Loo collection, in Volume III, Fig. 149.[1]

FIGURE 18
Bodhisattva from the Hōryūji frescoes.
— *From* Hōryūji

The "Romanesque" or "Gothic" character is even more striking in the Yumedono Kannon of Hōryūji, a wooden statue six feet six inches in height, the upper part of which we reproduce as Fig. 5.[2] The high open-work diadem, the sharply cut profile, the long, lean body, the scarfs falling in great angular points — all these traits accentuate the mystical quality of the statue. This work, which, like the last-mentioned, belongs to the school of Kuratsukuribe no Tori and therefore dates from the first twenty-five years of the seventh century, is, in our opinion, one of the finest works of that Chino-Japanese group which might be described as "Wei-Suiko" — always with the reservation that Korea has left a strong imprint upon the whole of this Tori school. Still more tall and slender is the wooden Kannon, about seven feet ten inches high, in the Kondō, Hōryūji (Fig. 6). The

[1] See the delicate wooden statue of Nikkō in the Hōryūji, in a different style, but with the same Wei inspiration, in *Hōryūji Ōkagami*, No. 18, Pl. 12–15; and in Langdon Warner, op. cit., Pl. 69. See also *Hōryūji Ōkagami*, No. 21, Pl. 8–11; No. 26, Pl. 6–9.

[2] See *Hōryūji Ōkagami*, No. 51, Pl. 9–14; No. 40, Pl. 1–7; and Langdon Warner, op. cit., Pl. 9.

FIGURE 19

Bodhisattva, from the Hōryūji frescoes.
— *From* Hōryūji

FIGURE 20

Bodhisattva, from the Hōryūji frescoes.
— *From* Hōryūji

statues of the famous Gothic church at Moissac, Tarn-et-Garonne, are the only thing in French Gothic at all comparable to this elongated body, whose form, so spare as to seem almost incorporeal among its drooping scarfs, seems to rise like an immaterial apparition and soar heavenward beneath its great pointed flame-like aureole. We may note that these Japanese works directly inspired by Wei art through Korean channels achieve immediate perfection in their own kind. Chinese statues of the Wei period are often more interesting from the religious than from the æsthetic point of view,[1] but almost all the corresponding works of the Suiko school at once stand out as masterpieces when judged by any artistic canon whatsoever; and they do so precisely because they are stripped of all superfluous ornament, preserving nothing but a moving simplicity which is a direct reflection of the Buddhism of the Mahāyāna (cf. also Fig. 7). This was to happen throughout the whole course of Japanese history, for while borrowing the motives and technical processes of her art from China at every period, Japan was in every instance to carry them to the highest perfection.[2]

The Suiko period (540–646) was succeeded by the age generally known as the Nara period, though it was not till 719 that Nara definitively became the capital. This period is accordingly divided into

[1] We may note, none the less, with Professor Pelliot, that the great works on the Wei bas-reliefs are splendid masterpieces.

[2] Professor Kyōsuke Ōguchi remarks that "the sculpture of the Suiko epoch had two different tendencies. One was represented by the sculptures belonging to the so-called Tori school, an extant example of which is the Buddhist triad in the main hall of Hōryūji Temple, while the other was represented by the Kokan (ancient Korean) school." With regard to the former, Professor Ōguchi points out that "this school came into existence as a result of formalization of the foreign methods of sculpture after a Chinese fashion as introduced into China in the second era (from the late fifth century to the early sixth century) in the history of sculpture of the Southern and Northern Dynasties period of China." But, according to Mr. Ōguchi, this process of formalization was by no means a mere imitation, but an idealization and a refinement in detail. "A remarkable example of this school is seen in the statue of Yakushi in the main hall of the same temple. A further development — indeed, the fullest development — of the Tori school would seem to have been reached in the above-mentioned Buddhist triad" (*Kokka*, No. 456, November 1928).

two secondary ones, the Hakuhō (646–710) and the Tempyō periods (710–94), both of which, moreover, represented the civilization of Yamato; for the chief temples of the Hakuhō period were built round Nara, including the Kōfukuji, erected in 670, and the Yakushiji, erected in 680, the former of which was moved into the town itself in 711, and the latter in 718 (Fig. 8).[1]

By the second half of the seventh century the influences coming from China underwent a visible change in character. Instead of Wei art, Buddhism brought in its train that of the Sui type. As we see, there is here a slight chronological discrepancy of about forty years, but this discrepancy, due to distance, will always be noticeable between any given stage in the development of Chinese art and the corresponding one in Japan.

As we may remember, Chinese art under the Sui dynasty and the earliest years of the T'ang emperors had been characterized by a return to favour of plastic methods of sculpture, though always subject to the limitations of the religious ideals by which it was inspired, and subordinated to a dogmatic ideal, for which very reason it harmoniously blended material beauty with a lofty spirituality. The conventionalized forms of Buddhist " Romanesque " were followed by a Gothic amplitude. And the Japanese sculpture of the second half of the seventh century, and even of the Tempyō era, shares in the same characteristics.[2]

To form an idea of the advance made, we have only to compare

[1] The Hakuhō period, which extends in the history of art from 646 to 710, is the term applied, in its strict historical sense, to the reign of the Emperor Temmu (673–86). In the same way the Tempyō period, which, from the point of view of civilization, is regarded as covering the years 710–94, takes its name from the years of the Emperor Shōmu's reign (724–48).

[2] See Professor Seiichi Taki: "The Fine Arts of the Tempyō Era," *Kokka*, No. 453 (August 1928). Professor Taki shows that "the idealism of the art of this period is due to the popular faith in the Kegon Scriptures, and that the extant works of Tempyō art bear indications of the realization of this idealism." As illustrations he refers to such works as the statue of Vairocana Buddha in the main hall of Tōshōdai-ji Temple, the statue of Kannon in the Sangatsu-dō Hall of the same temple, and some other works, all of which Mr. Taki considers to be "typical works revealing the effect of that idealism carried out in art."

FIGURE 21
Detail of Figure 19.

FIGURE 22

Bodhisattva from the frescoes of Ajaṇṭā, India.
— *Photo, Goloubew. By courtesy of M. Van Oest*

Figs. 6 and 7 with Fig. 9, the latter representing the Nyoirin Kannon, or Miroku Bosatsu (Maitrēya, the Buddhist Messiah), a wooden statue just over four feet three inches in height, dating from about 650 and preserved in the Chūgūji at Nara. As seen in profile (Fig. 10), the statue still has something of the austere spareness of the Miroku reproduced in Fig. 7, and the attitude, too, is exactly the same; but for the very reason that the seated posture (*āsana*) and the finger-gestures (*mudrā*) are identical, we may estimate the advance made

FIGURE 23
Flying genius, from the Hōryūji frescoes.
— *From* Hōryūji

within the space of a few years. The head has a fullness of life and a sweetness of expression hitherto unknown. The pure profile, which is still Indo-Greek in its correctness, is lit up as with the inner light of lofty meditation. The noble construction of the face is to be seen again in the nude torso, with its harmonious proportions, rising with tranquil grace from among the rounded waves of drapery handed down from the later days of Wei art.[1] The melting, lissom smoothness of the nude body, the broad shoulders, with their suave contour, and

[1] See Vol. III, Fig. 150 and 151 (the trinity from the Gualino collection and the Louvre Buddha, both formerly in the Vignier collection).

the slender waist all belong to a style familiar to us and are the heritage, not, this time, of the Greco-Buddhist art of Gandhāra, but of Gupta India.[1]

As we have shown before, in Volume II of the present work, Buddhism in central Asia started by importing the Hellenistic art of Gandhāra, from which, passing through a phase of " Romanesque " and mystical development, it evolved into the early Wei art of China and that of the Suiko period in Japan. It was not till later, towards the sixth and seventh centuries, that the living æsthetic ideal of Gupta India replaced the outworn Hellenistic models in central Asia. It was this fresh influx of vigour, flowing northwards from the Ganges valley, that gave rise to the Sui renaissance in China described in Volume III of this work, from which were derived in turn the great Japanese schools of Nara. But once again, by virtue of her vigorous artistic originality, Japan succeeded in casting in a supreme and unsurpassable form the metal and motives supplied to her. Of all the works inspired by the Indian canons of art coming from the Ganges valley, none, perhaps, is more powerful than the Nyoirin Kannon mentioned above (Fig. 9–10). This Buddhist statue of Meditation is directly akin — though with a gentle power

FIGURE 24
Portrait of Shōtoku-taishi, seventh century.
— *Preserved in the treasury of the Imperial House*

[1] See Vol. II, Fig. 41, 42, etc.

peculiar to itself alone — to the Maheśamūrti of Elephanta, or even, strangely enough, to the Zeus of Mylasa or the *Penseur* of Rodin.[1]

Thus it was the privilege of Japan to carry to their highest pitch of perfection the foreign types of art which she received from Asia, and to hand down to us an India and a China which were often superior to their originals, while at the same time creating out of these apparent borrowings a Japanese art of profound originality. The secret of this revivification of Sino-Indian themes by the spirit of Japan may no doubt be found in the fact that, being endowed with a keen and almost Hellenic sense of human personality — a sense unknown either to China or to India — Japan imparts this personal quality to all her works. Indian or Chinese Buddhas are often, so to speak, interchangeable and what we may almost call collective in character. But Japanese Buddhas and bodhisattvas possess the privilege, which they share with their Khmer brethren alone, of standing out among a mass of similar figures with a distinct individuality, as portraits of a soul within the limits of a personality. In many respects Japanese art may be simply defined as the introduction of the individualist temperament into the æsthetic ideal of the Far East.[2]

Again, it is a purely Indian influence — and more particularly an Indo-Gangetic or Gupta influence — which asserts itself in the Yakushiji trinity, dating from about 717 (Fig. 11).[3] In the seated central Buddha, indeed, the Gandhārian character of the general architectural construction and drapery is softened by the harmonizing and unifying quality of the melting Gupta softness; but the two standing

[1] Compare the various statues in this attitude (representing Miroku or Nyoirin Kannon) reproduced in Professor Langdon Warner's fine volume *Japanese Sculpture of the Suiko Period*, Pl. 47, 48, 52–68.

[2] "The fine arts of the Tempyō era were not mere imitation of the continental fine arts, but rather creations of originality under continental influence." See Professor Seiichi Taki: "The Fine Arts of the Tempyō Era," Pt. II, *Kokka*, No. 454 (September 1928).

[3] *Selected Relics of T'ang and Sung Dynasties*, Vol. V, Fig. 3; O. Kümmel, op. cit., p. 115; and Curt Gläser: *Ostasiatische Plastik*, Pl. 81–82, 83–84. Compare also certain bodhisattvas on the Tun-huang banners, illustrated in Vol. III, Fig. 205 of the present work; and the celebrated Korean relief of 750 from Sekkutsuan, frequently reproduced after the Chōsen Koseki, notably by Otto Kümmel, op. cit., Fig. 190, p. 189.

FIGURE 25
Bodhisattva, statue in painted wood, about 2 ft. 6 ins. in height.
— *Henri Vever collection, Paris*

bodhisattvas which flank it (Gakkō and Nikkō), with their nude torsos, their almost sensuous modelling, their slight sideward sway of the hips, and the sinuous elegance of their double scarfs, are in every way characteristic of Gupta, Sui, and T'ang days. The Gakkō and Nikkō of the Yakushiji at Nara already stand for a reversion to plastic treatment, an implied suggestion of tropical ardour so pronounced as to suggest to us, beneath the very chastity and sexless reserve of the bodhisattvas, something of the carnal mysticity of Krishnaism. The slightest tendency to fullness in the forms reveals, perhaps, the heaviness into which the powerful plastic technique of T'ang art finally degenerated. But with this reservation the two great bronzes in question, about five feet in height, are directly akin to those central Asiatic works in which Gupta tendencies are present.[1] The little bronze Amitābha trinity, about nineteen inches high, also dating from the early seventh century, now at the Hōryūji, suggests T'ang influences of a more tranquil sort; the head of Amitābha, incomparable in its fullness and softness,[2] shows us how the Apollo type, having travelled from Gandhāra to the far extremity of Asia, assumed a new spirituality beneath the chisel of this privileged race.

FIGURE 26
Kannon of the Kanshinji.
— *Photo*, Shimbi Shoin

This impression becomes more striking than ever before in the Bonten (Brahmā), a statue in dry lacquer,[3] some seven and a half feet in height, which stands to the right of the great Kannon of the

[1] Cf. the Samantabhadra of the painting brought back from Tun-huang by Professor Pelliot, now in the Musée Guimet, Vol. III, Fig. 203.

[2] Curt Gläser, op. cit., Pl. 87.

[3] Cf. Pelliot: "*Note sur la laque sèche,*" in *Journal asiatique*, April–June 1923.

FIGURE 27
Demons from Tun-huang.
— *Pelliot collection, Musée Guimet*

FIGURE 28
Shōtoku-taishi in the Ninnaji, Kyōto, ninth century, attributed to Kanaoka.
— *From* Japanese Temples

Sangatsu-dō in the Tōdaiji, Nara (Fig. 12). This work, which dates from the middle of the eighth century, is ascribed to the bonze Ryōben (689–773), who was, indeed, the head of the Tōdaiji; so that the school to which it belongs was able to draw plenteous inspiration from the realism of T'ang art in general, as well as from the harmonious and melting fullness of the works produced at T'ien-lung-shan in particular (cf. Vol. III, Fig. 164, 165, 166). Indeed, the Bonten of the Sangatsu-dō presupposes artists who had a knowledge of all these schools. Its perfect construction and the faultless classicism of its lines recall the Greek canon; its simple, tranquil forms might almost trace descent, through the T'ien-lung-shan school, from the melting softness of Gupta art, while its nobility recalls the best works of the Sui period. But these are but the component elements in the work, which is itself perfect in its unity. Or, rather, we see in it, even better than in earlier works, how out of these multifarious foreign elements Japan had created an art which, while specifically Japanese, raised each of these alien styles to its highest power. This is why the Japanese school succeeded in going back to the original sources underlying the second-hand versions which reached it. In the gentle strength of its rounded forms, and the

Figure 29
Jizō (Kshitigarbha). Louvre.
— *Photo, Giraudon*

calm, simple lines of its draperies, this Bonten rediscovers and revives the miracle of Greece. Indeed, for the attainment of such natural dignity and serene grandeur we should have to go back to the Greece of the fifth century; and, as a matter of fact, that harmonious union of pure Hellenic beauty with the great peace of Buddhism

FIGURE 30

Śrī (Kichijōten), wooden statue 3 ft. 3 ins. in height, in the Jōruriji, Kyōto, twelfth century.
— *Photo*, Shimbi Shoin

which the art of Gandhāra had striven in vain to achieve, and no Indian, central Asiatic, or Chinese copy had succeeded in realizing, was now effected by Japan almost at the first attempt, and without effort.

In the Bonten of the Sangatsu-dō the object aimed at by the Greco-Buddhist school is for the first time fully achieved; it is, moreover,

FIGURE 31
Paradise of Amida.
— *Musée Guimet*

a perfect fusion of the Hellenic canon with the Gupta ideal, and at the same time one of the most strongly national masterpieces of the native genius.

The same impression of pure Greco-Roman classicism emanates from a number of statues of monks carried out in the dry lacquer process and dating from the first half or the middle of the eighth century; we may mention in particular the standing figures of the monk Subhūti and a number of other disciples of Śākyamuni in the Kōfukuji, Nara, draped, as in a toga, in their monastic cloak or *saṃghāṭi*.[1] The simplicity and dignity of the attitudes, the natural arrangement of the drapery — which leaves the right side, or the breast only, uncovered — and the realistic directness with which the shaven heads are treated, all remind us of the best Roman portraits, dating from about the opening of the Christian era.[2] The same may be said of the commanding power and cold dignity, as well as of the tranquil classicism of the draperies, in the seated statue of the bonze Ryōben, preserved in the Tōdaiji, Nara, founded by that great organizer about 800.[3] The Greco-Roman models, which had

FIGURE 32
Statue of Maitrēya, lacquer on clay, in the Kōryūji, Kyōto, eleventh century. — *Photo*, Shimbi Shoin

[1] *Selected Relics* . . . , Vol. X, Pl. 4; O. Kümmel: *L'Art de l'Extrême-Orient*, Pl. 19; Curt Gläser, op. cit., Pl. 115.

[2] See the striking portrait reproduced in *Hōryūji Ōkagami*, No. 3, Pl. 3–5, which is worthy to compare to the portrait statues of Memphite Egypt — for instance, the Louvre scribe seated upon the ground.

[3] O. Kümmel: *L'Art de l'Extrême-Orient*, Pl. 23; *Selected Relics* . . . , VI, 4. See also

FIGURE 33
Amida, gilt wood, second half of the twelfth century.
— *Photo, Louvre*

degenerated into commonplace and found their way, in an incomprehensible, belated, and almost mummified version, across central Asia and China, now at last, on reaching the end of their long journey and touching the soil of Japan, the new Hellas, cast off the mortuary bands which swathed them, awoke to life, regained consciousness, and became vivified with a new vigour. For there was, so to speak, a predestined harmony between Greece and Japan. The Bonten reproduced as Fig. 12 has shown how the spirit of Japan discovered within itself an Attic beauty and nobility of rhythm. It was sufficient for a distant reminiscence of Greece to be transmitted to the Japan of the Nara period for this contact to reveal to her the Greek genius latent in her own soul. The ten disciples of the Buddha in the Kōfukuji show how she further discovered within herself the sober realism, the often cold, severe dignity, which constitute the beauty of the Roman portrait. This feeling for portraiture is, indeed, yet another point in which the Japanese taste for individualism in art, to which we referred above, finds expression. As early as the seated portraits of Ganjin and Gyōshin in the Tōshōdaiji and the Hōryūji at Nara, dating from the eighth century,[1] we see this side of the national temperament asserting itself unrestrained and, by creating a realism of almost crude simplicity in which to express itself, making these statues into psychological and social studies of a penetrating intensity.

It was at this stage in the revelation of their national genius under the stimulus of foreign importations that the Japanese of Yamato came in contact with the epic style. They had received from central Asia and T'ang China the type of the "kings of heaven (*lokapāla, t'ien-wang, shitennō*)," martial divinities whose function it was to

---

the wooden statue of Giyin Sōjō, Ryōben's master, in the Okadera Temple, Yamato Province, reproduced in *Selected Relics* . . . , XVIII, No. 5.

[1] Curt Gläser, op. cit., Pl. 119–122; and *Hōryūji Ōkagami*, No. 8, Pl. 4–6; ibid., No. 7, Pl. 10–17 are in the same style, and so is the extraordinary terracotta statue representing a bearded Vimalakīrti of the Tempyō period, also at Hōryūji, reproduced ibid., No. 9, Pl. 9–11.

protect the Church of the Buddha against all attacks, whether terrestrial or infernal.[1] These Buddhist St. Michaels and St. Georges were promptly transformed by Japan into figures worthy of her own

FIGURE 34

The moon-goddess. Painting attributed to Takuma Ihōga (1192), in the Kyōwōgokokuji Temple, Tōji, Kyōto.
— *Photo*, Shimbi Shoin

FIGURE 35

Portrait of a Tendai priest, in the Ichijōji Temple, Harima, about twelfth century.
— *Photo*, Shimbi Shoin

genius. We need only compare the four *shitennō* of the Tōdaiji (Fig. 13–15) with the finest statues of a similar nature from cen-

[1] Notably the *tennō* of the North, the king of the *yakshas*, Vaiśravaṇa, Japanese Bishamon. For the iconography of the subject, see the Buddhist dictionary *Hōbōgirin* (Tōkyō, 1929), I, p. 79, *s. v.* "*Bishamon.*"

tral Asia or T'ang China (cf. Vol. III, Fig. 184) to realize how great is the contribution of the Japanese genius. In China the power which was the characteristic feature of T'ang art was losing its vigour and clumsily degenerating into empty and declamatory gesticulation. Japan revived this art with tenfold vigour, breathing into it the soul of the samurai, with its concentrated violence and love of action. In the sketch of the evolution of Chinese art which we attempted in Volume III of this series, we showed how the immense potential energies latent in the Chóu bronzes found concrete expression, first in the art of the Han and afterwards in that of the Six Dynasties, reaching its full expansion in T'ang sculpture, only to lose its impetus and become, as it were, finally paralysed in the ostentatiously powerful style of its later forms. After the T'ang dynasty the plastic power of Chinese art was dead. But this power, which in China was in future to go to waste, was now inherited by Japan, where it set in motion an energy of unexpected scope, so that the plastic power which might have been considered to have lost its vigour for good was born again to a career which was to know no limits. The *shitennō* of the Tōdaiji, with their firm, commanding pose and their formidable armour, their terrible expression and gestures — those menacing faces with their wrathful glance, like forces held in check and ready to leap into action — warn us that a new force was now rearing its head in the east of Farthest Asia and laying claim to the heritage of a tottering China in the history of art just as it was to do in the history of the world. An epic Buddhism was now about to make its appearance, akin to the epic Christianity of the crusades.[1]

And here we may once more note how Buddhist art, which in all other lands was collective and " monistic," became in Japan an individualist art, both in the strongly personal stamp impressed upon it by the artist and in the intense personality of the work itself.

Lastly, the example of these famous statues shows us the first be-

[1] See *Hōryūji Ōkagami*, No. 34, Pl. 6.

ginnings of what was to develop into a secularized art growing up in the heart of Buddhism itself. Nor did this comparative seculariza-

FIGURE 36
Humorous scenes attributed to Toba-Sōjō, in the Kōzanji.
— *Photo*, Shimbi Shoin

FIGURE 37
Humorous scene.
— *Photo*, Shimbi Shoin

tion of art, which arose out of the very triumph of Buddhism, fail to find expression in architecture as well. Professor Elisséev points out, in fact, that the temples of the Tempyō period — such as the Tōdaiji, built between 741 and 747 (Fig. 4), the Tōshōdaiji, dating from 759, the Yumedono, Hōryūji, dating from 759, and the Shin-Yakushiji, dating from 747 (Fig. 8) — were now not merely sanctuaries, but also political and intellectual centres, having schools, universities, or dispensaries attached to them, as the case might be; moreover, he

FIGURE 38
Portrait of Gembō, by Kōkei, in the Kōfukuji, Nara.
— *Photo*, Shimbi Shoin

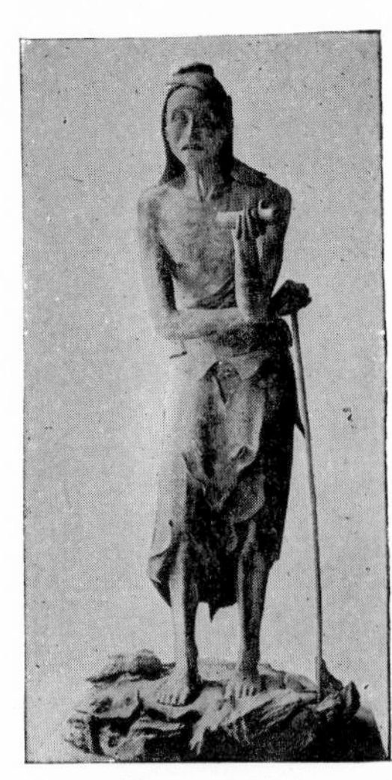

FIGURE 39
The hermit Bashisen, by Unkei, in the Sanjūsangendō, Kyōto.
— *Photo*, Shimbi Shoin

adds, " the spirit inspiring their conception is rationalistic rather than mystical: thus, for example, they avoid the dim light beloved of primitive temples."

The Nara period was drawing to its close; but in the days of its early ardour it had enriched the Buddhist world with what are its most marvellous masterpieces, after the Indian paintings of Ajaṇṭā: the frescoes of Hōryūji.[1]

[1] See *Hōryūji Ōkagami*, *Supplement*, *Frescoes of the Kondō Temple;* especially *Supplement*, No. 1, Pl. 1–4, 9, 12; No. 2, Pl. 6, 7; No. 3, Pl. 18, 21, 22; No. 4, Pl. 15, 16; also *Supplement*, I, Fig. 22, which might be a drawing of Leonardo's.

Even today the exact date of these frescoes is still a problem. The Kondō, or Golden Temple, of Hōryūji, the walls of which they adorn, was completed towards 607; tradition has it that it was seriously damaged by fire in 670 and considerably restored between 708 and 715. The question still to be solved is whether the frescoes date from the original building of the edifice or from its reconstruction.

FIGURE 40
Asaṅga, or Hsüan-tsang, by Unkei (1209). Wooden figure about 6 ft. 2 ins. in height, in the Kōfukuji.
— *Photo*, Shimbi Shoin

FIGURE 41
Detail of Figure 40.
— *Photo*, Shimbi Shoin

Whatever may be the solution of this problem — which involves a variation in the date of these mural paintings as great as from the beginning or middle of the seventh century to the beginning of the eighth — it is extremely probable that the frescoes should not be ascribed to a Japanese hand at all, but to Chinese or central Asian artists so saturated with Indian influences as to paint in the Indian style. Indeed, one may search them in vain for any Chinese characteristics. These paintings are derived from Ajaṇṭā, through the frescoes of Khotan, Kuchā, and Tun-huang, and the Korean tomb of Sammyori. The types, the costumes, the attitudes, the expressions — all are Indo-Gupta and go back to the style of Cave I at Ajaṇṭā, dating precisely from the first half of the seventh century. To convince ourselves of this we have only to compare the bodhisattvas illustrated in Fig. 16–21 with Fig. 43 and 47 in Volume III of this work, and 203 and 205 in Volume III, or, again, the flying genius in Fig. 23 with that from Tun-huang reproduced as Fig. 115 of Volume III.[1]

But just as we have seen above that the sculpture of Nara produced the purest masterpieces, and, if we may use the expression, the ultimate achievement of Greco-Buddhist and Indo-Gupta sculpture, so the frescoes of Hōryūji are a revelation of an Ajaṇṭā purified of its instinctive tropical paganism and raised to a purely ideal plane. It is true that the " beautiful bodhisattva " of Cave I at Ajaṇṭā, illustrated in Volume II, Fig. 47, bending over the suffering world with a gesture of infinite pity, was already a supernatural vision. But perhaps the very fact that the divine figure is rendered so profoundly human by this almost suffering pity erred precisely in bringing the divine too much down to our level. And if, on the other hand, the glance of the " beings of wisdom " was lost in a metaphysical meditation of unfathomable profundity, this detached superiority appeared to remove them far above all earth's vicissitudes (Fig. 22). The bodhisattvas of Hōryūji seem to stand half-way between these two philosophical attitudes. In spite of the " gentle strength of compassion " which is their whole *raison d'être,* they will not suffer themselves to be distracted from their transcendental reverie, though they still remain the incarnation of salvation and refuge (Fig. 19–21). These heroes of holiness, unearthly in their beauty beneath the huge aureole which surrounds their face with its glory and beneath their

[1] We may add the flying genii of Bāmiyān (Godard and Hackin: *Antiquités bouddhiques*, Pl. XVI–XVII), those of Qizil (see the photographs taken by Professor Pelliot reproduced in the same work, Pl. XLIV–XLVI), and those on the Korean frescoes of the sixth century (Eckardt: *History of Korean Art*, Fig. 217). See *Hōryūji Ōkagami, Supplement*, No. 4, Pl. 21; *Selected Relics . . . ,* VI, 10 (Angel, wall painting in the Hōkaiji, Hino, near Kyōto).

Figure 42

Heiji Monogatari. Roll in the Boston Museum.
— By courtesy of the Museum of Fine Arts, Boston

Figure 43

Grooms breaking in a horse. Beginning of the Kamakura period.
— Ulrich Odin collection. By courtesy of Messrs. Odin and Van Oest

Hindu tiara of chased gold, or flower-decked *mukuṭa,* still possess all the ineffable grace which clothed them on Indian soil. The Apollo-like nobility of their features and the tranquil suavity of their expression in no way diminish their quality of Olympian strength — as is also true of their counterparts at Ajaṇṭā. Like their common spiritual father, Śākyamuni, they are still " lions among men." Perhaps by accentuating the Aryan purity of their profiles Japan has even emphasized their voluptuous gravity, like that of charming princes. There is a triumphant elegance in their Indian pose with the sideward sway of the hips, as also in the play of contrast between the richness of their necklaces and bracelets and the lustreless quality of the flesh; while the nude shoulders, bust, and torso, which, though at times less slender, are even more meltingly soft than at Ajaṇṭā, are full of a virile sweetness.

Above all, in these beautiful bodies, at once haughty and tender, in these Olympian figures of an idealist religion, the pride of eternal youth is so deeply impregnated with intellectual gravity, so filled with a sense of the vanity of all things, so ripe with the experience of an ardent piety and mysticism, that at times a sort of weariness of life emanates from it. As at Ajaṇṭā, the meditative curve of the brows, traced like a bow across the whole forehead, is like a spreading of wings for metaphysical soarings. And, as at Ajaṇṭā again, we ask ourselves what inward mystery is concealed beneath these slightly drooping eyelids, from between which there none the less steals a glance of unfathomable mystery, or what word it is that trembles upon these lips which, in their consciousness of the vanity of all things, preserve a gentle, expectant, compassionate silence.

The gestures, above all, have a grace that thrills with mystical feeling and is almost haughty in its purity.[1] There is the gesture of the long, slender arm, with the delicate open hand on a level with the hip, holding a great flowering lotus-spray which springs up from it

[1] See *Hōryūji Ōkagami, Supplement,* I, Pl. 6, 11, 14.

in one long, spontaneous line (Fig. 16, 19). Or there is the finger-gesture of "reassurance," or "absence of fear," which in these great unearthly figures, worthy of Leonardo, is so intensely significant of salvation and repose (Fig. 16, 17). And, lastly, there are the gestures of the hands in prayer — not clasped, as in our Christian art,

FIGURE 44
Portrait of Yoritomo, by Takanobu (1141–1204), in the Jingoji.
— *Photo*, Shimbi Shoin

FIGURE 45
Portrait of Michizane, attributed to Tosa Tsunetaka (about 1240).
— *Ulrich Odin collection. By courtesy of Messrs. Odin and Van Oest. Photo, Laniepce*

or with palm resting against palm, as in the *añjali mudrā* (gesture of salutation), but simply crossing the tips of the fingers with infinite delicacy in this final pause (Fig. 20). Such are the typical gestures of the Hōryūji figures — gestures with a contemplative detachment and tenderness in which the whole spirit of the Mahāyānist age is expressed.

From the technical point of view, here again the secret of this art is perhaps to be sought in its perfect union between the constructive skill of the Gandhāra school and the spiritual qualities, the tenderness and mysticism, of the Gupta canon (cf. Fig. 20).

If the workmanship of the Hōryūji frescoes is Indian, that of the famous " portrait " of Prince Shōtoku-taishi and his two sons (Fig. 24) — apparently a work of the second half of the seventh century — is entirely Chinese — " a good example of the painting of the Six Dynasties," to quote Professor T. Naitō. It is interesting to compare this painting, too, with the Korean ones dating from the second half of the sixth century in the tomb of the " two pillars " (Ssang-yung-chung) near Phyŏng-an, mentioned in Volume III, page 273.[1] The fashions and costumes are different, but the technique is somewhat similar, notably in the treatment of the delicate, shining faces. There is, moreover, a tradition which attributes the portrait of Shōtoku-taishi to the Korean prince Asa. In reality all these works, whether Chino-Korean or Chino-Japanese, are connected with the ancient " civil " (or Confucian) school of Chinese painting, as to whose nature the roll of Ku K'ai-chih in the British Museum and a few fragments brought by the Pelliot mission from Tun-huang are among the few pieces of evidence (Vol. III, Fig. 215, 221).

THE HEIAN PERIOD

THE REIGN OF THE EMPEROR KAMMU (782–805) MARKS THE OPENing of a new era. In 794 this prince, who was one of the strong personalities of his dynasty, moved his residence from Nara to Kyōto, or rather Heian-kyō, as it was first called, which was to remain the imperial capital from 794 to 1868. The great period of Kyōto, where literature is concerned, is known as the Heian period (from about 794 to 1192). But from the point of view of the history of art, the

[1] Reproduced in Andreas Eckardt: *A History of Korean Art* (1929), p. 135.

earlier part of it is known as the Jogan period, lasting from 794 to 889.[1]

The transference of the capital to Kyōto, writes Mr. Anesaki Masaharu, was ordered by Kammu partly to escape from the supremacy which had been gained by the Buddhist clergy in the Nara

FIGURE 46
Noblemen at the theatre. Tosa school, about twelfth century.
— *Ulrich Odin collection. By courtesy of Messrs. Odin and Van Oest. Photo, Laniepce*

region. A first attempt at reform, aimed against this Church, which had already become over-tainted with worldliness, was instituted by Dengyō daishi (767–822). In 802, by order of the Emperor Kammu,

[1] From the purely political point of view, the Jogan period consists more particularly in the period 859–76, the years of Seiwa-tennō's reign.

Dengyō visited China, from whence he brought back the monist doctrine of the Tendai sect. The seat of this new sect, which gave a powerful impulse to Buddhist metaphysics, was the temple of Enryakuji, built by Dengyō in 788 on Mount Hieizan, to the north-east of Kyōto.

FIGURE 47
Amida, painting on silk in the Konkaikō-myōji, Kyōto (twelfth century).
— *Photo*, Shimbi Shoin

The importance of Dengyō's reform has been well brought out by Professor Anesaki. Rejecting the dogma professed by the ancient Church at Nara, which believed the possibility of Buddhahood to be reserved to a select body of saints, Dengyō discovered that the " Buddha nature " is inherent in all beings, and that all are destined for the perfect Illumination.[1]

FIGURE 48
Kannon, by the Shōgun Sanetomo (1204–19).
— *Ulrich Odin collection. By courtesy of Messrs. Odin and Van Oest*

In 804, following the example of Dengyō, his pupil Kōbō daishi, another great monk (744–835), went to China to study Buddhism,

[1] For Dengyō daishi as an artist see the wooden image of Ekādaśa mukha Avalokitēśvara attributed to this priest in the Kannondō Temple, Ōmi, reproduced in *Selected Relics* . . . , V, Fig. 7.

following in particular the mystical doctrines of the Shingon sect. In 816 Kōbō daishi established the seat of this new sect on Mount Kōyasan, where he founded the Kongōbuji temple.[1] The Shingon doctrines, even more than the Tendai, professed a mystical monism, which found its application in a sort of cosmic charity. In this system the Buddha when regarded as a metaphysical entity — *Mahā Vairocana,* the "Great Illuminator"; in Japanese, *Dainichi Nyorai*

FIGURE 49
Portrait of Ashikaga Yoshimasa, in the Ginkakuji, end of the fifteenth century.
— *Photo,* Shimbi Shoin

FIGURE 50
Monju (Mañjuśrī), by Chōdensu.
— *Odin collection. By courtesy of Messrs. Odin and Van Oest*

— was conceived, to quote Professor Anesaki, as "the all-comprehending soul and at the same time the all-creative force of the universe, all beings, whether divinities, angels, men, or beasts, being manifestations of his power and intentions.[2] Thus the body and life of the Great Illuminator may be discerned even in a grain of sand

[1] See *Art Treasures of the Kōyasan Temples* (Kokka Publishing Co., Tōkyō, 1908). For Kōbō daishi as an artist, see a kakemono in the Kyōwōgokoku Temple (Tōji), Kyōto, representing the bodhisattva Nāgārjuna and attributed to Kōbō daishi. Reproduced in *Selected Relics . . .* , XII, 4.

[2] See a wooden image of Mahā Vairocana in the Chūsonji Temple, Rikuchū, said to be by Unkei (twelfth century), in *Selected Relics . . .* , V, 9.

or a drop of water. His body, word, and actions make up the life of the universe, both as a whole and in every one of its parts."

Kōbō daishi's mystic poems enable us to form an estimate of this grandiose monism, in which, through Buddhism, the soul of Japan came into contact with the powerful pre-Buddhist systems of China and India:

> The lustral waters of the esoteric teachings have washed the dust,
> Now is the store of mystical words thrown open
> In which all hidden treasures come to light,
> In which all virtues and powers find concrete form.
> The Buddhas in the countless Buddhist kingdoms
> Are but the one Buddha in the depths of our souls;
> And the golden lotuses, as many as the drops of water in the ocean —
> These are our body.
> In every one of the sacred characters myriads of figures are contained.
> In every production of the brush, the chisel, or metal
> The vital force of the universe is made manifest,
> In which the real entities of the virtues are present in myriads;
> And by this way every man is called to the knowledge
> Of his own glorious personality even in his physical being.

It is impossible not to be struck by the analogies offered by such conceptions as these with those of Taoism in China, or of the Upanishads, the *Bhagavadgītā,* and the Vedānta in India. The ideal of Buddhism was shifting its focus. It was no longer the purely negative doctrine of renunciation, charity, and tenderness, but at the same time of disillusionment, of the earliest missionaries of the Hīnayāna, or "Lesser Vehicle." Beneath the externals of Buddhism it was developing into a monistic theology, by which the Absolute was restored to its position at the heart of things and beings: an ardently mystic theology, in the eyes of which the universe, illuminated by an esoteric doctrine accessible to all the faithful, became one vast symbol of the Divine.[1]

[1] See Anesaki Masaharu: *Buddhist Art in its Relation to Buddhist Ideals*, ch. ii.

This ideal was the same as that of Brahmanical India, of Śivaism and Krishnaism, a picture of which was drawn in Volume II of the present work. It is true that Japan did not obtain its knowledge of these doctrines, as such, directly and formally; but, just as it had rediscovered the Hellenic genius through the distant medium of Gandhārian art, transmitted through that of the Wei period, just as at Hōryūji it had rediscovered Ajaṇṭā through the medium of the art of Tun-huang, so now it was reinventing Hinduism through the agency of the Hindu elements which the Buddhism of the Mahāyāna unconsciously bore within it. Thus it will be no surprise to find the esoteric doctrines of the Tendai and Shingon sects transposing the values of Hinduism into those of Japanese Buddhism, especially when we consider that the " red sects " in Tibet were to produce exactly the same phenomenon (see below, chapter ii, page 266).

FIGURE 51
Kannon, formerly attributed to Chōdensu. — *Odin collection. By courtesy of Messrs. Odin and Van Oest. Photo, Laniepce*

One living confirmation of this statement is that, in the ninth and tenth centuries, Heian art rediscovered the principles of mediæval Hindu art. In this connexion nothing could be more typical than the well-known six-armed seated Kannon, a wooden statue more than a yard in height in the Kanshinji, Kawachi, dating from about 900 (Fig. 26), or, again, the standing Kannon " of the eleven heads," a slightly smaller wooden figure in the Hokkeji, Nara, also dating from the tenth century.[1] As Professor Elisséev has remarked, in such works as these sculpture is no longer treated " in terms of individuality," but from the point of view of its philosophico-religious significance. The multiplicity of arms in the former statue, or of heads in the latter, all of which possess a symbolism quite opposed to the Japanese instinct for moderation and pure anthropomorphism, illustrates the abrupt invasion of Hindu tendencies. But at this point it would be as well to consider the dates. As we have just seen, we have now arrived at the beginning of the tenth century or later. If these statues point to an Indian influence — as they obviously do — from what Indian school could this have come, if not from the very one which, not so long before, had produced in the south of India the sculptures in the caves of Ellora (the Kailāsa, dating from about 757 to 783) and Elephanta (dating from about 850 to 900),[2] as well as from the

FIGURE 52
Peach-tree in bloom, by Soga Jasoku. — *Odin collection. By courtesy of Messrs. Odin and Van Oest*

[1] See *Selected Relics . . .* , II, 3; and the remarkable study by Professor Yutaka Tasawa: "An Interpretation of the Sculpture in the Jogan Era," Pt. V, in *Kokka*, No. 435 (February 1927).

[2] See Vol. II, pp. 234–48.

north, where, between 750 and 1060, the metaphysical and plastic complications of the Pāla school, the precursors of all the tantrist versions of Hindu subjects which were to appear in Nepal and Tibet,[1]

FIGURE 53
Figure in meditation, gazing into space, Chinese landscape in the Konchiin, Kyōto, attributed to the Sung emperor Hui-tsung.
— *Photo*, Shimbi Shoin

FIGURE 54
Summer landscape, by Soga Jasoku.
— *Prince Tokugawa's collection*

were developing out of Gupta art? But if we examine into the characteristics of this Hinduistic or tantrist Buddhism, as opposed to the Indian art of Gupta Buddhism, we shall see that they consist in substituting for the human and anthropomorphic character of Gupta art

[1] See Vol. II, p. 273, and chapter ii of the present volume, p. 271.

FIGURE 55

Portrait of Lu Tung-pin, attributed to T'eng Ch'ang-yu, a Chinese painter of the ninth century.

— Formerly in the Goloubew collection. Photo, Goloubew

a cosmic conception of the divine which is sometimes transcendental and sometimes monstrous. Going beyond the human form, sculpture becomes depersonalized, or impersonalized, in order to attain to the Absolute in its entirety, in accordance with an incommensurable ideal. God is no longer an individual, but the realization of a metaphysical abstraction. This being so, it matters little that in the length of the right arm, descending below the knee, the eleven-headed Kannon in the Hokkeji shows an evident lack of proportion which could not have failed to shock the old masters of Nara. In this connexion we should think, not of Nara, the Oriental counterpart of Athens, but of the Pāla, Nepalese, and Tibetan Avalokiteśvaras which we shall soon be considering.[1] And, similarly, if the six-armed Kannon of the Kanshinji were to seek its kin, it might be referred to some cosmic vision such as the Śiva of Ellora or of Elephanta. See, for instance, Volume II, Fig. 81 and 83 (the central head of the Maheśamūrti), with which may be compared Fig. 26.

FIGURE 56

The *arhat* (Buddhist saint) Vanavāsi in a state of ecstasy, attributed to the Chinese painter Mu Ch'i (about 1250). — *Iwasaki collection. Photo,* Shimbi Shoin

The influences coming from " Chinese China " were not calculated to counterbalance those transmitted by an " Indianized China."

[1] See below, chapter ii, p. 267.

FIGURE 57

Śākyamuni as an ascetic, painting attributed to the Chinese artist Liang Ch'ai (thirteenth century). — *By courtesy of the* Shimbi Shoin

FIGURE 58

Saigyō Hōshi, by Soga Jasoku. — *Odin collection. By courtesy of Messrs. Odin and Van Oest*

In China, indeed, we have seen in what lifeless conventions the sculpture of the late T'ang, Five Dynasties, and Sung periods became immobilized. The complete triumph of a forcefully plastic convention and of an ostentatious realism made the muscles heavy, set, and clogged, and swamped all individual expression. This heaviness, it is true, is infinitely less noticeable in Heian than in Sung sculpture, for nothing could have been more repugnant to the precision, nervous vigour, and congenitally individualistic temperament of the Japanese artist. Hence great charm and suavity are still present in the two Kannons mentioned above, and still more so in another tenth-century painted wooden Kannon with six arms, just under a yard in height, seated in a pose of meditation, in the Murōji, Yamato.[1] Again, there is great force of personality in the seated wooden portrait of the priest Chishō daishi in the Onjōji, Ōtsu, in which the force of cosmic meditation is expressed and sustained by the full-blooded physical temperament.[2] It is none the less true that in these figures we are already some way from the anthropomorphism, full of moderation and balance, in which the spirit of Japan had proved itself the Oriental counterpart of the Greek spirit since its very earliest productions.

On the other hand, the statuary of the Heian period is of capital importance in the history of Far Eastern thought. Even if we were unaware of the mighty speculations of the Tendai and Shingon sects, this art alone would suffice to show us that Japan was now for the first time grappling with the problems of metaphysics.[3]

In many instances the painting reveals the same tendencies, showing us visions of remarkable power, which sometimes almost cause us a certain metaphysical malaise — as, for instance, the Fudō in colour on silk, about five feet five inches in height, in the Manshuin (or Manjuin), Kyōto, or the red Fudō of Kōyasan.[4] But in these

[1] Otto Kümmel: *L'Art de l'Extrême-Orient*, Pl. 28.

[2] Curt Gläser, op. cit., Pl. 142.

[3] See Professor Yutaka Tasawa: "An Interpretation of the Sculpture in the Jogan Era," Pt. III, *Kokka*, No. 425 (April 1926), and Pt. IV, *Kokka*, No. 432 (November 1926).

[4] Otto Kümmel: *L'Art de l'Extrême-Orient*, Pl. 29–31.

paintings there is no further cause for surprise, or, rather, we find in them the avowal of those tendencies of which we already had an inkling; for Fudō is the Japanese form of the god Śiva. Thus in taking him as one of the manifestations of the supreme Buddha Vairocana, the Shingon system deliberately associated Śivaism with its Buddhism; or, rather, in this system Buddhism had by that time be-

FIGURE 59
Bodhidharma, by Soga Jasoku, in the Jōtoku-in, Kyōto.

FIGURE 60
Bodhidharma, by Soga Jasoku. — *Odin collection. By courtesy of Messrs. Odin and Van Oest*

come no more than a vehicle for the whole spirit which underlay the religious tenets of India. Indeed, as we showed above, Śiva Bhairava, the god of terror, appearing amid flames among the peaks of the Kailās, is, as it were, the spirit of Ellora and Elephanta come to haunt the cloister of Kōyasan.[1] In order to obtain a better understand-

[1] Cf. Vol. II, pp. 188–9, 195–202. See *Art Treasures of the Kōyasan Temples* (Kokka Publishing Co., 1908), Pl. 18, 20, 40; *Kokka*, No. 240 (May 1910), Pl. I, p. 335 (Fudō of the Onjōji Temple, Yamashiro, eleventh century).

ing of the works of this school it should, moreover, be remembered that the Chinese Buddhist painting of the Six Dynasties and the first half of the T'ang period possessed "a strong character of religious magic."[1] The state of mind which during that very age was giving rise to the tantrist cults of Pāla Bengal, Nepal, and Tibet was generally prevalent throughout the Buddhist world of the day, as is further shown by the demon scenes of Tun-huang in Fig. 27.[2]

FIGURE 61
Tokusan, by Soga Jasoku, in the Daitokuji, Kyōto.

Such notions as these were leading Japanese painting and sculpture towards modes of expression which were almost diametrically opposed to the natural genius of the race: towards a seeking after "monumental" effects and a contempt for plastic methods as tending to set limits to the personality of the god, whereas the object was, on the contrary, to produce an impression of impersonal and unlimited force; towards rich colours chosen, not for their harmonious æsthetic effect, but, as in Tibet in later days, for their religious symbolism or some similar reason. All these characteristics, which have been so well analysed by Professor Elisséev, cause Heian art to stand apart, outside the general evolution of Japan.[3]

[1] Professor Pelliot's lecture of June 16, 1927, on Chinese Art, at the École des Hautes-Études Chinoises.

[2] See *Art Treasures of the Kōyasan Temples*, Pl. 46, 61, 69, 73.

[3] We may add that during the Heian period Japanese art also underwent the influence of Sāsānid Persia, which came by way of Khotan and Kuchā and can be noticed especially in the representations of certain Buddhist divinities of warlike aspect, such as Bishamon (Vaiśravaṇa). Cf. Yeiichi Matsumoto: "The Historical Origin of Tobatsu Bishamonten," *Kokka*, No. 471 (February 1930).

FIGURE 62
Portrait of the priest Jichin, fifteenth century.
— *Louvre, Charles Gillot donation. Photo, Giraudon*

There are many famous names among the Heian painters, especially that of Kudara Kawanari, who died in 853, and Kose Kanaoka, who flourished during the reign of the Emperor Uda (889–97). The name of Kanaoka has been connected with a great number of works, but none of them can be ascribed to him with any certainty, not even the portrait of Shōtoku-taishi as a child, in the Ninnaji, Kyōto (Fig. 28), though, whoever the artist may have been, this is an admirable work, with its calm, broad simplicity, purity of line, majesty and sweetness of expression, not to speak of the powerful personality of which it conveys an impression, or the magic of its sombre greens and faded pinks, which carry us far away from the tantrist ideal of the age of Kōbō daishi.[1] The same remarks — though for other reasons — apply to the Jizō Bosatsu in the Louvre, formerly attributed to Kanaoka (Fig. 29): a work in this style (which has, moreover, its counterpart in the Berlin Museum) [2] must surely be assigned to about the thirteenth century.[3] It has to be admitted that it is as difficult to assign a due place to the great name of Kanaoka in the development of the national canon of art — in so far, at least, as we are able to reconstitute it — as it is to do the same thing for the great name of Wu Tao-tzŭ in relation to Chinese art. On the other hand, tradition has handed down a number of legends about Kanaoka. One of these relates how a horse which he had painted in the Ninnaji Temple, Kyōto — a Shingon temple, as it happens — used to escape from the picture every night and scour the neighbourhood, a miracle which was repeated until somebody scratched out the eyes of the painting. Such a legend is quite in conformity with the old Chinese belief, adopted by Buddhism, that art confers a sort of life upon the painted figures. This magic conception of the work of art is, moreover, as old as art itself, and no doubt explains why it appeared at

[1] *Selected Relics . . .*, II, 9.

[2] Otto Kümmel: *L'Art de l'Extrême-Orient*, Fig. 38.

[3] See also the waterfall of Nachi, a kakemono in the Tetsuma Akaboshi collection, said to be by Kose Kanaoka, in *Selected Relics . . .*, XVII, 7.

all. In the archaic age of China, for example, the representation of a creature was considered to have taken shape so soon as the pupils of the eyes were painted in; and this, according to Professor Pelliot, explains the custom of the dot, standing for the eye, on the funeral tablets representing the dead man. But it is particularly interesting in this connexion to see these ancient animistic beliefs obtaining the support of the esoteric Buddhism of the Tendai and Shingon sects.[1]

FIGURE 63
Return of the junks on Lake Tung-t'ing, makimono attributed to the Chinese painter Mu Ch'i (*c.* 1250?).
— *Matsudaira collection, Tōkyō. Photo,* Shimbi Shoin

The literature of the Heian period (794–1192), even more than that of Nara, was a society and court literature. Feminine influence predominates in it. "It abounds," says Aston, "in descriptions of scenes of domestic and court life, and of amours and sentimental or romantic incidents." The most celebrated work of this period is the anthology known as the *Kokinshū,* or "poems ancient and modern,"

[1] Among the painters of this period we may also mention Eri Sōzu, who died in 936, a priest of the Tōji Temple, Kyōto, to whom is attributed in particular the celebrated kakemono representing Yama-deva, preserved in that temple (the Kanchi-in). Cf. *Selected Relics . . . ,* XII, 6. The middle of the Heian period also saw the appearance of the school known as the *Yamato-e,* which will be discussed in more detail in connexion with the Fujiwara period. We need only mention here the famous scroll illustrating the *Genji Monogatari* (the romance of Prince Genji), and some other works of a tranquil character belonging to the Heian period. We may also point out that the end of the same period saw the appearance of another feature of *Yamato-e* pictures — they began, that is, to assume a "character of motion and briskness." See the scroll pictures of the Shinki-zan Temple, on the foundation of the temple, and Professor Ozaki Natsuhiko in *Kokka,* No. 442 (September 1927).

collected between 905 and 922. The delicacy and even preciosity of most of the pieces contained in it make it an excellent picture of this period of refinement, during which the moral sensibility of Buddhism became so happily fused with the deep feeling of the Japanese people for nature: "Shall we call that only a dream which we see while asleep? This vain world itself I cannot regard as a reality." Or: "The hue of the flowers mingles with the snow, so that it cannot be seen; but their presence may be known were it only by the perfume." Or, again: "This night of spring, of formless gloom, the colour of the plum-flowers cannot, indeed, be seen; but how can their perfume be hidden?" [1] We may note the nature of this poetry. The *naga-uta,* or "long poems," of the Nara period are now replaced by *tanka,* or "short poems," confined to thirty-one syllables. From the point of view of subject-matter, too, they tend to enshrine an emotion, delicate or profound, a sensation, powerful or fleeting, within the narrow limits of the brief avowal of a personal experience or of a rapidly sketched miniature. It is curious to compare these short poems, so striking in their briefness and concentration, with the T'ang poetry of China and its full-bodied, orchestral harmonies. The preface of the *Kokinshū,* written by Ki no Tsurayuki, who died in 946, shows us how, as early as this period, Japanese taste and poetic sentiment had already found their classic perfection.

This sentiment is characterized by a sense of moderation which shrinks from everything overstepping the limits of humanity, and is in equal contrast with Indian rhapsodizing and with the impassioned exaltation of the Chinese soul. We shall find the same fellow-feeling for humanity, the same sense of moderation and craving for finish, in the Japanese art of the Heian period — as, indeed, in the whole æsthetic ideal of the country in later days. The same innate classicism inspires the novels of the period; for example, the *Ise Monogatari,* dating from the beginning of the tenth century, and the *Genji*

[1] W. G. Aston: *Japanese Literature,* pp. 60, 61.

Monogatari, composed about the year 1000 by Murasaki Shikibu, one of the court ladies, who relates in a style at once high-bred and full of melancholy, and with infinite delicacy of feeling, the love-

FIGURE 63 b
Bamboos on the shore. Drawing in wash, probably of the Yüan period.
— *Musée Guimet*

adventures of a charming prince, Genji, the son of the Emperor by a favourite.[1] We may also mention the *Pillow-sketches* (*Makura no sōshi*), from the pen of Sei Shōnagon, another lady of the court and

[1] Translated by Arthur Waley, *The Tale of Genji* (London, 1925).

Japanese poetess, who lived about the year 1000. In these two works we are initiated into the pastimes of one of the most refined societies which the world has ever known: scenes of court life, in a setting of marvellous costumes and noble attitudes; subtle shades of feeling touched in with an exquisite delicacy; occasional verses or love-poems; moral reflections marked by a fine understanding of psychology and often by a humour very similar to our own; and, as a background to these scenes of social life, fresh glimpses of nature in Japan: " In spring, I love to watch the dawn grow gradually whiter and whiter, till a faint rosy tinge crowns the mountain's crest, while slender streaks of purple cloud extend themselves above. In summer, I love the night, not only when the moon is shining, but the dark too, when the fireflies cross each other's paths in their flight, or when the rain is falling. In autumn, it is the beauty of the evening which most deeply moves me, as I watch the crows seeking their roosting-place in twos and threes and fours, while the setting sun sends forth his beams gorgeously as he draws near the mountain's rim. Still more is it delightful to see the lines of wild geese pass, looking exceeding small in the distance. And when the sun has quite gone down, how moving it is to hear the chirruping of insects or the sighing of the wind! "[1]

The whole fragrance of the Heian period is revived by the tones of these poetesses of the year 1000, as Sei Shōnagon herself expresses it in one of her comparisons: " The kimonos are perfumed and laid away in cupboards, and time goes by. The day before yesterday, yesterday, today . . . days . . . months . . . they are utterly forgotten. One day the whim seizes one to take out once more the forgotten garment, all steeped in the perfume of the past, which rises about one and diffuses itself through the air. . . . The fragrance of the past is something far more delicious and subtle than the perfume of the present."[2] Or let us listen to the tones of the night-piece composed by

[1] W. G. Aston: *Japanese Literature*, p. 106.

[2] The *Pillow-book* of Sei Shōnagon has been translated by Arthur Waley (London, 1928). See also Nobuko Kobayashi: *Sketch-book of the Lady Sei Shonagon* (London, 1930).

the tender Murasaki Shikibu in the imperial palace, in her journal, written between 1007 and 1010: [1] "As the autumn season draws nigh, the tops of the trees beside the pool, and the bushes on the banks of the stream, are tinged with varying tones whose hues grow deeper in the mellow sunset light. All through the night the murmur of the

FIGURE 64
Sesshū. Spring landscape.
— *Kuroda collection, Tōkyō. Photo,* Shimbi Shoin

FIGURE 65
Sesshū. Summer.
— *Kuroda collection. Photo,* Shimbi Shoin

waters mingles with the ceaseless recitation of the Buddhist *sūtras,* which appeal more and more deeply to the heart as the breezes freshen. The ladies in waiting upon the Empress chatter idly. It is still the middle of the night. The moon pales and darkness lurks beneath

[1] See "The Diary of Murasaki Shikibu," coloured rolls said to be by Fujiwara Nobuzane (who died in 1206), now in the Hachisuka collection. *Selected Relics . . .*, IV, 17; "The Diary of Murasaki Shikibu," *Kokka,* XX, 239 (April 1910); *Year-book of Japanese Art, 1929–1930,* Pl. LXVI.

the stars. We hear an officer of the court cry: 'Open the outer gates of the Empress's apartments; the maids of honour are not yet here; let the secretaries come forward!' While this order rings out, the three-o'clock bell begins to toll, sending a vibration through the air. Prayers begin at once at the five altars. The voices of the priests are solemn indeed as they recite in a very loud voice, vying with one another from near and far. The abbot of the temple of Kannon-yin, accompanied by twenty priests, comes from the east of the palace to pray. Holy are their footsteps, as they echo along the gallery. I follow them with my eyes, as their sacred forms, clad in spotless white robes, cross the majestic Chinese bridge and proceed along the path."[1] But perhaps Sei Shōnagon, wittier, less sentimental in her melancholy, and more of a woman of the world than Murasaki Shikibu, paints an even better picture of the life of the great nobles, writers, and lovely women who formed the court of Kyōto at the beginning of the eleventh century.

FIGURE 66
Sesshū. Landscape.
— *Tanaka collection, Tōkyō.*
Photo, Shimbi Shoin

Love-poems, Buddhist piety, and the caprices of fashion were the chief interests of this select society, which gave Japanese manners their inimitable politeness. Witness this page from Sei Shōnagon: "On the sliding doors of the northern front of the Mikado's private apartments there are painted fearful pictures of creatures that live in the wild ocean, some with long arms, others with long legs. . . . One day towards noon, while we were laughing and talking about them, say-

[1] Cf. Shepley Omori and Kochi Doi: *The Diaries of Court Ladies of Old Japan* (New York and London, 1920), with introduction by Amy Lowell.

FIGURE 67
Sesshū. Landscape.
— *Odin collection. By courtesy of Messrs. Odin and Van Oest. Photo, Laniepce*

ing what hideous things they are, and were engaged in setting great flower-pots of green porcelain by the balustrade of the verandah, and filling them with an abundance of the most delightful cherry branches five feet long, so that the blossoms overflowed to the foot of the railing, his Excellency the Dainagon [the Empress's brother] approached. He had on a cherry-coloured tunic, enough worn to have lost its stiffness, and dark purple trousers. His white underclothing, showing at the neck, displayed a gay pattern of a deep crimson hue. As the Mikado was then with the Empress, he seated himself on the narrow platform before the door and made some report to him on official matters. The waiting-women, with their cherry-coloured sleeveless jackets hanging down loosely by their sides, some dressed in *wistaria* [purple], some in *kerria* [yellow], and all manner of lovely colours, showed out from the screen of the small hatch. Just then dinner was served in the Imperial apartments. We could hear the trampling of the attendants' feet, and the cry 'Less noise' from one of the chamberlains. The serene aspect of the weather was exceedingly agreeable. When the last dishes had been served . . . the Mikado went away by the middle door, attended by his Excellency the Dainagon, who subsequently returned to his former place beside the flowers. The Empress then pushed aside the curtain, and came forward as far as the threshold to greet him. He remarked on the beauty of the surroundings and the good deportment of the servants, and ended by quoting the line of poetry which says —

> 'The days and months roll on,
> But the Mount of Mimoro remains for ever.'

I was deeply impressed, and wished in my heart that so it might indeed continue for a thousand years."[1]

While this high civilization was flourishing at the court of Kyōto, in the *Gosho*, or imperial palace built by Kammu in 794, the influence of the *kampaku*, or mayors of the palace of the Fujiwara family,

[1] Translated by W. G. Aston, op. cit., pp. 109–10.

was beginning to relegate the imperial dynasty to merely honorary functions. The Emperor Uda (889–97), aided by his counsellor Sugawara Michizane (cf. Fig. 45), tried to make a stand against this. His son Daigo (898–930) was weak enough to sacrifice Michizane, and so, in spite of the literary brilliance of these years, known as the Engi period (901–22), and the splendour of the court, the reign of Daigo witnessed the gradual spread of disorder in the

FIGURE 68
Landscape, by Sesshū.
— *Photo*, Shimbi Shoin

country. The provincial governors began to give up residing in the territories entrusted to them and came to live at court, where they, together with the officials of the central administration, formed the civil nobility known as the *Kuge*. The families of the military class began to substitute their own authority for that of the *Kuge* nobles in the provinces, and thus a process of feudalization gradually went on, analogous to that which marked the opening of the Middle Ages in western Europe. A split was bound to take place soon between this territorial nobility, which had now come to consist of the hereditary owners of the soil and of armed power, while remaining profoundly national and warlike, and the little civil society, with its Chino-Indian culture and ineffable refinement, which thronged about the *Gosho.*

THE FUJIWARA PERIOD (889–1192)[1]

THE ELEGANT SOCIETY, WITH A PASSION FOR CONFUCIAN CEREMONIAL and Buddhist gentleness, which gathered at the *Gosho* and in the monasteries of Kyōto, could not stand out indefinitely against the warlike temperament of the race. It was too fine a flower, blooming prematurely under foreign influences, and soon found itself overgrown, though not yet smothered, by the rank weeds of primitive passion. It still survived, however, with diminished vigour and within a restricted territory — the Gokinai, or region of Kyōto — while the rest of Japan was entering upon a sort of mediæval feudal stage which, like that of western Europe, was an age of brutality and violence, but at the same time of heroism and chivalry.

As early as the eleventh century the *kampaku,* or mayors of the palace belonging to the Fujiwara family, who wielded power in the name of the dilettante emperors, found themselves overwhelmed by the growth of feudalism. The great noble houses broke up the fine Chino-Indian structure by which the Nara emperors and the Fujiwaras of Kyōto had replaced the rule of the clans. The unitary empire subsisted in theory, but the sovereignty of the emperor became converted into a mere suzerainty. Thus the administrative and centralized régime of the eighth century gave place to a military society, based upon hereditary office, the grant of fiefs to the warriors, and the splitting up of the territorial sovereignty. Each of the *myōdens* or *daimyōs* — that is, the great barons — considered himself absolute master in his own domains. In theory they all recognized the Kyōto

[1] The Fujiwara period is generally divided into two parts, especially where the history of art is concerned: the first part, 889–1069, and the second part, 1069–1192. For all these divisions of the history of art we follow the table indicated by Professor Seiichi Taki at the end of the *Year-book of Japanese Art, 1929–1930*, p. 173.

emperor as supreme pontiff and temporal suzerain, but as a matter of fact, from behind the walls of their *shiros,* they defied alike the fulminations of the emperor and the attacks of their peers.

The *shiros,* or fortresses, were powerful, commanding masses, built of cyclopean blocks fitted together without mortar, and keeping

FIGURE 69
Landscape, by Sesshū.
— *Daté collection, Tōkyō. Photo,* Shimbi Shoin

FIGURE 70
Landscape, by Sōami.
— *Abé collection. Photo,* Shimbi Shoin

watch far and wide over the plain. Before their walls lay a whole system of moats and water-channels intended to protect the owner of the castle against the surprises of feudal war.[1] The great lord's men-

[1] See Shin Ōrui: "Some Artistic Aspects of Japanese Castles," in *Kokka,* No. 236 (January 1910), p. 205.

at-arms, or *samurai,* formed a regular chivalry hereditarily devoted to his service.[1] The law of the samurai was the *bushidō,* or code of chivalrous honour, according to which a desperate bravery, an abso-

FIGURE 71
Landscape, by Sōami, in the Daitokuji, Tōkyō.
— *Photo,* Shimbi Shoin

[1] For the equestrian sports of this Japanese chivalry see the "Picture of the Inu-ō-mono in the possession of the Imperial Household," by Mugaishi, in *Kokka,* No. 436 (March 1927). The Inu-ō-mono was a ceremonial sport in which the samurai, riding on galloping horses, shot with bows and arrows at a dog in rapid flight along the racecourse in the enclosure.

FIGURE 72
Landscape, by Sōami.
— *Abé collection. Photo,* Shimbi Shoin

lute contempt for suffering and danger, and an unshakable loyalty to the family of his lord were the most ordinary virtues of the samurai. In the observance of his oath he was bound to defend the honour of the clan to his last breath, and to wipe out in blood any insult to the arms of the house he served. Rather than submit to dishonour, he was bound to have recourse to the heroic form of suicide known as *hara-kiri*. The *bushidō*, which was chivalrous honour raised to a religion,

FIGURE 73
Lao-tzŭ, Confucius, and Śākyamuni, by Kanō Masanobu.
— *Henri Rivière collection*

lent the manners of mediæval Japan a character of nobility and courtesy which recalls the mediæval European romances of chivalry.

The samurai resembled the Western knight physically as well as morally. He wore a helmet of *cuir bouilli*, surmounted by a crest and warlike horns, a tunic of the same, protected by plates of steel, a corselet, shoulder-plates, arm-guards, thigh-pieces, greaves, and gauntlets of metal. His offensive weapons consisted of immense bows, which he used with amazing skill, a two-edged sword, a sabre, either straight or sickle-shaped, an ax, and a halberd. Between the horns of the helmet, above the visor, he wore the *mon*, or badge of the clan.

FIGURE 74
Landscape by Kanō Motonobu. Reiun-in Temple, Myōshin-ji, Kyōto.
— *Photo*, Shimbi Shoin

Under the feudal régime, indeed, heraldic art developed considerably, though it was now based upon floral or geometrical motives rather than upon animal totems. The most famous Japanese coats of arms known to history were the paulownia-blossom and the sixteen-

FIGURE 75
Landscape by Kanō Motonobu. Reiun-in, Kyōto.
— *Photo*, Shimbi Shoin

petalled chrysanthemum belonging to the imperial family, the spray of wistaria for the Fujiwara family, the butterfly with outspread wings for the Taira family, the three gentian-flowers above five bamboo-leaves for the Minamoto family, the three triangles for the

FIGURE 76
Snow-storm, by Kanō Motonobu. Tokaian, Kyōto.
— *Photo*, Shimbi Shoin

Hōjō family, the paulownia for the Ashikaga family, the three asarum-leaves in a roundel for the Tokugawa family, etc. The standards of the great seigniorial houses, adorned with the arms of the clan, guided the samurai in the midst of the mêlée, while the generals had as the emblem of their command an iron fan, which they held in one hand while they wielded the sword with the other.

Even the Buddhist Church found itself drawn into the fray. In defiance of all the *sūtras,* the monks donned helmets and threw themselves into the struggles between the clans, waging war in the inter-

FIGURE 77
Landscape, by Motonobu.
— *Ulrich Odin collection. By courtesy of Messrs. Odin and Van Oest*

vals of preaching. At last these ancestors of Friar John began to scandalize the devout. The monks of Enryakuji, belonging to the Tendai sect, which had its seat on the heights of Hieizan, and those of the Kōfukuji, at Nara, kept up considerable armies, which became the terror of Kyōto. It is one of Japan's not least original feats to have given the world a Buddhism of the cloak and sword in the shape of these surprising prelates. As a matter of fact, the whole of Japan, from the princes of the blood down to the lowest of the *rōnin,* or robber knights, from the secular barons to the abbots of the great monasteries, now knew but one religion — the *bushidō*, or code of knightly honour.

The whole of the Japanese Middle Ages, from the eleventh to the twelfth centuries, was filled by great feudal wars, the incidents of which remind us in every feature of the similar struggles in western Europe. The first of these, out of which sprang all the rest, was that between the Taira and the Minamoto families.

The Tairas and Minamotos were two great apanaged houses founded by younger sons of the imperial house in the ninth century,

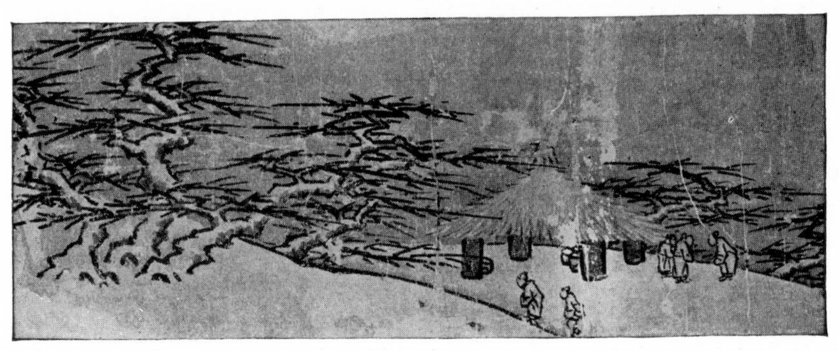

FIGURE 78
Among the pine-trees, landscape attributed to Kanō Motonobu.
— *Ulrich Odin collection. By courtesy of Messrs. Odin and Van Oest*

and both were desperate fire-eaters. While the emperors, the heads of the elder branch, were devoting all their activity to improvising poems or choosing schemes of decoration, their cousins of the collateral branches seemed to have inherited all the energy of the race. Always on horseback and sheathed in steel, they were impatient of the civil government — the Chinese bureaucracy of the Fujiwara mayors of the palace — and even less ready to tolerate the pretensions of the rival clan.

As early as 939 Taira Masakado broke into revolt in the Kantō. He was defeated and put to death, but his example was to be followed by all the ambitious members of both families, especially in the choice of the Kantō — that is, the region round what is now Tōkyō — as the centre of their operations. There was a solid body of knightly families in that part of the country, whom it was easy to stir up with the object of conquering the rich imperial provinces of the Gokinai — that is, the region of Kyōto — and whom both the Taira and Minamoto clans tried to win over to their cause. There are, moreover, certain figures in this epic age who are still surrounded by a veil of legend, such as Minamoto Yorimitsu (944–1021), who by his fabulous exploits cleared the outlying quarters of Kyōto of the brigands by whom they were infested. Equally famous in story and legend is Yorimitsu's grand-nephew Minamoto Yoshiie (1041–1108), who was, like him, a paladin with a love of redressing injustices.

The duel between the Taira and Minamoto clans entered upon its decisive phase with Taira Kiyomori (1118–81) and took the form of the two wars known as that of Hōgen, in 1156, and that of Heiji, in 1159, in the second of which Kiyomori's great rival, Minamoto Yoshitomo, was defeated and slain, Kiyomori remaining master of Kyōto, where he acted as lawgiver. Indefatigable as a soldier, and a powerful leader of men, he was implacable and cruel in his policy, and his proscriptions recall those of Sulla. For more than twenty years (1159–81) the country was crushed beneath an iron tyranny, and any attempt at revolt was at once wiped out in blood.[1] Kiyomori did not spare even the monasteries that opposed him, but caused them to be burnt by his bands. Nor did he show the conventional respect for the person of the emperors affected even by the lowest of the troops, but was seen not only eclipsing them by his luxury, but deposing and imprisoning them, or forcing his daughters upon them as wives, till in the end he succeeded in placing his own grandson upon the throne. But it was these very excesses which, for all his genius, prevented his work from having lasting effects and made it possible

[1] See S. Goto and M. Prunier: *Episodes of the Heiji Monogatari* (1930).

FIGURE 79
Screen of the Portuguese, Kanō school.
— *Musée Guimet*

FIGURE 80
Japanese Buddha, sixteenth–seventeenth century.
— *Musée Guimet. Photo, Pivot*

for fortune suddenly to take a turn favourable to the Minamotos.

In the midst of his proscriptions the dictator had committed the strange imprudence of sparing the sons of Minamoto Yoshitomo, Yoritomo and Yoshitsune, together with their cousin Yoshitaka.[1] Arrived at man's estate, these young men made their escape, accompanied by a series of romantic adventures, from the monastery where they had been imprisoned. Kiyomori died of rage in 1181 on hearing of their initial successes. Once he was gone, the three Minamotos, who had gathered about them the forces of the Kantō, seized Kyōto in 1183, and the Tairas fled towards the south-west. Two furious engagements, one in 1184 at Ichinotani, in Settsu, and the other in 1185 at Dan-no-ura, in Nagato, ended in decisive victories for the Minamotos, as a result of which the Taira party, and the whole clan, were annihilated. Yoritomo took a savage revenge upon them, by turning the laws made by Kiyomori against the dictator's own kin and systematically exterminating the population of the whole region.

The triumph of the Minamoto and the extermination of the Taira clans marked the triumph of the north over the south.

[1] See the splendid equestrian portrait of Yoshitsune by Itcho Hanabusa in the Iwasaki collection, in *Selected Relics* . . . , XIII, 35.

The warriors of the Kantō had defeated the men of the Gokinai and Kyūshū, and for seven centuries the Kantō was to preserve the hegemony thus won.

FIGURE 81
Stag belling at the moon. Gold lacquer, fifteenth–sixteenth century.
— Henri Vever collection. Photo, Laniepce

Yoritomo, the elder of the Minamoto brothers, had directed the events which ended in the triumph of his party with consummate skill. More adroit in handling men than in strategy, he had left the command of the troops to his younger brother, Yoshitsune. But now that success was in his grasp, Yoritomo got rid of his brother, whom he forced to commit suicide in 1189, when he was left as sole master of Japan.

These events marked the end of the Fujiwara period.

During this age of iron the soul of Japan had sought consolation in Buddhism, the esoteric and already somewhat Tibetanized Tendai and Shingon doctrines having been succeeded by quite a new form of them, almost amounting to a new religion: Amidism, or the cult of Amida.[1]

Amitābha, the "Infinite Light" — in Japanese, Amida (Fig. 33, 47, etc.) — is a bodhisattva of the Mahāyāna form of Buddhism who did not begin to play a prominent part until the earliest centuries of our era, in the Indo-Scythian or Kushān Empire, lying on the borders of India, Iran, and central Asia.[2] It is possible, indeed, that this divinity was of Iranian origin and should be regarded as the Buddhist version of some spirit of light belonging to the Persian pantheon.[3] It was, in fact, a Parthian prince, known in Chinese as Ngan Shih-kao, who introduced Amidism into China between 148 and 170 of our era. He was the first to preach in Farthest Asia the creed of a merciful bodhisattva reigning over a wondrous paradise, the Land of the West, or Blessed Land (*Sukhāvatī;* in Japanese, *Jōdo*), an abode of beauty and virtue in which pure souls were to be born again at the feet of Amida.[4] But though Amidism had spread through China

[1] See the very important article: "Amida" in *Hōbōgirin, an Encyclopædic Dictionary of Buddhism,* published under the editorship of Sylvain Lévi and J. Takakusu, Pt. I (Tōkyō, 1929), I. p. 24; Hans Haas: *Amida Buddha, unsere Zuflucht* (Leipzig, 1910); D. T. Suzuki: *The Eastern Buddhist,* No. III, 2.

[2] See Vol. II, chapter i, p. 81.

[3] While Amitābha made the conquest of China and Japan, another Iranian divinity, Mithras, almost anticipated Christianity in its conquest of the Roman Empire, in which case Christendom would have been a "Mithradom" instead.

[4] See Vol. II, chapter i, p. 81.

Figure 82
Young nobleman on prancing horse. Tosa school, fifteenth–sixteenth century.
— *Henri Vever collection. Photo, Laniepce*

as early as the second century of our era, it was not till rather late that it developed to any great extent. In the early Middle Ages, at the opening of the T'ang period, it was Maitrēya, the Buddhist Messiah,[1] whose name the seventh-century pilgrim Hsuan-tsang invoked and in whose paradise he hoped to be born again. A little later, in

FIGURE 83
Fighting horseman, attributed to Tosa Mitsuyoshi.
— *Louvre. Photo, Giraudon*

the ninth and tenth centuries, the paintings at Tun-huang show another bodhisattva playing a leading part — the Indian Avalokitēśvara, who became the Chinese Kuan-yin and the Japanese Kannon; while the art of the Nara and Heian schools, inspired by that of the

[1] In Chinese, Mi-lo Fu; in Japanese, Miroku. Cf. Fig. 7 and 31.

T'ang dynasty, also reveals the popularity of the same divinity (Fig. 5, 48, etc.). In fact, the importance of Amitābha did not begin to assert itself in China till the end of the seventh century and did not triumph till the second part of the T'ang period. It was not till then,

FIGURE 84
Horseman and footman in single combat, attributed to Tosa Mitsuyoshi.
— *Louvre. Photo, Giraudon*

and under the Five Dynasties and the Sung, that the theory of the paradise of Amitābha became thoroughly popular.

This success, as Professor Pelliot has pointed out, has a logical explanation. Emotional exigencies prevented some of the faithful from contenting themselves with Nirvāṇa and caused them to seek personal consolation in an after-life of bliss; they therefore imagined the existence of paradises, the rule over which was first assigned to Maitrēya, the Buddhist Messiah; [1] but it was no doubt seen that there was some incompatibility between his Messianic functions and this celestial role. On the other hand, Amitābha was able to devote himself entirely to the vocation of presiding over paradise. Thus he became the centre of a new cult, which became all the more widely spread because it was better adapted to the requirements of Chino-Japanese pietism. In the popular distress which accompanied the great civil wars of the Fujiwara period all tender souls and simple hearts turned towards this divine saviour, who required nothing but a little confidence and love to induce him to pour forth his grace.

There could, indeed, be no more consoling doctrine. Though Amidism had as its starting-point the same mystical monism as had the Tendai and Shingon systems, it based upon it, not, this time, an esoteric doctrine expressed in terms of energy and with a taint of magic, but a delightfully soothing pietism, of a quietistic tinge, resting upon a foundation of faith — a religion instinct with tenderness, according to which all beings form part of the *dharmakāya* or mystical body of Amida Buddha, who regards all living creatures as parcels of his own nature, and loves them as parts of himself. Though, as we see, Amidism was based upon a metaphysical monism, in practice it really amounted to a theism. Amida does not seem to have been at all a vague and absolute divinity; there could have been no more personal god, nor one in closer contact with humanity, than this compassionate redeemer. The communion of the soul with him fills the whole of this religious creed with a sense of peaceful confidence and ineffable joy. In order to be saved it was sufficient for believers to pronounce his name a single time. An act of repentance, a sincere desire for betterment — and all sins were wiped out. But, above all, what entirely transformed the Amidist religion was the belief in the paradises of purity. In future, Japanese painting was to delight in

[1] See Max Wegner: "*Ikonographie des chinesischen Maitreya*," in *Ostasiatische Zeitschrift*, 1929, p. 156.

representing the splendours of that after-world of light in which, under the eyes of Amida, souls were born again, spotlessly white, in the mystic lotus (Fig. 31).

One of the first great preachers of Amidism in Japan was the monk Ryōnin, or Shō-ō daishi (1072–1132), who started his career on Mount Hieizan, in the Tendai sect, afterwards going off and founding the temples of the Raikōin at Ōhara in Yamashiro, and of Dai-nembutsuji at Sumiyoshi in Settsu in honour of Amida. But it was Hōnen-shōnin whose name will go down in history as the apostle *par excellence* of Amidism.

FIGURE 85
Kannon Reichojō. Kanō school, perhaps by Eitoku. — *Odin collection. Photo, Laniepce*

Like Ryōnin, Hōnen-shōnin (1133–1212), otherwise known as Genkū, started his career on Mount Hieizan, in the monastery of Enryakuji, belonging to the Tendai sect.[1] But having discovered an Amidist work, he embraced the new doc-

[1] See Rev. H. H. Coates and Rev. Ryugaku Ishizuka: *Hōnen Shōnin Gyojo Ezu: Hōnen, the Buddhist Saint, his Life and Teaching* (Kyōto, 1925). The biography of Hōnen was represented in a series of paintings by Tosa Yoshimitsu (fourteenth century) in a scroll now in the Zōjōji Temple, Tōkyō. See *Year-book of Japanese Art, 1929–1930,* Pl. LXVII.

trines, split off from the Tendai sect, and went to live, first in the hermitage of Kurodani, and afterwards in the retreat of Yoshimizu, "the Fountain of Joy," where he founded the sect of the Pure Earth (*Jōdo-shū*) in 1174. "The Fountain of Joy," writes Anesaki, "became a true source of peace and inspiration to many a starved soul —

FIGURE 86
The priest Kisen, attributed to Kōetsu.
— *Odin collection. Photo, Laniepce*

to monks who could find no satisfaction in the scholastic philosophy of the schools or the mysteries of ritual; to nobles and ladies of the court whose lives had been thrown out of gear by the abrupt decline in the luxury of the imperial capital, and who now sought happiness in a sphere that was not of this world; to warriors weary of the sword

FIGURE 87
Deer, lead upon lacquer, by Kōetsu.
— *Henri Vever collection. Photo, Laniepce*

and longing for eternal peace; to poor people whom the aristocratic Church had held at arm's length, and who hoped at last to slake their spiritual thirst. . . . Among the followers of Hōnen were to be found the humblest among men, including prostitutes and thieves, side by side with the highest ministers of state." [1]

Moreover, the rapid spread of the gospel of Hōnen was facilitated by its simplicity. Faith in Amida, hope in Amida, and love of Amida were sufficient, as we have said, to secure the redemption of man — indeed, of all men. "Just as a heavy stone," taught the apostle, "when placed on board a ship, can cross the sea and make a voyage of a thousand leagues without sinking, so, in spite of our sins, which are as heavy as stones, those of us who are borne by the ship of Amida's prayers may make the voyage of eternal Bliss without foundering in the sea of births and deaths." In fact, Amida showed the tenderness of a father for his children towards all mankind. There is a poem of Hōnen which describes the full extent of this divine solicitude:

> There is no hamlet so tiny, in any land,
> Nor so hidden, that the silver moon
> Fails to reach it with its rays. Even so, if a man
> Open wide the windows and gaze long out,
> The heavenly truth will enter and dwell within him. . . .
> In spring the morning mist veils the light
> Of the new-born day and grudgingly lets pass
> A few yellow rays, as though
> The pure light did not exist. And yet, behind the veil,
> Behold the sun flooding the universe with its white light.

This transparent imagery is used to clothe lessons of fervent charity, which go back behind the cold metaphysics of the "Greater Vehicle" in its later forms and give us back the true soul of the primitive Buddhist Church: "Think with love and sympathy," says

[1] Anesaki: *Quelques Pages de l'histoire religieuse du Japon,* pp. 71, 74.

Hōnen, " of all beings, whosoever they may be, that cherish a deep desire for the land of Bliss and pronounce the name of the Buddha;

FIGURE 88
Lacquer writing-desk, sixteenth century.
— *Henri Vever collection. Photo, Laniepce*

think of them as though they were your relatives or children, in whatsoever land they may be living, even outside the cosmic systems."

This religion of the heart, this religion of abandonment to the

Deity and utter confidence in him, rendered the complicated practices of the Tendai or Shingon ritual useless: " Our pious practices," taught Hōnen on his death-bed, " do not consist in meditation according to the counsels of the sages of old. Our prayer is not the fruit of the enlightenment which science or wisdom can give. When we invoke the Buddha and call upon him by name in the firm confidence that we shall be born again in his paradise, we may be sure of being received by him one day; to this end there is no other mystery save that we should pronounce his name in faith. Whatever understanding of the doctrines of Śākyamuni we may possess, every man, from the moment when he puts his faith in the salvation of Amida, should regard himself as on an equality with the ignorant who do not understand a single letter. We must put our whole heart into the method which consists in pronouncing the name of the Buddha in company with the ignorant and in putting off entirely the ways of the wise."

It is not surprising that the ancient Tendai Church, whose authority was undermined by this quietism, should have procured the exile of the apostle, who was banished to Sanuki in 1207 in spite of his seventy-four years. He accepted persecution smilingly, saying: " Nobody has power to check the spread of the gospel," and he watched the approach of death with resignation:

> What matter that our bodies, frail as dew,
> Should melt now here, now there, and vanish into nothingness?
> Our souls shall meet again in happier days
> In the same lotus-bed in paradise.

His last words were a salutation to the light of this longed-for paradise, which he now saw at last, and a foreshadowing of Amida Buddha's coming:

> His light is diffused through the worlds in all directions,
> His grace fails not him who calls upon it. . . .

Amidism, as understood and propagated by Hōnen, calls for two comments: in the first place we should insist once more upon the amazing powers of insight and rediscovery possessed by the Japa-

FIGURE 89
Japanese lacquer, late sixteenth century.
— Henri Vever collection. Photo, Giraudon

nese genius. As we have seen, Buddhism was transmitted to Japan from the continent in the form of the Chinese Mahāyāna system of the Six Dynasties and the T'angs, which, though no doubt a powerful metaphysical and theological structure, was rather remote from the simplicity of the primitive gospel. But it was this latter that the soul of Japan rediscovered in Amidism, finding within itself the fresh well-springs of *ahiṃsā,* the infinite sweetness of the *sūtras* of the Blessed One. It freed the pure treasure stored up for sixteen centuries past in the holy scriptures from later accumulations of scholastic systems. Beneath the body of the Church it discovered, with infinite joy, the very soul of Buddhism, the doctrine of universal charity.

But more than this: in the process of rediscovering primitive Buddhism Japan added something all its own — its humanism. Indian Buddhism, sprung from a land steeped in subtropical languor and born of the longing for a way of escape from reincarnation — that is, from the forced labour of eternal life — was in many respects a negative doctrine, one of whose dogmas was the negation and destruction of the personality. To the Japanese mind, compact of moderation, possessing a bent towards the personal and a joy in living, and harmoniously reflecting the sweetest land that ever existed, this could not possibly remain the essential form of the religion. It is true that, for the Japanese Buddhist, as for all the followers of Śākyamuni, the Buddhist dogmas continued in force theoretically; but in practice Nirvāṇa was replaced by the Amidist paradise, in which the souls saved by the bodhisattva were to prolong their personal existence indefinitely. Thus we have, on the one hand, a return to the pure charity which was the whole of primitive Buddhism, but had been overlaid by Chino-Indian metaphysics; and, on the other hand, a practical restoration of human personality by grace of the new Amidist beliefs; and lastly, as the medium in which these heterogeneous elements were fused, a religion all trust and tenderness, expressed in an exquisite poetry full of heart.

There was another cult, developed in the same spirit as that of

Amida: that of another bodhisattva, Kshitigarbha — in Japanese, Jizō — whom we have already met at Tun-huang as the kindly judge of souls,[1] and who was to become in Japan the special protector of children, travellers, and women with child, being "represented in the guise of a bonze with shaven head, holding a precious stone in one hand, and in the other a staff, to the tip of which are attached metal rings" (Fig. 29).[2]

The influence of Amidism very soon made itself felt in art. We may cite as an example the Byōdō-in of Uji, to the south of Kyōto, a temple built in 1053. In this sanctuary the angels represented as grouped round the Buddha on the tops of the columns are derived from Amidist conceptions — for Amidism, like Franciscanism, was to be distinguished in art by its bands of angels, full of a candid fervour. Amidism is also the creed inspiring the Konji-kidō, built in 1121, the sanctuary of which contains the trinity of Amida with six figures of Jizō; as well as the Amida-dō in the Hokkaiji of Yamashiro, possibly dating from the end of the twelfth century, with its frescoes of angel musicians. As Professor Elisséev has pointed out, the fact that the sanctuary is simply indicated by columns, and not fenced off from the crowd, shows what a revolution had been effected by this popular pietism of the Amidist cult, as distinguished from the esoteric Tendai doctrines.

Moreover, tradition has preserved the names of a number of Amidist monks who had distinguished themselves in sculpture and painting, such as Eshin (942–1017), the precursor of the Jōdo sect.[3]

[1] Vol. III, Fig. 206, 207, 210.

[2] M. W. de Visser: "The Bodhisattva Ti-Tsang (Jizō) in China and Japan," in *Ostasiatische Zeitschrift*, Berlin, 1915.

[3] See the pair of kakemonos, in colour on silk, said to be by Eshin, representing twenty-five bodhisattvas, the central figure being that of Amida, in the Jōfukuji Temple, Kyōto, reproduced in *Selected Relics* . . . , XIX, 7; ibid., Vol. IV, Pl. 8, picture of Hachiman-kō, Kōyasan; and the Welcoming Amitāyas, a kakemono said to be by Eshin Sōzu, belonging to the Annyōji Temple, Fukui, Echizen, reproduced in *Selected Relics* . . . , XII, 7; the Amitāyas of the Zen-rin-ji, Kyōto, ibid., I, Pl. 8; the descent of

FIGURE 90
Kannon, seventeenth century.
— *Henri Vever collection.*
Photo, Laniepce

Another sculptor who was also a bonze, Jōchō, who died in 1057, set up a gilt wooden figure of Amida, nearly six feet high, in the Byōdō-in, which is still in existence,[1] and whose calm simplicity is in contrast with the exaggerated violence of Shingon works in the Heian period. The same softened, tranquil simplicity can be seen in the seated wooden Dainichi, about two feet six inches in height, in the Chūsonji, dating from the first quarter of the twelfth century: this bare tranquillity, which verges almost upon the pretty in the treatment of the nude torso, with its elegant scarfs and shoulder-straps, is all the more remarkable because here we have a Vairocana, the universal adi-Buddha of the Shingon system of former days. The fact that this divinity, with his tendency to tantrist violence, is here reduced to the proportions of a statue of almost feminine elegance, shows to what an extent the softening influence of Amidism had made itself felt. There is the same absolutely feminine charm in the various statues of Kichijōten — that is, Śri, or Lakshmī, the Indian goddess of fortune and beauty — for instance, the painted wooden Śri, about three feet six inches in height, at Hōryūji, dating

Amitāyasa from paradise, in the Chion-in, Kyōto, ibid., XIV, 6; and, lastly, the Yamagoshi Amida in the Riitchi Veno collection, Ōsaka, for which see *Kokka*, 302 (July 1915).

[1] Otto Kümmel: *Kunst Chinas, Japans und Koreas*, Fig. 111, and Curt Gläser: *Ostasiatische Plastik*, Pl. 143.

Figure 91
Landscape, by Kanō Sansetsu.
— *Odin collection. Photo, Laniepce*

from 1079; [1] and that in the Jōruriji, Kyōto, also in wood, about three feet three inches in height, dating from the twelfth century, reproduced as Fig. 30.[2] These two delicate figures, with their ripe, blooming beauty, their expression of subtle intelligence, their graceful attitudes, and their handsome court costume, are indeed, as Herr Otto Kümmel remarks, just like the ladies forming the society of the Fujiwara period, fine flowers of the Gosho. A comparison between them and the Indian Lakshmī, reproduced as Fig. 101 of Volume II, has a certain piquancy. The object of both figures is to represent the Oriental Aphrodite, sea-born like her Greek sister.[3] But on the one hand we have a Dravidian type of nude, the all too intoxicating fruit of a tropical soil, with the full, rounded curves of a young, lissom, swaying body, enmeshing the beholder in its graces; and on the other hand a lady of high rank, delicate and reserved in her handsome robe and profusion of ornaments — a reminiscence, perhaps, of some poetess of the previous generation, some Sei Shōnagon or Murasaki Shikibu. The two figures are an illustration of Indian and Japanese society respectively, and of the position occupied by women in both, and at the same time of two conceptions of feminine beauty and two ideals of art, the product of two races of contrasting temperament and moral atmosphere.

This preoccupation with sweetness of expression and elegance of form and attitude due to the influence of Amidist Buddhism in Japan of the eleventh and twelfth centuries was not without its drawbacks. As Professor Elisséev has pointed out, the often exaggerated violence and breadth of works of art inspired by the Tendai and Shingon doctrines died away perhaps too rapidly. Amidist art certainly approximated more closely to the human; the divine came down to earth. The faces of the bodhisattvas bear the imprint of a soothing and facile

[1] Otto Kümmel: *L'Art de l'Extrême-Orient*, Pl. 43. See in the same style a Benzaiten (the goddess Sarasvatī), a picture of the eighth century, in the shrine of Kichijōten, in the School of Fine Arts, Tōkyō, reproduced in *Hōbōgirin*, p. 64, Pl. 8.

[2] *Selected Relics . . .* , VI, 6.

[3] Cf. Vol. II, p. 172.

FIGURE 92
Landscape, by Tannyū.
— *Vever collection. Photo, Laniepce*

humanity. Instead of losing itself in cosmic reveries, their glance mildly invites the faithful to salvation won without effort.[1] But it is evident that such a conception is naturally exclusive of any sort of vigour. Its rather conventional sweetness soon verges upon insignificance of expression, just as its often studiedly childlike simplicity is in danger of becoming a mannerism. On the whole, however, it is a charming type of art, with visions of tenderness and wonder sometimes worthy of the paradises of Fra Angelico, as can be seen in the celebrated group of Amida surrounded by twenty-five bodhisattvas in the Kōyasan.[2]

We here reproduce a few well-known works inspired by this artistic canon. Among the statues is one of a seated Maitrēya, in dry lacquer on a core of clay, in the Kōryūji, Kyōto, dating from the eleventh century (Fig. 32),[3] and a gilt wooden Amida in the Louvre, belonging to the second half of the twelfth century (Fig. 33); among the paintings we have one of the moon-goddess Chandra in the Kyōwōgokokuji, dating from the end of the twelfth century (Fig. 34),[4] and a portrait of a Tendai priest in the Ichijōji, which, in spite of the sect to which he belonged, is more akin to the Amidist figures (Fig. 35),[5] not to speak of the Jizō figures formerly ascribed to Kanaoka, which we mentioned above (Fig. 29).

The same tradition is to be traced in the Amida (" Amitayus and the Ten Worlds ") of the Konkaikō-myōji, Kyōto, with the upper part of the body appearing in the heavens behind Mount Hieizan, between Kannon and Seishi (Fig. 47), though this belongs to a later date. To quote Herr Kümmel's words, it is an " apparition of

[1] See the Amida Nyorai in the collection of the Jōfukuin Temple, reproduced in *Art Treasures of the Kōyasan Temples*, Pl. 60.

[2] Reproduced by Otto Kümmel: *Kunst Chinas, Japans und Koreas*, Fig. 112, and in *Art Treasures of the Kōyasan Temples*, Pl. 72. See also ibid., Pl. 57, the famous "Amida in his Paradise" (*Taema mandara*) of the Kamakura period, in the collection of the Shōjōshin-in Temple, of which there is a good reproduction in the Musée Guimet, Paris.

[3] *Selected Relics* . . . , V, 6.

[4] Ibid., VI, 13.

[5] Harima province. *Selected Relics* . . . , XIII, 6.

FIGURE 93
Landscape, by Kanō Naonobu.
— *Henri Rivière collection.*
Photo, Laniepce

FIGURE 94
Landscape, by Kanō Naonobu.
— *Henri Rivière collection.*
Photo, Laniepce

more than earthly grandeur, dazzling with gold and of supernatural brilliance: it is Amida rising up behind the sacred mountain. He has come to seek the faithful soul and lead it into the heavenly kingdom. . . ." [1]

But this pietistic art had its moments of relaxation and monastic recreation, of which the painting of Toba-Sōjō was a manifestation. This Buddhist bishop (1053–1114) was the creator of the humorous *genre* and of caricature, which were so often practised since. In his miniature compositions, with their astounding vigour and lightness of touch, he shows us rabbits, frogs, and monkeys parodying the acts and gestures of men (Fig. 36), and in particular the occupations of the good monks among whom he and his imitators lived (Fig. 37).[2] His was an art full of subtlety and freshness, reminding us of the spirit of La Fontaine in the sly humour of its psychology, the speaking way in which it depicts the animals to the very life, and the delicacy with which the rustic setting is touched in.

THE KAMAKURA PERIOD (1192–1333 OR 1337)

AS WE MAY REMEMBER, IN 1189 YORITOMO, THE CONQUEROR OF THE Taira clan, which he exterminated, had removed all possible competitors in his own family by getting rid of his brother Yoshitsune. In this position, exempt from all rivalry, he showed himself one of the greatest statesmen in Japanese history (Fig. 44). With his practical sense of reality, he knew how to profit by the experience of his predecessors and opponents. A more profound statesman than Kiyomori, and a better dissembler, more prudent, but equally implacable, this great, silent hero made no sacrifices to vanity, but reorganized the State

[1] The whole triptych, of which we give only the central figure, is reproduced by Kümmel in *Ostasiatische Kunst*, Pl. 40. This triptych was formerly said to be by Eshin Sōzu. Cf. *Selected Relics* . . . , XIII, 7.

[2] Cf. *Selected Relics* . . . , I, 15; XIII, 8; *Year-book of Japanese Art, 1929–1930*, Pl. LX, LXI, LXII (sketches of animals and birds in the Kōzanji Temple, Kyōto, Exhibition of Famous Japanese Art and Treasures).

from top to bottom. He began by establishing the power of his house on a solid territorial basis; and his ancestral fief of the Kantō, which had secured the victory of the Minamoto cause, shared in the triumph

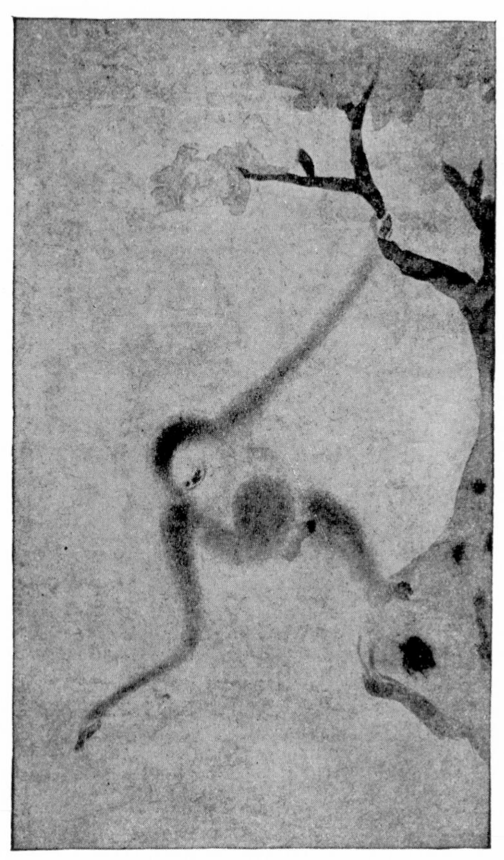

FIGURE 95
Monkey, by Sōtatsu.
— *Odin collection. By courtesy of Messrs. Odin and Van Oest. Photo, Laniepce*

of his family. It was at Kamakura, in the Kantō, that he established his capital, with the title of *shōgun,* or supreme military chief, conferred upon him by the Emperor in 1192. The government which he organized there was known as the *bakufu* — that is, "the government of the tent, or camp," as opposed to the "civil" régime of the imperial court at Kyōto. The shōgun had his military representative,

FIGURE 96
Autumn visions, by Sōtatsu.
— *Odin collection. By courtesy of Messrs. Odin and Van Oest. Photo, Laniepce*

permanent garrison, and fiscal agent in every province, side by side with the former civil governor, who was now deprived of his powers.

Thus the Japanese Japan of the Kantō kept the Chinese Japan of the Gokinai in a state of tutelage, without, however, destroying it.

The Gosho could not be touched; the dictator Kiyomori had made as though he would attempt to do so by installing himself at Kyōto at the side of the Emperor, whom he treated as a useless figure-head — a sacrilegious attitude which may be compared to that of Cæsar when he reduced the Senate to insignificance and aspired to the crown.

FIGURE 97
Pine-trees, by Kōrin.
— *Ulrich Odin collection. By courtesy of Messrs. Odin and Van Oest. Photo, Laniepce*

Like Cæsar, the Taira clan had fallen beneath the blows of the outraged aristocracy. Yoritomo was taught by their experience. Just as, after the murder of Cæsar, his heir Augustus heaped civilities upon the Senate and kept himself in the background, leaving the administration of civil affairs in its hands, so now Yoritomo, who reminds us of Augustus in the prudence and simplicity of his life, in his administrative talents, but also in his dissimulation, hypocrisy, and perfidy, adopted the same attitude towards the traditional authorities as Augustus had done. The Emperor had no more respectful subject than he was; nor was anything changed in the civil administration of Japan, which continued to go on side by side with the régime of the *bakufu,* just as the institutions of republican Rome had been maintained under the Empire. Yoritomo did not touch the privileges of the *kuge* class, the former imperial nobility, which had become a mere civil nobility since the development of the military régime. It is true that he established a garrison of his own near Kyōto, under the orders of his father-in-law, Hōjō Tokimasa, lord of Izu. But he was careful to keep this garrison out of sight in the suburb of Rokuhara, and affected to leave the administration of the capital and the provinces of the Gokinai to the imperial officials. For his own part he gave himself out as no more than a simple military leader, living as modestly, soberly, and frugally as the least of his samurai, and unassuming both in tone and bearing. Kyōto continued to be the seat of the Gosho, the capital of the emperors by right divine. Yoritomo took care not to compete on their own ground with the dynasty descended from the sun. His own capital was Kamakura, in the Kantō, at the entrance to the Gulf of Tōkyō. Thus the military colony of the Kantō played somewhat the same part as that of Macedonia in ancient Greece, Prussia in Germany, or Piedmont in Italy. There was a military head of the samurai at Kamakura, and a civil and religious sovereign of the *kuge* at Kyōto. Thus, in spite of all Yoritomo's protestations of loyalty, the separation of the two powers was quite definite, and so was their respective importance: Kamakura was everything, while Kyōto no longer counted.[1]

[1] As a living illustration of the warlike genius of this period I would merely cite the two painted wooden statues of Baira and Anira, two of the twelve guardian deities of Yakushi Buddha, in the Kamakura style, reproduced in *Kokka,* No. 451 (June 1928), Pl. I and II, treated in a realistic vein characteristic of the age, with a noble unity of execution.

Based on these foundations, the political structure set up by Yoritomo, consisting in the *bakufu* and the shōgunate, lasted for six centuries, twice as long as that established by Augustus. But though

FIGURE 98
Lacquer by Kōrin.
— *Vever collection. Photo, Laniepce*

the work of the great Minamoto shōgun survived him for so long, his own family did not benefit by it, for twenty years after his death it was overthrown by a fresh palace revolution.[1]

[1] See James Murdoch: *A History of Japan*, I, 412–90 ("The Kamakura Bakufu").

Yoritomo died in 1199. His widow, the energetic Masa-ko, who belonged to the house of Hōjō, had borne him two sons, Yoriie and Sanetomo. At the death of their father these two princes were still minors. The elder, Yoriie, was none the less proclaimed shōgun under the guardianship of his maternal grandfather, Hōjō Tokimasa, lord of Izu.

The Hōjō clan, who now appeared for the first time upon the stage of high politics, were quite minor barons whose ancestral home was in the Kantō, and who had only risen in the world as hangers-on of the Minamoto family. The head of the house, Hōjō Tokimasa, a practical and not too scrupulous intriguer, had all the qualities necessary for coming to the front, provided always that he was prepared to sacrifice his own grandsons, the sons of the great shōgun Yoritomo. Nobody knew the workings of the *bakufu* better than the Hōjō who had done so much to establish it. Once Yoritomo had gone, he saw no reason why he should not step into his shoes. It is true that the army of the north remained attached to the shōgun's family and true to the badge of the Minamoto clan. But though the whole of Japan was fanatically devoted to its divinely descended emperors, the shōgun Yoritomo had succeeded in stripping the emperors of all their power without raising any protest, so long as he maintained them in their titles, honours, and privileges. The Hōjōs now determined to turn against the heirs of Yoritomo the treatment meted out by him to the imperial dynasty; all they had to do was to set the shōgun beside the emperor amid the pomp of the court. Thus Japan would have two honorary sovereigns — the emperor, its spiritual sovereign, and the shōgun, nominal head of the armies — but in reality a single master: the minor baron Hōjō.

Moreover, in the school of Yoritomo, Tokimasa had learnt all the secrets of Japanese Machiavellianism. It so happened that Yoriie, the nominal shōgun, was a pleasure-loving, frivolous young man who had no understanding for the subtle policy of his maternal grand-

FIGURE 99
Lacquer of the seventeenth century.
— *Vever collection. Photo, Laniepce*

father. At the instigation of the Hōjōs, his counsellors persuaded him to cede part of his domains to his younger brother Sanetomo — and the power of the Minamotos was broken. When Yoriie saw what an error he had been made to commit, he threatened to massacre the Hōjōs; but it was he who was deposed, tonsured, shut up in a monastery, and assassinated in 1204, before he had had time to appreciate the charms of monastic life, his brother Sanetomo being proclaimed shōgun in his stead by the all-powerful Hōjōs. The new shōgun was a painter of taste (Fig. 48), and a charming poet, who made verses which might have been the despair of the emperors themselves.[1] "From the Hakone road," he wrote one day, "the Gulf of Izu appears before me, and beyond it the open sea, the little islands, and the waves, which seem to press one upon the other. If only this lovely world could remain unchanged!" These were harmless pastimes. The Hōjōs left him to dream at leisure in his villas on the Gulf of Sagami and had themselves nominated *shikken,* or regents, having all the effective power in their hands. A few years later, in 1219, Sanetomo perished in a brawl from a blow of his own nephew's, after which none of the Minamoto family was left.

The house of Hōjō resisted the temptation to proclaim themselves shōguns and prudently conferred this dignity upon a member of the Fujiwara family, who was proclaimed a descendant of the Minamotos for the occasion; and in future they kept this line of shadowy shōguns as heads of the Kamakura government. In reality the Hōjō family, under the modest name of *shikken* — mayors of the palace or regents — were the sole heads of the *bakufu.* The son of Tokimasa, Hōjō Yoshitoki, who succeeded him, and occupied his place from 1205 to 1224, established the position of his house still more firmly. An energetic emperor, Go-Toba, who tried to profit by circumstances and attempt a legitimist restoration, was defeated and exiled by the

[1] See Professor Wada Hidematsu: "The Ye-awasé, an ancient custom to give comments on pictures by comparison," in *Kokka,* No. 449 (April 1928).

Figure 100
Lacquer, end of the seventeenth century.
— *Doucet collection.*

Hōjōs in 1221, and in future their power met with no further opposition in the archipelago. From their stronghold of Kamakura they were able to govern Japan as absolute masters for a hundred and thirty years.

Whatever judgment may have been passed by Japanese historians on the irregular methods by which Tokimasa gained possession of the shōgunate of Minamoto, the government of the Hōjōs was far from being devoid of benefit to the country. The sixth of the *shikken,* Hōjō Tokimune (1256–84), had the glory of saving Japan from invasion by the Mongols.

This was, in fact, the period at which the Mongols, having conquered China, were casting their eyes upon the neighbouring countries, which they regarded as natural dependencies of the Celestial Empire. Kublai, the grandson of Jenghiz-Khan, and Mongol emperor of China, called upon the Japanese to submit to him and upon their refusal to do so sent an expedition against them.

Never had Japan been in such danger. She alone of all the Asiatic nations had hitherto been immune from the Turko-Mongol invasions. And now that these had triumphed over the rest of Asia, Japan would have to meet the attack of the whole of Asia, for it never entered the head of the Japanese to submit to the yoke. The whole country rose as one man to reject Kublai's insulting demand. Hōjō Tokimune, " the great chevalier of Kamakura," as he was called from that day onward, summoned the people to arms. Japan now experienced a few days similar to those through which she lived while awaiting the arrival of the Baltic squadron in 1905. Or, rather, it was as critical an hour for her as the days of Marathon and Salamis can have been for the Hellenic world. On the one side stood the " conquerors of the world," as the Mongols called themselves; on the other side the island power of Japan.

In 1274 the first Sino-Mongol expeditionary force made an attempt to land upon the coast of Chikuzen, in Kyūshū. In spite of the surprise created by the Chinese fire-arms, the attack failed, and the Mongols had to retreat on board their ships. In 1281 they returned with a formidable fleet carrying, it is said, a hundred thousand men. But since the last attempt the Japanese had had time to fortify the coasts of Hizen and Chikuzen, which were now manned by defenders.

FIGURE 101
Deer, by Kōrin.
— *Vever collection. Photo, Laniepce*

Thrilling with patriotism, the people thronged the sanctuaries of Isé, and from the depths of his retirement in the Gosho the Emperor invoked the intercession of his divine ancestors and implored Amaterasu and the *kami* not to permit the barbarians to profane the sacred archipelago. The gods heard his prayers, and on August 14–15, 1281 not only was the Mongol army driven back from the coasts of Kyūshū, but the fleet was also destroyed by a terrible typhoon.

When the sea subsided, not a trace was left of the dread armada which had set forth from all the ports of Korea and China to reduce the land of the Gods to servitude. The island empire of the Japanese had defeated the Conquerors of the World.

It was Hōjō Tokimune, the "Great *Bushi*" of Kamakura, who reaped the benefit of this victory. After the expulsion of the Mongols, Japan hailed him as her liberator. His son, Hōjō Sadatoki, who succeeded him as *shikken*, and held this position from 1284 to 1311, showed himself as worthy of the dictatorship as his father had been. But in 1311 the rank of *shikken* passed to an incompetent prince, Hōjō Takatoki, whose weakness threatened within a few years to ruin the work of his forebears.

For a long time past, the rank of shōgun enjoyed by the Minamoto family had been no more than an empty title. If, then, owing to the incompetence of Takatoki, the function of *shikken* now became a mere honorary charge, divorced from all power, on whom was the burden of government to rest in future? The government of Japan threatened to lapse — or, rather, the agents who had been entrusted, one after the other, with carrying it on were gradually breaking down, so that it only remained for the real head of it, the true master of the land, to resume control. The emperor's rights over the Empire were imprescriptible. He might leave to others the task of managing his property, delegating his powers to them for many years, or even centuries, and apparently ceasing almost entirely to interest himself in political questions; ever since the days of Nara and Heian the dynasty tracing its origin back to Amaterasu, the dynasty descended from the sun, might withdraw into the mysterious seclusion of the Gosho, just as a god returns to heaven after completing his life upon earth; but it was none the less incumbent upon this dynasty to appear once more before the eyes of men and show itself to the people when, in course of time, the safety of the people should require it. Such, at least, was the view taken at the beginning of the fourteenth century by a remarkable sovereign, the emperor Go-Daigo, or Daigo II, who ascended the throne of the Rising Sun in 1319.[1]

The ruling passion of Go-Daigo seems to have been his sense of the dignity and sacredness of his mission. Few Japanese sovereigns had such a consciousness of their divine origin and of the radiance shed upon them by their solar origin. As descendant of a line of emperors dating back ten centuries and tracing their origin back to Amaterasu — as an authentic son of the gods, himself a god and high priest of a religion a thousand years old, whose whole being was still steeped in the mythical and fabu-

FIGURE 102
Fallow-deer, by Sosen.
—*Vever collection.*
Photo, Laniepce

[1] Portrait of Go-Daigo in the Shōjōkōji Temple, Fujisawa, Sagami, reproduced in *Selected Relics* . . . , VI, 22. Other portraits of Go-Daigo in the Daitokuji, Kyōto, *Selected Relics* . . . , X, 13; and *Kokka*, No. 237 (February 1910), Pl. I; ibid., No. 307 (December 1915), p. 140.

lous past of his race — Go-Daigo judged that the time had come to overthrow all the intermediate repositories of power whom his ancestors had allowed to set themselves up between them and their people, and to address his people face to face.

Go-Daigo's son, the heroic prince imperial Morinaga (1308–35), entered ardently into his views. He enlisted the co-operation of the second great moral force at that period — the Buddhist Church — in the projected work of restoration, and the rich monasteries of Hieizan and Nara rallied to the legitimist side. His task was, by the aid of the monks of Hieizan and of the *kuge* class, to expel the garrison of the *bakufu* from Kyōto, to deliver the Gokinai and call the samurai of the south to arms. The Emperor soon collected a small army, at the head of which were the Prince Imperial, Morinaga, and his worthy comrade the chivalrous Kusunoki Masashige, the "Bayard of Japan" (1331).

FIGURE 103
Monkeys, by Sosen.
— *Henri Rivière collection. Photo, Laniepce*

But the *bakufu* was too strong to be overthrown at a single blow. Neither the samurai of the Kantō nor all the clans of the north in general could acquiesce in an imperial restoration the first act of which would be to abolish their own hegemony. They therefore rallied round the house of Hōjō and descended in a body upon Kyōto. This time again the north got the better of the south. Go-Daigo was captured, imprisoned, and exiled to the little island of Okishima, far out at sea off the coast on the Korean side. But once the imperial idea became diffused among the masses, it made great headway and led to a general readiness to make sacrifices for the cause. Morinaga and

FIGURE 104
Monkeys, by Sosen.
— Henri Rivière collection. Photo, Giraudon

Masashige maintained their position among the mountains of Yamato, to the south of Kyōto and Ōsaka, fortifying the great monasteries of those parts and repulsing several attacks on the part of the government of Kamakura. The news of their fidelity reached the emperor Go-Daigo on his island. He made his escape and after a romantic Odyssey landed on the coast of Sanindō, where he was joined by Morinaga's army. The sovereign's misfortunes and exile had roused intense emotion among the whole people, and his return assumed the proportions of a triumph. The divine monarch, who was elevated almost into a martyr by the treatment of the Hōjōs and whose return seemed due to a miracle, was greeted by crowds wild with enthusiasm. He profited by his popularity to overthrow his enemies. Once restored to the throne of his fathers, and acting in his capacity as supreme pontiff of the traditional Shinto religion, he proclaimed the Hōjōs guilty of rebellion and sacrilege. The heads of the two chief northern clans, Yoshisada, head of the house of Nitta, and Takauji, head of the house of Ashikaga, rallied to his side, and Takauji handed over to him the impregnable Rokuhara, the last stronghold of the *bakufu* at Kyōto, while the Nittas made it their task to oust Hōjō Takatoki himself from his castle of Kamakura. In 1333 the fortifications of Kamakura were stormed by Nitta Yoshisada, and the Hōjō clan exterminated.

For the first time in five centuries Japan had no master save her Emperor. The masses of the people, for whom the emperor was still the descendant of Amaterasu and the high priest of the native religion; and the Confucian *literati*, who were devoted to the idea of a Son of Heaven on the Chinese model, saw their prayers at last realized. The legitimate master of the Empire having deigned to resume possession of his patrimony, the era of the great civil wars seemed to be closed for ever. After four centuries of governments with no basis in law, the country returned to the legitimate régime. "For a moment the mass of the people was filled with boundless hopes."

FIGURE 105
Landscape, by Konoe Yorakuin (1666–1736).
— *Ulrich Odin collection. Photo, Laniepce*

But though feudalism was legally abolished, its habits lingered on.[1] "The military caste, though deprived of its head, remained all-powerful." If he was to deter it from fresh revolutions, Go-Daigo ought to have done what the emperor Mutsuhito did five centuries later — proclaim himself head of the samurai and boldly transfer the seat of government to the Kantō. Unfortunately the artificial education which he had received in the Gosho made any real contact

FIGURE 106
Fuji-san among the clouds, by Ōkyo (1733–95).
— *Odin collection. Photo, Laniepce*

between the Emperor and the outer world impossible. After his heroic feats in 1333, he allowed court life to regain its hold on him, in the belief that his victory was final, and that it only remained for him to enjoy its fruits. He would have no dealings with any but the civil government and behaved in all things as if the government of the *bakufu* had never existed. His hereditary tendencies and education

[1] See *The Documents of Iriki, Illustrative of the Development of the Feudal Institutions of Japan*, translated and edited by K. Asakawa (New Haven: Yale University Press, 1929).

gained the upper hand to such an extent that he even abandoned for new friends those who had stood by him in the struggle, so that the samurai who had shed their blood for him saw the lettered class, the useless *kuge* about the court, preferred above themselves. His son Morinaga, it is true, received the title of shōgun, and his chief lieutenants were rewarded with vast fiefs, Masashige in the region of Ōsaka and Nitta Yoshisada on the western coast. But these two faithful serv-

FIGURE 107
Moonlight on the river, by Ōkyo.
— *Matsusaka collection. Photo,* Shimbi Shoin

ants did not receive half as much as was granted to the Ashikagas, whose loyalty was far less secure, but who were more adroit and in higher favour at court.

The hereditary domains of the Ashikagas were situated in the province of Shimozuke, to the south of Nikkō, and it was here that Ashikaga Takauji set to work to extend his power. He persuaded Go-Daigo to grant him the larger part of the Kantō, and after that the province of Tōtōmi, on the Tōkaidō coast, the possession of which gave him the command of the road to Kyōto. By creating this enormous fief for the benefit of the least faithful of his vassals Go-Daigo undid all the good of his victory. Outwitted by the Ashikagas, he did not see that he was reviving for their benefit the military principate

FIGURE 108
Landscape, by Buzen (1734–1806).
— Odin collection. Photo, Laniepce

of the house of Hōjō; for by the very nature of things he who was master of the Kantō was sure sooner or later to be led on to place himself at the head of the northern clans with the object of reviving the *bakufu*.

Go-Daigo's son Morinaga, being more clear-sighted than his father, saw the danger and determined to resist, even at the risk of a revolt against his father's authority. Realizing whither his father's blindness was leading the dynasty, he summoned his trusty followers to arms in his capacity as shōgun, a vigorous proceeding which, by making the Emperor's own son the head of the *bakufu,* would have brought the whole military party into the service of the Empire. But Go-Daigo was so blinded by weakness that he lost sight of his own interest and disowned his son, who was captured by the Ashikagas

FIGURE 109
Fuji, by Tani Bunchō (1763–1842).
— Odin collection. Photo, Laniepce

and shortly afterwards murdered, in 1335. Once rid of the young Prince, whose presence was an obstacle to his projects, Ashikaga Takauji judged that the moment had come to throw off the mask. He established himself in Kamakura, occupied the other fortresses in the Kantō, and, summoning all the samurai of the north, assumed the title of shōgun and, in 1335, proclaimed the re-establishment of the *bakufu.*

This dramatic step at last opened the eyes of Go-Daigo. Furious at having been duped by a rogue, and bitterly regretting the death of his son, he charged Nitta Yoshisada to avenge him without fail. But it was too late. The Ashikagas had had time to gather round them all the clans of the north, and, descending upon Kyōto at their head, they took it by surprise.

The loss of Kyōto marked the irrevocable failure of the imperial restoration. But it is characteristic of the samurai to sacrifice himself for a lost cause, and the Japanese had no more thoroughgoing samurais than Masashige, the Bayard of the imperial cause, and his son Masatsura. The decisive battle between the army of the Ashikagas and the imperial troops under the command of Masashige was fought near Kōbe in 1336. Masashige was slain at the very beginning of the action, and his death involved the ruin of his party. Ashikaga Takauji made a triumphal entry into Kyōto, where he solemnly re-established the government of the shōguns and the *bakufu.*

Go-Daigo, who had showed such weakness when in power, once more excited the popular pity by his misfortunes. Legend took possession of him on the very morrow of his death, and his memory, embellished and idealized, kept up the courage of the defenders for a long time to come. Led by Masatsura, who had inherited the chivalrous character of his father, Masashige, they continued to hold the islands of Kyūshū and Shikoku, as well as certain points in Hondo. His heroic death at the battle of Shijōnawate, in 1348, was the final blow to the imperial cause. If the legitimist party maintained a footing in the south for a few years longer, this was due not so much to its own strength as to the dissensions of its opponents.

The Kamakura period, lasting from 1192 to 1333, of which we have briefly related the history, witnessed the final emancipation of the Japanese genius. The individual character of the race now emerged, forged once and for all in these bitter feudal wars. The military dictatorship which, from the fortified town of Kamakura, imposed its will upon the feudal nobles of Nippon focused the scattered forces of the country and made the race conscious of its worth;

FIGURE 110
Beauty stretching her arms. Ming style.
— *Gunpei collection. Photo,* Shimbi Shoin

FIGURE 111
Beauty playing the flute. Ming style.
— *Kinzaburo collection. Photo,* Shimbi Shoin

and it is not without significance that this great age ended with the epic spectacle of the Japanese victoriously holding their own against the conquerors of Asia.

It was now, too, that Japan defined her position for good, in religion as well as in politics. This was the time when the *Shinshū* and the *Nichirenshū* were taking form, and Zenism was at its height.

The Shinshū sect, or Jōdo-Shinshū, which means the " true sect of Jōdo," was a reforming movement affecting the type of Amidism known by this name and carried out by the celebrated apostle Shinran-shōnin (1173–1262).[1] Having received his initiation into the Tendai and afterwards into the Jōdo sect, Shinran resolved to found a new school of his own in 1224. He accepted the Amidist pietism of the Jōdo sect, but rejected its practices. Its clamorous prayers and litanies of the name of Amida seemed to him mere verbalism, and in their place he inculcated the doctrine of the " Only Thought." For acts of piety and even for the monastic virtues he substituted the ardour of faith. Thus he condemned the celibacy of the bonzes and set an example by marrying the daughter of Fujiwara Kanenori. At the same time he carried Amidist quietism to extremes, teaching that deeds are as nothing in comparison with the mercy of the Buddha, by whom we are predestined to salvation. " And so," to quote Anesaki, " the key to salvation is to lose oneself in the grace of the Buddha by a full and self-forgetting faith in his redeeming power alone." The order founded by Shinran, which assumed the character of a " third order," owing to the general practice of marriage by its members, none the less remained strongly organized, especially as his descendants formed a sort of hereditary papacy. In spite of the piety of its founder, the Amidist papacy, established as early as 1272 at the Honganji Temple, Kyōto, and having a married order at its command, gradually developed into a political power,

[1] See Gesho Sasaki: *A Study of Shin Buddhism* (Kyōto: Eastern Buddhist Society, 1925).

FIGURE 112

Woman selling fans, by Kanshi, end of seventeenth century.

— *Ulrich Odin collection. Photo, Laniepce*

FIGURE 113

Portrait of a woman, by Miyagawa Choshun (about 1720).

— *Odin collection. Photo, Laniepce*

a state within the State. In the fifteenth century the Honganji was to become a regular fortress, harbouring an army of soldier monks. Here again the martial temperament of Japan was at work, producing the phenomenon of a militant Buddhism, with organizations rather recalling the western European militant orders in the Holy Land and the Baltic regions. The transformation is all the more

FIGURE 114
Courtesan and servants, by Eishi (end of eighteenth century).
— *Odin collection. Photo, Laniepce*

striking because it was carried out in the most pious and quietistic of all the religious fraternities. We may hasten to add that, in spite of this passing secular phase, the Honganji remained a fine school of piety and moral grandeur.

The same reawakening of Japanese energy after the mildness of the early forms of Amidism appears in the life and teaching of Nichiren

(1222–82).[1] Nichiren, " the lotus of the sun," was born in the village of Kominato, in the province of Awa, of a once noble family which had come down in the world and earned a living by fishing. When quite a young man he entered the monistic and " energetist " Shingon sect as a bonze. Under the influence of an ancient Sanskrit work, *The Lotus of the Good Law,* he was led to break not only with the Shingon, but with all other contemporary sects, and found a new doctrine, the *Hokkeshū,* which likewise had as its basis a grandiose monism, the aim of the believer in this creed, as in those above mentioned, being to identify himself with the nature of the Buddha — that is, with the cosmic soul.

FIGURE 115
Tayu dancing, by Kitao Keisei Masayoshi (died 1824).
— *Odin collection. By courtesy of Messrs. Odin and Van Oest*

This son of a poor fisherman had in him something of the prophet Isaiah or of Savonarola. Once in possession of the truth, he went to Kamakura, the political capital of Japan, and began to preach against the depravity of society and the unworthiness of the other sects, presenting remonstrances to the government and proposing a project of reform for the State. In 1260 he even went so far as to predict the Mongol invasion, which was, in fact, not far off.

" Woe unto them! " he said of his enemies. " They have failed to

[1] See Masaharu Anesaki: *Nichiren, the Buddhist Prophet* (Cambridge: Harvard University Press, 1916).

enter in at the door which leads to true Buddhism, they have fallen into the dungeon of false doctrines. . . . O men of little faith! Turn your souls without delay towards the only Truth of the straight way!"

The answer of the Hōjō government was to exile the apostle to Itō, on the wild shore of the peninsula of Izu, where he completed the development of his doctrine, with which apocalyptic foreshadowings now began to mingle, for he believed his words to be addressed to

FIGURE 116
Moronobu. Cavalcade of Amazons.
— *Vever collection. Photo, Vever*

humanity in its last days. On his return from exile in 1263, he began to travel about the country preaching his gospel everywhere. The visionary became an agitator, and his prophecies met with all the more credence because the country was living in dread of the approaching Mongol invasion. This time he was condemned to death, and in 1271 he was just about to suffer execution when a miracle caused the sabre to fall from the hands of his executioner. Hōjō Tokimune commuted his sentence to one of rigorous banishment, and he was sent to the island of Sado, off the north-east coast of Nippon, where he spent the winter in a desolate spot amid snow and ice (Fig. 158). But nothing would induce him to renounce his teaching.

This doctrine assumed more and more the form of a mystical

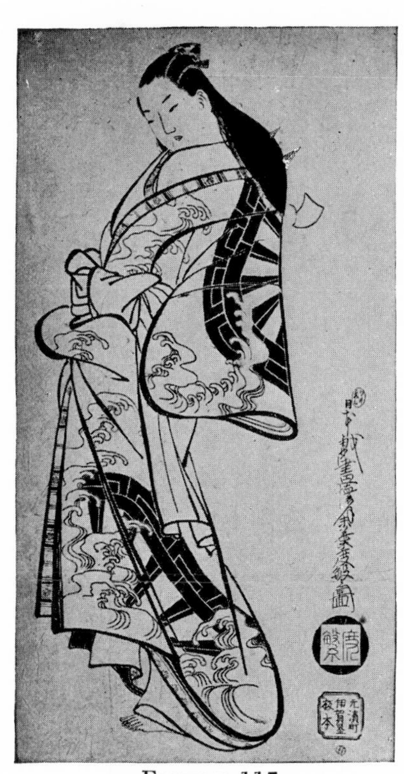

FIGURE 117
Kaigetsudō. Courtesan.
— *Vever collection. Photo, Pivot*

FIGURE 118
Print by Toyonobu.
— *Vever collection. Photo, Pivot*

monism, stated as follows by Anesaki:[1] "The Supreme Being is the Buddha, in his capacity as the true essence of the universe, the cosmic soul in full possession of the whole truth of existence. In other words, the person of the Buddha, in its eternal reality and full significance,

[1] In *Quelques Pages de l'histoire religieuse.*

is identical with the universe itself. The Buddha nature, on the other hand, is inherent in every human or celestial being, and even in

FIGURE 119
Harunobu. Looking out at the snow.
— *Vever collection. Photo, Giraudon*

animals and demons. Thus, if illuminated by the Buddha, every creature lives in real communion with all other beings, for the same Buddha nature lies at the root of all existence and every action."

Figure 120
Harunobu. Women washing their hair.
— Vever collection. Photo, Giraudon

Having been recalled from exile, Nichiren returned in triumph to Kamakura, where he was an " anxious spectator " of the drama of the Mongol invasions in 1274 and 1281, for he was not only a prophet, but at the same time an ardent patriot, who loved Japan as the land predestined to become the fostering-ground of universal redemption. It was in this high hope that he died, in 1282, reciting the *Lotus of the Good Law.* His order, that of the *Hokke,* had as its permanent seat the Kuonji, the monastery which he had himself built at Minobu, in the province of Kai.

The powerful personality of this tumultuous genius, sprung from the heart of the people, had a profound influence upon the development of Japan. His stern preaching roused the country from its facile pietism, and in every sphere Japan was recovering her fierce energy.

The influence of the Zen sect worked in the same direction.[1] After several less successful attempts this famous sect, an outgrowth from the *Dhyāna* — that is, from the Indian theories of contemplation, or, rather, mental concentration — was finally propagated throughout Japan from 1192 onwards by the monk Eisai, who had gone to China to obtain his initiation into it and on his return founded the monastery of the Shōfokuji at Hakata in Chikuzen. A still more famous preacher of Zenism was the bonze Dōgen (1200–53), who had entered the monastery of the Hieizan as quite a young man, but, having failed to find satisfaction in the doctrines of the Tendai sect, likewise went to China in 1223, bringing back with him in 1228 the Sōtō doctrine, a reformed type of Zenism, which had its centre at the Eiheiji, in Echizen.

" Zenism," writes Professor Anesaki,[2] " was an intuitive method

[1] See Daisetz Taitaro Suzuki: *Essays in Zen Buddhism* (London, 1927); Arthur Waley: *Zen Buddhism and Its Relation to Art* (London, 1922); K. Nukariya: *The Religion of the Samurai* (London, 1912); Anesaki: *Buddhist Art in Its Relation to Buddhist Ideals* (Boston, 1915), ch. iv.

[2] In *Quelques Pages de l'histoire religieuse.*

Figure 121
Harunobu. Couple in the snow.
— *Vever collection. Photo, Laniepce*

of spiritual exercise, the followers of which had as their aim to attain purity of soul, and having acquired it, to keep themselves apart

FIGURE 122
Koriusai. Women reading.
— *Vever collection. Photo, Pivot*

from the unrest of human life. . . . In defiance of reason and logic, the Zenist endeavours to emancipate himself from the usual processes of thought, and always refuses to formulate his doctrine, for to reduce a doctrine to formulas paralyzes life and renders the soul

FIGURE 123
Koriusai. Study of birds.
— *Vever collection. Photo, Pivot*

inert. . . . The object of Zenism is to make us intuitively sure that we have discovered in the depths of our soul the entity which goes beyond and takes the place of all individual differences and temporary changes. This entity is known as spirit, or soul, or as the fundamental nature of the universe and the spirit. It implies the supreme unity of existence, a latent unity which permeates individual beings and their changing forms, a unity which should not be sought in the outer world, but can be found directly within ourselves. So soon as the discipline of Zen has endowed one with the consciousness of this fundamental nature or primordial quality of the self and of the universe alike, one has absorbed the universe into oneself, which amounts to saying that one has identified oneself with the cosmos."

Though, as Professor Anesaki points out, this doctrine, which the Japanese had sought in the Sung China of the Hang-chou period, was included under the designation of Buddhism, it was deeply impregnated with the mighty Taoist speculations of ancient China. Through this medium the monism of Lao-tzŭ and Chuang-tzŭ now flooded the Japanese soul with its unrivalled force, its philosophy of nature, and its sense of the life that is in things. "These Buddhist Taoists," as Anesaki justly calls them, were, in fact, mystical nature-philosophers, impassioned lovers of forests and waters, of far distances and mountain peaks. Their communion with nature was complete, but it involved no abdication of the personality or false sensibility — on the contrary: for, though a thoroughgoing nature-philosophy, Zenism is a system of mental concentration with a view to action, a doctrine of action, intense, unlimited, and superhuman, a cult of energy for its own sake, and even, in reality, a pure doctrine of energy. The Zenist, as Anesaki notes, placed himself above good or evil, above pleasure or pain. The soul, which has become the universe, dominates itself and the universe alike. The Zenist is "an immovable rock" against which the tempests dash themselves in vain. We can see why, amid the tumult of the great civil wars of the Japanese Middle Ages, amid the convulsions of a society as tough

FIGURE 124
Shunchō. Women smoking by the waterside.
— *Vever collection. Photo, Pivot*

as steel, this iron doctrine at once became the religion of the samurai — a school of personality, an anvil on which to forge the ego. It was

FIGURE 125
Shunchō. Three courtesans.
— *Photo, Giraudon*

a knightly Buddhism, far more useful to them than the effeminate Buddhism of the Amidists. Their paradise no longer had any affinity with those of Fra Angelico, but was overshadowed by the sword. As early as the thirteenth century Hōjō Tokiyori and his son Hōjō Tokimune, the conqueror of the Mongols and the "great *bushi* of Kamakura," were fervent Zenists, and, following their example, many of the Japanese military leaders of the thirteenth and fourteenth centuries drew their superhuman courage from the transcendental calm of the Zenshū. The famous *bushidō,* the samurai's code of chivalry, was no more than the practical application of the same doctrine.[1]

FIGURE 126
Bunchō. Young woman.
— *Vever collection. Photo, Pivot*

We shall meet with the same conceptions in the æsthetic ideal of the day, and notably in the landscapes in wash. Since, according to the Zenist creed, the soul was identified with the universe, the harmony between these created a vast symbolism in which states of mind were expressed in landscape, and landscapes were expressive of a state of mind. "Moonlight came to signify spiritual limpidity, rock firmness of soul, and snow a coldly resolute spirit." And as a symbol of the soul which has attained complete liberty by its absolute purity, Dōgen was to describe a boat floating in the immensity of space:

[1] See Inazo Itobe: *Bushidō, the Soul of Japan* (Tōkyō, 1901).

On the tranquil water, without so much as the vestige of a ripple,
In the air calm as though dead, at the midnight hour serene,
A boat floats free.
Lo! the moon's pure brightness filters through air and wave,
And the boat is bathed in the purity of the pale light.

After such doctrines as these we need not be surprised to see a transformation in the Japanese æsthetic ideal. It now became animated with a prodigious energy both of spirit and of action, and a totally new feeling for nature was revealed to it.

A direct Zenist inspiration, as Professor Elisséev notes, is to be traced in the architecture, " with its temples strong and sober in form, built on a square plan with four great round columns " — such as the Engakuji at Kamakura, built in 1282 by Hōjō Tokimune.[1] This vigorous Zenist simplicity is in contrast with the complications of the Shingon style, which can still be perceived in the Ishiyamadera, in Ōmi, rebuilt under Yoritomo with its ground-floor on a square plan, and the rest, from the first roof upwards, on a circular plan.

In the plastic arts[2] Zenist inspiration appeared in the form of realism.[3] As we have seen, Zenism took a practical interest above all in " the realization of man." Aiming as it did at modelling and, if we may use the expression, carving in the heart the statue of ideal man, it was to develop plastic methods of a powerful, commanding, and sober realism. Kōkei, who flourished at the end of the twelfth century, and his son Unkei, who lived from about 1150 to 1220, two

[1] The great roof of the Engakuji is of a later date. We may add, moreover, that it was also at the opening of the Kamakura period that the celebrated Tōdaiji Temple was rebuilt by the monk Chōgen in the new style known as *tenjiku-yō*. See Yutaka Tazawa: "The Fine Arts of the Early Kamakura Era and the Buddhist Monk Chōgen," in *Kokka*, No. 462, 464, 466, 467 (May–October 1923).

[2] See Hamada Kosaku: "Japanese Fine Arts of the Kamakura Period: Sculptures," in *Kokka*, XX, No. 239 (April 1910), p. 305.

[3] See Kumagaye Nobuo: "Portrait Painting of the Yamato-e Style," Pt. V, in *Kokka*, No. 446 (January 1928).

masters of genius worthy of Donatello and Verrocchio, who had as their successors Unkei's son and grandson, Tankei and Kōen, filled

FIGURE 127
Kiyonaga. Young women.
— *Vever collection. Photo, Laniepce*

the temples of Nara and Kamakura with their works. In the statues of this school, which were executed in painted wood and did not exceed six feet six inches in height, we are dealing with true portraiture.[1] "The forms become individualized," to quote Professor Elisséev, "and the love of strongly characterized personalities lends the statue intensity of life."[2] In these works, indeed, the whole "personalism" of Nippon is brought into play, and leaves its hallmark upon them. The Zenism which inspired them may have come from China; but Japanese power and individualism here assert themselves triumphantly. Moreover, at that date Chinese sculpture was a dead thing; while on Japanese soil, on the other hand, Zenism found the powerful tradition of sculpture connected with the Shingon school. But in sculpture, as in metaphysics, the Shingon sect moved in the sphere of the cosmic and the infinite. Japanese Zenism, on the other hand, gave concrete, real, and individual expression to this overflowing energy. Its sculpture represented human beings, living with an intensely individual life, in which, moreover, the imprint of social conditions, vulgarity of physique, or the signs of age — that caricature of himself which can be seen in every man when regarded from a certain angle — merely serve to bring out his spiritual personality. All this realism remains, in fact, curiously sober and strong because it is uplifted by the spirit — or, rather, the intensity of the realism is no more than the expression of a spiritual intensity, the physical portrait has such a speaking quality only because it is, above all and directly, an intellectual and moral portrait.[3]

1 See the wooden images of Nārāyana and Vajrapāṇi by Jōkei in the Kōfukuji, Nara, with their strong suggestion of Michelangelo. *Selected Relics . . .* , XIII, 12.

2 Professor Elisséev, lecture at the École du Louvre, Paris, 1929.

3 The same tendency to free individuality in the pictorial art. In a remarkable article in *Kokka*, No. 439 (June 1927), Professor Seiichi Taki says that "before the Kamakura period the portraits belonging to the Yamato-e school had a dual character, containing both religious and artistic elements. Influenced by these two conditions, these portraits had too great a character of artificiality. During the Tempyō and Heian eras, preceding the Kamakura age, Japanese portraits faithfully observed the conventions of the Chinese portraits of the T'ang dynasty. In the Fujiwara age, pictures of this type took on an ornate and formal character under the necessity of infusing solemnity into them, as in the case of Buddhist pictures. And it was indeed during the Kamakura age that the portraits began to be made free from this religious meaning and with an independent

FIGURE 128
Kiyonaga. Woman playing with a baby.
— *Vever collection. Photo, Laniepce*

In the Kōfukuji at Nara there is a portrait in this style by Kōkei of the priest Gembō, kneeling, with his hands together, a wooden figure about two feet six inches in height (Fig. 38),[1] showing an old man's thin, shrunken face, seamed with wrinkles — a monkish physiognomy with a cold penetrating glance which might indicate cunning, but is really nothing but pure spirituality and fervour and reminds us of Donatello's Zuccone or Poggio. In two other wooden statues by Kōkei in the Kōfukuji, one of the monk Gempin, with his simian type of face, and the other of Gyōga, with his cold, commanding, priestly energy,[2] the realism of the portraiture is equally intense, though, as in that of Gembō, it stops at the point where it might become too brutal, and obscure the moral personality. In the Sanjūsangendō, Kyōto, there is an amazing masterpiece of Unkei's — the painted wooden figure, about five feet ten inches in height, of the hermit Bashisen, or Vasubandhu.[3] By courtesy of the *Shimbi Shoin* we reproduce the front view of this famous work (Fig. 39).[4] No words can express the striking effect of this lean old man's body, nude to the waist, with the loins and thighs swathed in a few rags, which seems to shiver as he stands on his thin legs, leaning with his right

---

content. In the Kamakura age even works with Buddhist subjects came to contain many human elements in their attempt to express the idea of Buddha. Let us take, for instance, the portraits of *Kami*, made in connexion with the theory that *Kami* and Buddha are one and the same being, differently embodied in India and Japan. These latter pictures foreshadow the coming of ordinary portraits as a result of the development of the art of characterizing individuality in pictures which were the copies of human figures, side by side with the custom of making memorial pictures of the ceremonies held at court since the closing years of the Fujiwara age. The transition came about when the Yamato-e pictures began to concern themselves with the scenes in which men play a part, and moreoever began to assume a secular character in depicting the Divine Being." Seiichi Taki: "Pictures of the Yamato-e Style," *Kokka*, 439.

[1] Front view of the same statue in Curt Gläser: *Ostasiatische Plastik*, Pl. 156. Cf. *Selected Relics* . . . , X, 9.

[2] Curt Gläser, op. cit., Pl. 157, 158.

[3] This is the traditional attribution. Herr Otto Kümmel considers that the work ought perhaps to be ascribed to Tankei (*Kunst Chinas, Japans und Koreas*, Fig. 130). Cf. *Selected Relics* . . . , VIII, 15 and 16.

[4] The profile view will be found in Curt Gläser, op. cit., Pl. 156. See *Selected Relics* . . . , IV, 13.

FIGURE 129
Kiyonaga. On the quay of the Sumida.
— *Vever collection. Photo, Pivot*

arm upon his long pilgrim's staff, and holding out some prayer-roll in his left hand. The front view of the head, in particular, absolutely fleshless and shrunken in aspect, would be almost tragic and corpse-like if it were not for the two strangely living eyes cut in it like two slits; while, seen in profile, with its long, drooping nose and little pointed beard, it is almost drivellingly senile. Yet a fiery energy streams from this wasted form!

And since we have mentioned Donatello, this figure suggests St. John in the Museo Nazionale, Florence; while, on the other hand, the Asaṅga, or, rather, the Hsüan-tsang, by Unkei in the Kōfukuji (Fig. 40–41) suggests rather the beauty and nobility of the St. Mark in Or San Michele.[1] Here again, it is true, the priestly stamp, the episcopal physiognomy, are strongly marked. This head, as well-knit, balanced, and powerful as a Roman head, suggests at once a broad grasp of ideas, a power of handling men, a strong faculty of administering philosophical systems and politico-religious institutions, and a knowledge of human nature, unmixed with illusions, together with a mind accustomed to dwelling on the loftiest problems. It is the eternal type of the ecclesiastic. But a lofty serenity emanates from the personality of these portraits and transcends it. This sober realism forms the approach to a powerful idealism. The perfect harmony between the material envelope and the spiritual content fills us with an impression of majesty, calm, and perfect beauty. The amplitude and noble simplicity of the drapery are, moreover, worthy of the finest statues of all time, the Sophocles or Demosthenes in the Vatican or the figure of God at Amiens. And to realize to what an extent this school of sculpture is a school of portraiture we have only to look at Unkei's statue of Asaṅga's brother Vasubandhu, by his side; the construction and drapery are the same, but the thickening of the features, the brow, steeped in wisdom and high intellectual power,

[1] Attribution rectified by O. Kümmel, *Kunst Chinas, Japans und Koreas*, Fig. 129, p. 154.

FIGURE 130
Kiyonaga. Terrace at the edge of the sea.
— *Vever collection. Photo, Laniepce*

but contradicted by the heaviness of the jowl, proclaim the sensual monk.[1]

Among the anonymous works of the same school we may mention the statue of the priest Eison, a wooden figure just under three feet in height, dating from the late thirteenth century, in the Saidaiji, Nara.[2] This figure, as ugly and simian in type as St. Vincent de Paul, is a caricature both of the priestly type in general and of the Japanese physiognomy; but at the same time it has an extraordinary expression of psychological subtlety and kindliness, like that of " Monsieur Vincent." And, lastly, we have the portrait of the bonze Shungō, a wooden figure some half-inch shorter than the one last mentioned, carved about 1200 for the Tōdaiji, Nara.[3] The monk is seated in the Japanese fashion — a centenarian, whose face is a network of wrinkles and whose bald, narrow head has a suggestion of fragility, while the skin is so tightly shrunk over the wasted frame that the nose, mouth, and chin already reveal the skeleton. He is telling his beads and seems to mutter a prayer. The expression is fixed and senile and at first sight almost devoid of intelligence; but here, again, on looking more closely we discern behind the mask of this wretched physiognomy a powerful personality lurking in the eyes, which follow one persistently with the force of an obsession.[4]

The same ideals inspire the painting of the Kamakura period.[5] Towards the end of the Fujiwara period, in the second half of the

[1] Curt Gläser, op. cit., Fig. 159; *Selected Relics . . .* , II, 15. See also the Vimalakīrti (Yuima), a wooden image also by Unkei, in the Kōfukuji, Nara, *Selected Relics . . .* , II, 16. Also II, 17, the two terrible deities Nārāyaṇa and Vajrapaṇi, wooden figures, also by Unkei, in the Tōdaiji.

[2] Otto Kümmel: *Kunst Chinas, Japans und Koreas*, Fig. 133, p. 157

[3] Otto Kümmel: *L'Art de l'Extrême-Orient*, Pl. 106.

[4] The decline of wooden sculpture in Japan only began at the end of the Kamakura age. In the opinion of Mr. Shōsaburo Maruo, the attempt at exaggeratedly realistic treatment characteristic of the Kamakura age was the death-knell of the spiritual qualities of sculpture in wood. Cf. Shōsaburo Maruo in *Kokka*, No. 467 (October 1929).

[5] Hamada Kōsaku: "Japanese Art of the Kamakura Period: Paintings," in *Kokka*, XX, No. 241 (June 1910), p. 369.

FIGURE 131
Kiyonaga. Courtesans on a terrace (detail of Fig. 130).
— *Photo, Musée Guimet*

twelfth century, the old national school of the Yamato-ryu or Yamato-e had already produced two masters with a highly personal style: Fujiwara Mitsunaga and Fujiwara Takanobu.[1] There are a few *makimonos* (paintings unrolled horizontally) representing historical scenes which are attributed to Mitsunaga. Such, for example, are the story of Tomo no Dainagon in the Sakai collection, Tōkyō, the scene representing a fire, and the group of wailing women — works of amazing dramatic intensity, with their surging crowds and poignant expressions of terror or suffering.[2] It is quite obvious that here we have specifically Japanese works, which no longer owe anything to Chinese inspiration. In the same vein are the three celebrated rolls ascribed to a certain Sumiyoshi Keion (1166–1237), who is otherwise unknown, illustrating the *Heiji Monogatari*, a phase in the struggle between the houses of Taira and Minamoto in 1159, and dating at least from the thirteenth century, one of which is now in the Boston Museum and the others in Japanese collections.[3] With its cavalcades of horsemen, its furiously galloping squadrons, its scene of the imperial palace in flames, its dashing attacks, jostling groups,

[1] According to Professor Nobuo Kamagaye, the earliest specimens of portraiture of the Yamato-e style are found in the work of Fujiwara Takanobu, now in the possession of the Jingo-ji Temple, and also in the portrait of the emperor Go-Shirakawa in the Myōhō-in Temple. These specimens are expressive of a strong penchant for the study of character, enriched by purely Japanese elements, instead of the more formal modellings of human figures that characterized the works belonging to the preceding ages. "It will be noted that in these specimens religious and lay subjects are treated differently, but it should none the less be pointed out that the general effect is produced in all cases by outline touches. The Yamato-e school took up this tendency at this point and developed it still further. Thus it came about that the Yamato-e pictures in a way answered the requirements of the age with regard to religious portraiture, and so the original style of that particular school came into pre-eminent existence." *Kokka*, 441 (August 1927).

[2] Otto Kümmel: *L'Art de l'Extrême-Orient*, Pl. 45–48; and *Year-book of Japanese Art, 1929–1930*, Pl. XLV.

[3] The scenes from the Boston roll are reproduced by Fenollosa: *Epochs of Chinese and Japanese Art*, I, p. 192, and by Otto Kümmel, both in *Kunst Chinas, Japans und Koreas*, Fig. 126, 127, and in *L'Art de l'Extrême-Orient*, Pl. 48–53. Part of one of the rolls in the Sakai Tadamichi collection was reproduced by the Marquis de Tressan in "*La Peinture en Orient et en Extrême-Orient*," in *L'Art et les artistes* for October 1913, p. 23. See the rolls of the Matsudaira collection reproduced in *Selected Relics* . . . , V, 12; and the roll in the Iwasaki collection, ibid., X, 10.

FIGURE 132

A tea-house at Shinagawa.

— *Vever collection. Photo, Laniepce*

mêlées, and massacres, it is a striking historical vision, an epic page written in characters of fire and blood. What is more, these tumultuous scenes of violent movement are treated by the most precise and coldly elegant brush that ever existed (Fig. 42). We may note the profound insight into anatomy revealed in the studies of horses prancing to be off or rushing away at a wild gallop after the deed has been done, and compare these nervous, elegant beasts with the stubborn little Mongol ponies which were afterwards popularized in China by the school of Chao Meng-fu.[1] The former style represents the Japanese epic, the latter the Mongol.

Another good specimen of this school is to be seen in Fig. 43, showing one of the palace grooms trying to break a horse which has become unmanageable and is viciously biting another groom in the arm. M. Odin, the owner of this fine makimono, rejects the attribution to Fujiwara Nobuzane, son of Fujiwara Takanobu,[2] but it is certainly a work closely akin to the *Heiji Monogatari*, and possessing the same fire, movement, and elegance of drawing.

In painting, too, the Kamakura period saw the development of non-religious portraiture, of which we here reproduce two masterpieces: the portrait of Minamoto Yoritomo by Fujiwara Takanobu (1141–1204), now in the Jingūji, Kyōto (Fig. 44), and, by courtesy of Messrs. Odin and Van Oest, the portrait of Sugawara Michizane attributed to Tosa Tsunetaka, dating from about 1240 (Fig. 45). In psychological intensity, power of evoking the historic past, cold nobility of pose, and breadth of design these are Japanese counterparts of the most powerful portraits by Titian or Velasquez. The same art, applied to action, is to be seen in the noblemen looking on at a theatrical performance from behind a screen, in the Odin collec-

[1] Vol. III, Fig. 242–249.

[2] Fujiwara Nobuzane painted a fine portrait of the emperor Go-Toba. See Kumagaye Nobuo: "On the Portrait Painting of the Yamato-e Style," III, in *Kokka*, 442 (September 1907). To him are also attributed the paintings for illustrating the *Diary of Murasaki Shikibu*, belonging to the Marquis Hachisuka. Cf. *Year-book of Japanese Art, 1929–1930*, Pl. LXVI.

tion, in which we may note the play of the faces, the surprise of the spectators, the long eyes with their intent expression, and the woman's smile (Fig. 46). In a portrait of a priest, representing the bishop Daitō-kokushi (1292–1337),[1] we have a type of a prelate, with a full, fat face, double chin, and small mouth, but remarkable for psychological subtlety and sureness of handling. In the same category may be placed the famous portrait of the priest Jichin, presented by M. Charles Gillot to the Louvre (Fig. 62). Though chronologically, no doubt, we have here a work of the fifteenth century, it belongs in every respect to the Tosa school of the Kamakura period. Here again we have the face of a churchman and spiritual director, accustomed to being a repository of religious confidences and to the healing of moral suffering, full of wisdom, prudence, authority, and kindliness. Add to this the splendour of the costume and stuffs, with their neutral tones of tobacco-brown and grey,[2] and the general impression is like that of a Holbein.[3]

We have mentioned the Tosa school in connexion with many of these works. This celebrated school, derived from the ancient national *Yamato-ryū,* first makes its appearance under its historic name in Tosa Tsunetaka, son of the Fujiwara Mitsunaga mentioned above. Tsunetaka, who was painting between about 1229 and 1255 (cf. Fig. 45), was the ancestor of a long line of painters whom we shall trace through the Ashikaga, Momoyama, and Tokugawa periods down to the middle of the nineteenth century.[4]

1 Kümmel: *L'Art de l'Extrême-Orient*, Pl. 73; *Kunst Chinas, Japans und Koreas,* Fig. 124.

2 Reproduced in colour as the frontispiece to Fenollosa, op. cit., Vol. II.

3 This may be compared, from the formal point of view at least, with the Zen patriarch Myoan (1480–1567) in Berlin (1546) reproduced by O. Kümmel: *L'Art de l'Extrême-Orient*, Pl. 75.

4 Before finishing this paragraph I feel bound to mention the two tendencies in the Yamato-e school distinguished by Professor Kumagaye Nobuo during this same period: "The Yamato-e pictures," he says, "which took on their definite character in delineating human figures in outline touches during the Kamakura age, began later to elaborate the details by a realistic method of sketching. This new tendency is evident in the portrait of the emperor Go-Toba by Nobuzane. On the other hand these outlines took a swifter

THE ASHIKAGA SHŌGUNS (1337–1573)

THE ATTEMPT AT AN IMPERIAL RESTORATION UNDER GO-DAIGO HAD as its sole result to change the depositaries of power. In place of the house of Hōjō the Ashikaga family now placed itself at the head of the *bakufu;* one feudal house was replaced by another, but apart from this detail the régime of the shōguns was restored in its entirety.

In fact, once Ashikaga Takauji was victorious, he immediately revived the administration of the *bakufu,* appointing as its titular head a branch of the imperial house, now relegated to a purely honorary role. The legitimists maintained themselves in the southern islands, however, under another branch of the imperial house, descended from Go-Daigo. The war dragged on for a long time as a result of this "great schism," which only ended in 1392, on the abdication of the last legitimist emperor of the line of Go-Daigo. But at the same time a split occurred in the Ashikaga family in turn. While the head of the family, Takauji, established himself as shōgun at Kyōto, the younger sons tried to make themselves independent in the Kantō. The disorder only came to an end when the shōgun Ashikaga Yoshimitsu (1368–1408) at last imposed his authority upon all the rival clans.

This Yoshimitsu was the most famous of the Ashikaga shōguns. As we have seen, it was he who put an end to the schism between the two branches of the imperial house by taking Kyūshū from the descendants of Go-Daigo in 1374 and bringing about the abdication of this line in 1392. Yoshimitsu was, moreover, a magnificent prince and a great patron of letters and the arts. He embellished his Kyōto residence, the Muromachi Palace, in which he had established the

---

tempo and diminished in their subjective significance. These outlines of course lent a vivacious effect to the whole, but were greatly simplified. The tendency reached its climax in the portrait of the emperor Hanazone executed by another Takanobu at the end of the Kamakura age." *Kokka,* 442 (September 1927).

shōgunal government in 1378, with marvellous decorations; besides which he also erected a number of celebrated buildings, such as the Buddhist temple of the Sōkokuji, Kyōto, in 1383, and the Kinkakuji, or golden pavilion, in an outlying part of the city. It was here that he retired after 1394, when he abdicated in order to become a bonze, though still continuing to direct affairs of state from his monastery.

FIGURE 133
Kiyonaga. A walk by night.
— *Vever collection. Photo, Laniepce*

But he was the last of the Ashikaga shōguns whose authority was strong enough to impose itself upon the growing insubordination of the daimyōs. Under the shōgunate of Yoshimasa (1449–90) (Fig. 49) feudalism triumphed. For more than ten years the quarrels of the clans stained even the city of Kyōto with blood in the course of the Ōnin war, which lasted from 1467 to 1477. During this time

Yoshimasa retired to the palace of the Ginkakuji, to the east of Kyōto, surrounded himself with a court of bonzes, poets, and actors in the *nō* dramas, and, neglecting the affairs of state, devoted himself to literature and art alone.[1] On his death the anarchy became complete, and Japan was split up among the great territorial houses under a feudal régime which came to an end only in the second half of the sixteenth century, thanks to the efforts of the three great statesmen of the Japanese Renaissance, Nobunaga, Hideyoshi, and Ieyasu.

Thus at the opening of the sixteenth century Japan resembled fifteenth-century Italy. The moral authority of the emperors descended from the sun had disappeared just as that of the Roman pontiffs had done. The military power of the Ashikaga shōguns, like that of the Germanic cæsars, had vanished. In Kyōtō, the imperial city, the emperor and the shōgun were held in check by the local clans, just as the pope had been in Rome. In place of these two great traditional authorities some ten principalities, as restless and ambitious as the houses of Rimini or Borgia, Visconti or Medici had been in Italy, divided up the archipelago among them, exercising a supremacy as sovereign as theirs. These great daimyōs of the sixteenth century should, indeed, be regarded something in the light of the princes of the Italian Renaissance, each pursuing a dynastic policy by force or cunning, and keeping up a regular system of mutual embassies, elegant social relations, and artistic intercourse — not to speak of espionage and treachery — and all swayed solely by the reason of state. But in addition to this they were splendid Mæcenases and great lovers of art and poetry, attaching the same importance to the acquisition of a kakemono or the composition of a *haiku* as to the winning of a battle.

In order to understand the development of Japan it is therefore necessary to know the chief of these baronial houses, which often

[1] See Yeisaku Toyama: "The Love of Landscape Gardening in the Ashikaga Shōgunate Family," Pt. VII, *Kokka*, No. 423 (February 1926).

FIGURE 134

Kiyonaga. Young women dressing after the bath.
— *Vever collection. Photo, Giraudon*

exerted as great an influence over the art of the day as did the central power. In the north, in northern Hondo, we may mention the principality of Sendai, belonging to the Daté family, which produced that prudent statesman Daté Masamune (1566–1636). In central Hondo we may mention three powerful rival houses, those of Uesugi, Hōjō of Odawara, and Takeda. The first-named were for a short time masters of the Kantō, but were driven out by the second towards the middle of the sixteenth century and reduced to the possession of the province of Echigo alone, though the famous Uesugi Kenshin (1539–78) afterwards restored the fortunes of his house. After his victory over the Hōjōs he was to find a rival worthy of his steel in the head of the third feudal house of central Hondo, Takeda Shingen (1521–73), daimyō of the province of Kai. The duel between these two paladins lasted for more than thirty years, from 1530 to 1560. More to the south, the region of Kyōto was the most debatable land in Japan, for the prestige of the imperial capital made it a bone of contention between all parties. During the sixteenth century Kyōto continued to be the residence of the Ashikaga shōgun as well as of the emperor (*tennō*). But tennō and shōgun alike had sunk into political impotence, and the city fell a prey to the rivalries between the nobles of the region, the Hosokawas, Miyoshis, and Hatakeyamas, not to speak of the bonzes of the Hieizan, who took part in the War of Ōnin (1467–77). To the south-west of Hondo the peninsula of Nagato, or Chōshū, belonged to the ambitious clan of the Mōri, the most celebrated members of which were Mōri Motonari (1497–1571) and Mōri Terumoto (1553–1625). Lastly, the southern islands were in the power of a few famous clans, such as the Chōsokabes of Tosa in Shikoku, the Ryūzōjis of Hizen in Kyūshū, the Ōtomos of Bungo, and, above all, the Shimazus of Satsuma. The highly particularist policy of the last-named family, tending towards maritime expeditions and relations with both China and Europeans, often anticipated the course of subsequent historical development.

This is not the place to describe in detail the maritime expeditions of the men of Satsuma and the other great families of Kyūshū. All that we need note — for this closely concerns the history of civilization — is that, during the whole of the sixteenth century, they never ceased making raids upon the coasts of central and southern China, while in the seventeenth century a number of these bold corsairs em-

FIGURE 135
Kiyonaga. The toilet.
— *Vever collection. Photo, Pivot*

barked upon expeditions to Formosa, Hainan, or the Philippines.[1] In the course of these voyages the sailors of Kyūshū came in contact with the Spanish and Portuguese conquistadores and later on with Dutch colonists. This was how Christianity made its way into the archi-

[1] See Y. Takekoshi: *Japanese Rule in Formosa*, with preface by the Baron Shimpei Goto (London, 1907).

pelago. On August 15, 1549 St. Francis Xavier landed at Kagoshima. He remained in Japan till November 20, 1551, chiefly at Hakata, Yamaguchi, and Funai, in Bungo. The daimyō at Bungo, Ōtomo Yoshishige (or Sōrin) (1530–87), offered him hospitality and listened to his teaching, to such good purpose that in 1578 he was baptized. Christianity thus gained a footing in the island of Kyūshū; but since its introduction had been favoured by political and feudal considerations, the daimyōs who adopted it regarding it only too often merely as a support against their neighbours, its success was likewise to remain subordinate to purely temporal considerations. And so it was bound to happen that, in spite of the political sense of the Jesuits, in the end they backed the weakest clans involved in the feudal conflict in Kyūshū. However this may have been, the Spanish missions in Japan are of interest in the general history of the world because they brought the civilization of the islands for the first time in contact with that of the West. The well-known " Screen of the Portuguese " in the Museé Guimet shows us better than any document what this sudden revelation of the West meant to the Japanese themselves (Fig. 79).[1]

The Ashikagas were splendid patrons of literature and the arts, their residence of Muromachi, Kyōto, having given its name to the literary period from 1392 to 1603. In 1397 the most famous of them, the shōgun Yoshimitsu, built to the north-west of Kyōto the Kinkakuji, or golden pavilion, in two storeys, to which he retired and surrounded himself with " a court of a subtle æstheticism."[2] Similarly, in 1473 his grandson, the shōgun Yoshimasa, caused a palace to be built for him to the east of Kyōto, with a " pavilion of silver," the Ginkakuji, and summoned the most skilful artists of the day to adorn it. One of the chief treasures of the Ginkakuji is a fine statue of Yoshimasa, some two feet nine inches high (Fig. 49), which is in some sense the equiva-

[1] Cf. I. Shimmura, translated by S. Elisséev: "*L'Introduction de la peinture occidentale au Japon*," *Revue des arts asiatiques*, IVth year, No. 4 (December 1927).

[2] U. Odin, *Ars Asiatica*, XIV, 10.

FIGURE 136
Sharaku. Portrait of an actor.
— *Vever collection. Photo, Pivot*

lent in sculpture of the portrait of Yoritomo painted by Takanobu, having the same breadth of conception, enhanced by the calm, regular arrangement of the planes and the simplicity of the masses. But of course there is a great difference between the personality of Yoritomo and that of Yoshimasa. The simplicity of the great Minamoto only lent greater power to the concentrated energy of that sombre figure. In Yoshimasa — the last of the Ashikagas who really wielded any power — this simplicity appears as no more than a supreme refinement of elegance (Fig. 44 and 49).[1]

In painting, too, the Ashikaga period is of great, and even capital, importance. As Professor Elisséev has shown, it is marked by a general secularization of art and a growing assertion of the national temperament. It was now that the genuinely Japanese Tosa school produced its most famous masters in Tosa Mitsunobu — who probably lived from about 1434 to 1525 — and Tosa Mitsumoto (1530–59), with his finished drawing and delicate feeling for colour.[2] The artists who still treated Buddhist subjects, such as Chōdensu, a bonze at the Tōfukuji, Kyōto (whose real name was Minchō and who lived from about 1352 to 1431), introduced into their work a previously unknown note, as may be seen in the Nawa Monju in the Odin collection (Fig. 50), which, though a " traditional presentation " of the subject — to quote Monsieur Odin — is " a work of rare originality in the spiritual individuality of the face and the charm of the expression, set off by the fine black of the hair, floating above the clouds." The same thing may be seen in the Kannon in the same collection reproduced as Fig. 51. Here again we have a representation of a traditional subject, for it is the same as the Sung version of Kuan-yin attributed to Mu Ch'i in Volume III of this work (Fig. 235), but with the addition of a truly Japanese wealth of individuality.

[1] *Selected Relics . . .* , VI, 27.

[2] *Collection Ulrich Odin*, *Ars Asiatica*, XV, Pl. XII (O Hina sama and branch of white peach-blossom), and the Kitano Jinja collection, Kyōto (Sugawara Michizane in a landscape setting), in Otto Kümmel: *L'Art de l'Extrême-Orient*, Pl. 60.

FIGURE 137
Utamaro. Woman making up.
— *Louvre. Photo, Giraudon*

Chinese influence was as little of an obstacle to the assertion of Japanese originality as were these Buddhist themes. The school of drawing in wash, known as the " Chinese school," founded about 1370 by the bonze Josetsu, while treating subjects which were certainly Chinese, developed a character which was quite uncompromisingly Japanese. To convince ourselves of this it suffices to recall the fact that Josetsu had as his pupils the two Shūbuns,[1] one of whom was in turn the master of Oguri Sōtan (1378–1464), the master of Soga Jasoku (who died about 1483), among whose pupils was Sesshū. No names could be more representative of the great national school of Japanese painting, for they are those of the very creators of the classic Japanese landscape. Yet this school of landscape-painting was based upon Sung models.

Though Japan has always been subject to Chinese influence, this has always displayed certain chronological discrepancies. Under the Ashikagas (1338–1573) the Chinese schools which made themselves felt in the archipelago were those of the Sung dynasty (960–1279). As we may remember, Chinese art in the Sung period had two most typical *genres:* on the one hand, " philosophical portraiture " — that is, the school of portrait-painting influenced by Dhyānist doctrines and expressing with an intensity hitherto unknown the illimitable power and all-pervading cosmic sense latent in the depths of the ego; and, on the other hand, landscape, again conceived not only as a psychic state, but as a symbol of the cosmic essence, as it were the very face of universal Being (cf. Vol. III, pp. 285, 307–8, and Fig. 63 of the present volume). We shall find the same metaphysical conception of art in the painting of the Ashikaga period. The landscapes of Shūbun, in particular, are inspired by the school of Hsia Kuei — to convince ourselves of which it will suffice to examine the two pictures signed by his name, one in the Fujita collection, Ōsaka, the other in the

[1] It was once held that one of the painters named Shūbun was identical with Gakuo, but it is now evident that this was not so. See *Kokka*, No. 440 (July 1927).

FIGURE 138
Utamaro. Portrait of a young woman.
— Vever collection. Photo, Laniepce

Uyeno collection in the same city, the former representing an autumn evening, and the second the pavilion of the sage.[1] Nobody can fail to see that these two compositions, and especially the latter, directly recall the old Sung master — for instance, his "autumn storm" in the Iwasaki collection, Kōbe,[2] or the Yüan landscape in his manner in the same collection, reproduced as Fig. 240 in Volume III of the present work. The gnarled tree in the foreground is the same, and so is the house of the sage, sheltered beneath it, or, again, the perpendicular crags, rising like menhirs or stalagmites, seen on the horizon through layer upon layer of mist.

The technique of Hsia Kuei is again recalled by the brush-work of Oguri Sōtan (1378–1464), as is proved by a much-reproduced landscape on paper in the Daté collection; [3] the treatment of the pine-trees, of the overhanging path climbing upwards along the coast, of the pavilions dreaming on the edge of the cliffs, and the haze which blurs the second plane, are all characteristic features borrowed from Chinese wash drawings, though the pine-trees or mossy rocks overhanging the sea have that individual character which is the rule in Japan for things both animate and inanimate and betrays itself in a detailed finish, in sharp contrast with Chinese landscape, which is monist in theory and synthetic in practice. Chinese landscape — or, at any rate, that of the Sung and Yüan periods — was essentially universalist; whatever spot or moment it might choose to select, it tended to assume first and foremost a general, philosophical character. A Japanese landscape, on the other hand, though inspired by the same ideal principles, was always some particular landscape or other; whatever symbolic significance it might bear, neither artist nor spectator would ever forget the local circumstances which gave rise to it;

[1] Reproduced in Grosse: *Le Lavis en Extrême-Orient*, Pl. 77, 78. See also *Selected Relics . . .* , VI, 24 (landscape in the Hachisuga collection; and *Kokka*, No. 305 (October 1915), 81 (on the standard of Shūbun's painting).

[2] Grosse, op. cit., Pl. 12, 13.

[3] Ibid., Pl. 79, 80.

FIGURE 139
Utamaro. Courtesan smoking.
— Vever collection. Photo, Laniepce

it was always localized and concrete, or was at least based upon some such scene. However much it might be inspired by the mountains and valleys of Cheh-kiang — the Holy Land of the Sung æsthetic canon, seen, like all other Holy Lands, through the medium of a traditional idealization, both mental and emotional — it none the less remained, either secretly or frankly, a Japanese landscape.

In Soga Jasoku or Dasoku (a pupil of Oguri Sōtan), who died in 1483, we may note a fresh advance, not only because Jasoku shows signs of a nervous power very superior to that of his master, but because, in our opinion, his work marks a date of capital importance in the relations between the two great cultures of the Far East. With him, in fact, it becomes obvious that the primacy in art has definitively passed from China to Japan. The true heirs of the Chinese Sung masters, who were to carry on, develop, and outgrow their work and conventions, were not the Ming landscape-painters, who were merely copyists lacking in originality, but the Japanese landscape-painters of the stamp of Jasoku, Sesshū, and Sōami.

With Jasoku Japanese technique took shape once and for all in accordance with the Japanese temperament. The flowering peach-tree in the Odin collection (Fig. 52) is drawn, it is true, with that almost sculptural modelling which we have seen in China in the works of Ma Yuan or the pseudo-Hui-tsung (cf. Vol. III, Fig. 231 and Vol. IV, Fig. 53); yet a " personal " quality can be felt in its branches which one would seek in vain in the Chinese model. Hui-tsung's pine-trees were always metaphysical symbols; but those of Jasoku assert themselves with an individual value of their own, like living persons. For the same reasons Jasoku's landscapes of winter and summer scenes, etc., in the Tokugawa collection [1] — so broad in spite of the small dimensions of the paper, which is little more than eighteen inches in height — are so specifically Japanese that they already

[1] Grosse, op. cit., Pl. 83–84. See in the same style two landscapes by Jasoku treated in a "hard" style in the Naonori collection, reproduced in *Selected Relics* . . . , IV, 22.

have more in common with a print of the popular school than with a Sung painting. It is true that the technique still borrows the processes of Sung art. The trees are treated by floating a mass of diluted ink so that the whole landscape takes on the appearance of a charcoal drawing in the style of Hsia Kuei and Chang Fang-ju. And yet, in spite of this vagueness, and the " pencilled " treatment which leaves the second planes vague while drawing in the foregrounds as though with charcoal, Jasoku's romantic " Summer," which we reproduce here (Fig. 54), can at once be distinguished from a Chinese picture of a similar kind, for it bears the stamp of the Japanese temperament, with its precise and finite quality. Whereas Sung landscape, while taking an individual and local scene as its pretext, stood for the infinite (Fig. 63), Japanese landscape, from the time of Soga Jasoku onward, while starting from a reverie which is in theory universal, stood for a well-defined spot of Japanese territory at a well-defined moment.[1] Japanese painting is, so to speak, the canalization in a concrete and particular form of what was universal and unbounded in Chinese art. Taking the estuaries of the Yang-tze or the Hoang-ho, those shoreless rivers which are arms of the sea, it reduced them to the modest proportions of the Sumida.

The same remarks may be applied to the " philosophical portrait." This *genre,* as we may remember, developed in the Dhyāna sect of Buddhism (Chinese *Ch'an,* Japanese *Zen*), an intuitionist sect which neglected the scriptures and aimed, like Chinese Taoism, at imparting the Buddha nature by a tremendous discharge of psychic force. According to this conception, the portraits of the Zenist saints were of a capital importance, for an active part in the propagation of the ineffable reality was assigned to them. In Volume III of this work we referred to the importance of this school in the Chinese art of the Sung dynasty; and as a reminder of what we said then we give here a

[1] See, for example, a picture of scenery by Soga Jasoku in the possession of the Shin-ju-an, Daitokuji, Kyōto, in *Selected Relics . . . ,* I, 16.

FIGURE 140
Utamaro. The young mother.
— *Vever collection. Photo, Pivot*

FIGURE 141
Utamaro. Mother and child.
— *Vever collection. Photo, Laniepce*

few reproductions of its chief works (Fig. 55–57), placing immediately beside them Japanese works of a similar character, and notably Soga Jasoku's portraits of ascetics (Fig. 58–61). From a comparison between these we may conclude that the portraits of ascetics by T'eng Ch'ang-yu, Liang Ch'ai, or Mu Ch'i possess a far greater majesty and cosmic power (Fig. 56, 57). All the same, in his Japanese versions of these subjects (Fig. 58 et seq.) Soga Jasoku has not made them insipid, for under his hands they are still striking in their psychological intensity; but he has humanized them, turning these metaphysical portraits into wonderful psychological studies. The Sung portraits of ascetics transcended humanity, giving us, through the human countenance, a direct glimpse of the Divine. The faces of these Japanese ascetics, on the other hand, are powerful and poignant studies of individual souls. It is impossible to forget the intellectual vehemence of the Bodhidharma in the Jōtokuin (Fig. 59), the haunting intensity of that in the Odin collection (Fig. 60), or the Tokusan in the Daitokuji (Fig. 61), one of the profoundest portraits of a thinker produced by the art of all time, and worthy of the Descartes of Frans Hals.[1] The reason is that they are portraits first and foremost — portraits of superhuman individualities, it is true, but still of individualities, and not, as in Sung works, of the cosmic force manifesting itself in the guise and under the pretext of a human being. Once more the Japanese genius, like that of Greece, has brought the cosmic within the reach of the human.

The great master of drawing in wash at this period is Sesshū, who lived from about 1420 to 1506 and was an eminent bonze at the Hōfukuji.[2] Between 1463 and 1469 he paid a long visit to China,[3]

[1] *Selected Relics . . .* , I, 13 a, b, c. See also the Bodhidharma in the Nanzen-ji, Kyōto, by Shōkei (fifteenth century), reproduced in *Selected Relics . . .* , VI, 25.

[2] Cf. *Masterpieces by Sesshū* (Tōkyō: Shimbi Shoin, 1910).

[3] Cf. a study by O. Kümmel in *Hirth Festschrift*, and another by Professor Seiichi Taki: "A Disquisition on the Movements of Sesshū during his Stay in China," in *Kokka*, 444 (November 1927).

and was received with favour at the court of the Ming emperors, a fact which is in itself a proof of his worth. Great as were the technical

FIGURE 142
Utamaro. Woman fishing for awabis.
— *Vever collection. Photo, Laniepce*

skill and artistic erudition of the Ming masters, the fact remains that they reduced the reverie of the Sung school to conventional formulas (cf. Volume III, pp. 341–2, 348). It remained for Sesshū to elevate it into a sort of personal romanticism. For one thing, though a Zenist, he almost entirely eliminated from his landscapes the intentional vagueness of the Sung metaphysical school — a sure sign, in our opinion, that he was affected by Ming influences. The commanding firmness of his brush but rarely admits of a vague line or an elusive contour. It is true that he very often preserves the layers of mist separating the planes, for this is one of the ordinary conventions of drawing in wash in the Far East, but he does so without in any way impairing the vigour of the forms which emerge from it (Fig. 67–69). On the contrary, in works of this character the line becomes harder, firmer, and blacker and widens into a patch of ink.[1] As we know, the Chinese origin of this style of workmanship can be traced back to the brush-work of Ma Yüan and his school, under the Sung dynasty of Hang-chou (see Vol. III, Fig. 23). In Sesshū we find the same gnarled trees, full of knots and abrupt angles, the same boles of trees modelled in such relief as almost to stand out in the round (Fig. 66 and 69), the same rocks suggesting monstrous beasts, the same perpendicular peaks with their wild, precipitous lines, sometimes hanging threateningly over the valley, the same fresh traces of cataclysms which have gashed and torn open the living rock (Fig. 64, 65).[2] But Sesshū has a rugged style, a romantic harshness, and, if we may use the expression, a blackness in his brush-work which distinguish him from his Chinese originals (Fig. 66, 67, 69).[3] At times his drawings might be taken for the most fantastic of Victor Hugo's productions (Fig. 64, 65).[4]

[1] Cf. S. Elisséev: "*Sur le paysage à l'encre de Chine du Japon*" (a study of Sesshū and his school), in *Revue des arts asiatiques*, IInd year, No. 2 (June 1925). See also the landscapes of Sesshū in the Manshu-in, Kyōto, *Selected Relics . . .* , I, 17.

[2] Cf. the landscapes in the Daté collection, in *Selected Relics . . .* , VII, 29; XIV, 17; and XVII, 20.

[3] There are other works of Sesshū which show how, by his own genius, he adapts and transforms the theme of the "birds and flowers of the four seasons," dear to the painters of the earlier Ming schools. See the paintings in the Marquis Mayeda Toshitame's collection, reproduced in *Kokka*, 444 (November 1927).

[4] Cf. the landscapes in the Kuroda collection, in *Selected Relics . . .* , X, 17.

FIGURE 143
Eishi. Courtesan.
— *Vever collection. Photo, Pivot*

But even in these romantic visions, in spite of the vapour rising from the surface of the water and clinging in a haze round the foot of the mountains (Fig. 69), the landscape still has an effect of solidity which makes it accessible, familiar, and even akin to us. Though as picturesque as could be imagined, it is none the less habitable for that, and for this very reason has ceased to have any metaphysical suggestion. Often, moreover, Sesshū's landscapes are not romantic at all, but simply " composed with an eye to the picturesque," as, for instance, in the " Winter " in the Kuroda collection,[1] or in certain broad panoramas in wash slightly enhanced with colour, such as the well-known " Mōri makimono "[2] and that in the Manjuin or Manshuin, Kyōto.[3] In the Mōri makimono and in that in the Manjuin the landscape has a panoramic continuity, a constructive power, and a decision of line — whether the strokes are vigorously laid on, with a brush full of ink, or merely scratched in with a light touch, according to the importance of the mountain ridges — which typify his individual genius better than all his other qualities. Here again, it is true, the origins of this manner might be found in certain landscapes by the Chinese painter Hsia Kuei, in the Iwasaki collection,[4] but in these works the turns in the line are drawn with a firmer brush, while in the angles, zigzags, and intersections of the strokes one is conscious of a greater violence and nervous vigour and a more personal temperament, which is, again, one of the typical qualities of Japanese art. Even in the greatest painters Chinese art was the product of a school, consecrated by collective and religiously inculcated traditions. But even in the works of those schools which share certain marked characteristics Japanese art reveals the irrepressible personality of the artist, impatient of restraint. So far as Sesshū is concerned, moreover, it should be recognized that the personal factor was bound to play a

[1] Grosse, op. cit., Pl. 111; *Selected Relics . . .* , IX, 19 and 19 b.
[2] Grosse, op. cit., Pl. 112–114; and *Selected Relics . . .* , IV, 24 and 29.
[3] Grosse, op. cit., Pl. 115, 116.
[4] Ibid., Pl. 11 and 12–13.

very prominent part in him; for he is one of the broadest and most vigorous landscape-painters of all time.[1]

FIGURE 144
Eisho. Young woman.
— *Vever collection. Photo, Pivot*

[1] On Sesshū as a portrayer of character and an intuitionist psychologist, see his splendid portrait of Dharma in the possession of the Baron Riuichi Kuki, Tōkyō, in *Selected Relics* . . . , XV, 23. In his portraits Sesshū displays the same romantic vehemence as in his landscapes.

Sōami, who lived from about 1450 to 1530, is a Sesshū bathed in mist and steeped in tenderness. We reproduce three of his drawings in wash (Fig. 70–72),[1] in which the branches and foliage of the trees in the foreground are no longer scratchy and " zigzagging " in the manner of Sesshū — which is, we may say, a little that of Daubigny and Théodore Rousseau — but merely indicated by " mists of greenery " in the manner of Corot. And, when all due reservations are made, Sōami almost reminds us of Corot — though of a Corot who loved the water even more than the land, or, rather, the point at which land and water melt vaguely into each other, as seen at certain dawn or evening hours among the mountains as one draws near to a river (Fig. 70, 72). In Sōami's works, indeed, this indefiniteness of form does not possess the strong power of suggestion belonging to Sung works of a similar nature. In the Japanese master's works the mist does not lead one to imagine a glimpse of an invisible Presence behind the veil. Its softness is inherent in itself. The charm of Sōami's studies of rain and snow in the Fukuoka collection, Tōkyō,[2] or in the Daisen-in Temple, Daitokuji,[3] has a directness which appeals to our sensibility without any metaphysical suggestion — the charm of rain veiling the river and blurring the opposite bank, with its line of misty trees; or of rain descending in a column upon the village which nestles in a corner of a bay and drenching the meadow which surrounds it — a scene redolent of grass, water, and space; or, again, the charm of snow-covered huts huddled at the foot of a few trees, whose branches, powdered though they are with snow-flakes, form the only dark mass on the white plain at the foot of the white mountains. We have an impression of a soft, sleepy life, " the peace of the earth asleep beneath the mists, the tender delicacy of the veiled and dreaming landscape." [4] Or, again, the charm of the moon rising

[1] *Selected Relics* . . . , X, 18.
[2] Grosse, op. cit., Pl. 99, 100.
[3] *Selected Relics* . . . , V, 22.
[4] E. Hovelaque: *Le Japon*, p. 219.

Figure 145

Eiri. Young woman.

— *Vever collection. Photo, Laniepce*

in the sky on a misty night, when nothing is to be seen but the moon herself and the foreground, with its perpendicular crags, its groups of trees, and kiosks lost in the mist.[1]

Sesson, on the other hand — who was still alive in 1572, though the other dates of his life are uncertain — while taking Sesshū as his model, developed a line that was even harder. The metallic precision of his touch is incompatible with misty effects. Even in the storm in the Satake collection, Tōkyō,[2] the ship tossing on the waves is drawn in firm, clear-cut lines, the wave assumes an almost animal form, like some many-headed serpent, while the leafless tree, with its angular branches, which seems to symbolize the resistance of the earth, is treated in a hard, linear way, with claw-like shoots that make it resemble some myriad-legged insect. For the rest, landscape seems to have less attraction for Sesson than the fowls of the air, which enable him to display the full violence of his touch and give vent to his fiery inspiration.[3] Thus he paints mighty birds of prey, falcons with metallic plumage, such as that in the Manjuin, Kyōto;[4] or magicians, such as the Lu Tung-pin in the Masuda collection, who, mounted upon a dragon of livid hue, soars straight up into the clouds, where another blazing dragon awaits him; or, again, studies of dragons treated for their own sake in the style of the Yüan school[5] (cf. Vol. III, Fig. 253).

Through Sesson the " Chinese " school is linked up with that of the Kanōs.[6] This celebrated school, the masters of which fill the his-

[1] See the picture in the Daisen-in, Kyōto; Grosse, op. cit., Pl. 97–98.

[2] Ibid., Pl. 127; *Selected Relics . . .* , VIII, 26; and the landscapes by Sesson in the Imperial Museum, Tōkyō, in *Selected Relics . . .* , VII, 27.

[3] See, in the same style, the willow-trees and herons in the possession of the Baron Iwasaki, Tōkyō, in *Selected Relics . . .* , XIV, 19.

[4] See also the beautiful birds and flowers of Sesshū's kakemonos in the Fine Arts School, Tōkyō, in *Year-book of Japanese Art, 1929–1930*, Pl. 71–72.

[5] Grosse, op. cit., Pl. 124–126; and *Selected Relics . . .* , IX, 21.

[6] An indispensable work on this subject is Professor S. Elisséev's "*Les Peintres de l'école Kanō*," in *Revue des arts asiatiques*, Vol. II (1925), No. 2, pp. 30–8 (with two plates).

tory of Japanese art from the middle of the fifteenth century till the Meiji revolution, is characterized by vigour of line, rapidity of execution, and synthetic simplification, all qualities which were present in the germ in the so-called Chinese school. The founder of the Kanō school, Kanō Masanobu, who lived from about 1453 to 1490, was, moreover, a pupil of Oguri Sōtan and a friend of Sesshū. But whereas these masters impose themselves upon us by their powerful and creative personality, the Kanōs were first and foremost members of a school, or, rather, apprentices of a master, whose officially recognized task it was to supply the court of the shōguns with drawings in wash; so that their style was necessarily characterized by a synthetic rapidity. Most of them, it is true, such as Masanobu, whom we have just mentioned, and his son Motonobu (1476–1559), possess an unrivalled talent, and " we find in them excellent composition and a technique as solid as it is brilliant." If we compare the Kanōs with such creative geniuses as Sesshū, we may be struck by a certain formalism, but in Masanobu, Motonobu, and Tannyū, at least, we find art of a very high order. " In execution," writes Fenollosa, " it is perfection itself; while its composition is full of plenitude." The art-critics of the present day give it a more qualified praise. " The work of Motonobu," writes M. Ulrich Odin, " is an epitome of all the successful features in the most ambitious of the Chinese masters; but, successful though his own work is, it no doubt displays just so much depth as he aimed at and no more. It is brilliant rather than concise. . . . Yet, having mastered all the conventions consecrated by the usages of the day, he adds yet others, thus proving his independence and his anxiety to leave on his work the stamp of his own thought. By his untiring efforts he rose to very great heights, and though he never attained to the power of Sesshū, yet, thanks as much to the ease with which his work is understood as to these efforts themselves, he none the less caused the Kanō school to dominate Japanese art for three hundred years." [1]

[1] *Ars Asiatica*, XIV, pp. 11–12.

To sum up, the Kanō school represents a Chino-Japanese academic style, but one full of strength, and is hence infinitely superior to Ming painting, with its weak academic quality. We reproduce a few paintings in monochrome or wash slightly enhanced with colour, which illustrate this definition. From the brush of Kanō Masanobu we give the representation of the "Three Sages" (Lao-tzŭ, Confucius, and Śākyamuni) in the Henri Rivière collection (Fig. 73),[1] a painting in which we find typical portraits of the sages, in the manner of the Sung masters mentioned above (Fig. 53–61); while from that of Kanō Motonobu we give two landscapes in the Reiun-in, Myōshin-ji, Kyōto (Fig. 74–75),[2] and a landscape in the Ulrich Odin collection (Fig. 77), in all of which the mastery of the Kanōs is displayed in ample panoramas of water, mountains, groves of trees, bridges and hamlets, mist and sunlight; a comparison of these few specimens will show better than any theory how, by utilizing elements drawn from the Sung tradition of China, and the discoveries of their great fellow-countrymen of the group of Sesshū, Sesson, and Sōami, the Kanōs brought discipline and order into the rules of classical landscape in Japan. No doubt a practised eye would find it possible to discern Sesshū's breadth in certain panoramas of mountains and creeks (Fig. 68 and 77),[3] Sōami's influence in certain vaporous or snowy effects (Fig. 70 and 75),[4] or an affinity with Sesson in the claw-like gesticulations of the leafless trees (Fig. 78).[5] Contemporary Chinese

[1] Cf. the similar painting by Kanō Motonobu in the Boston Museum; and, in the same style, "Feng-kan, Han-shan, and Shih-teh" by Kanō Motonobu, kakemonos in the Tetsuma Akaboshi collection, in *Selected Relics . . .* , XII, 24; or the three figures laughing at Hu-Hsi, in the Akimoto collection, in *Selected Relics . . .* , VII, 31; and, lastly, another admirable portrait of Hotei by the same Masanobu, again in the same style, in the Zenshirō Kuriyama collection, Tōkyō, a study of which by Professor Seiichi Taki is to be found in *Kokka*, No. 434 (January 1927).

[2] See *Selected Relics . . .* , IV, 28; and I, 19. Also the eight scenes on the rivers Hsiao and Hsiang, four kakemonos of the Tōkai-an, Myōshin-ji, reproduced in *Selected Relics . . .* , I, 18.

[3] Cf. also the landscape by Motonobu in the Tōkaian, Kyōto, reproduced by Grosse, op. cit., Pl. 142, and the "Seasons," by Sesshū, in the Kuroda collection, also in Grosse, op. cit., Pl. 110–111. The mountains, the peaks, the treatment of the trees, are the same.

[4] For snowy landscapes see Grosse, op. cit., Pl. 100 (Sōami) and 143 (Motonobu).

[5] Ibid., Pl. 133.

FIGURE 146
Hokusai. Boating scene.
— *Vever collection. Photo, Pivot*

schools were also laid under contribution. There is a crane in the Reiun-in, Kyōto,[1] perched on a gnarled branch bridging a torrent, which reminds us of some beautiful bird of the Ming school. But a knowledge of the sources of a classic school need not prevent us from enjoying it. It would be rather pointless to run down the art of the Kanōs because we can distinguish the elements which go to compose it. Their absolute mastery of technique, the professional and almost hereditary way in which they take possession, as it were, of the " picturesque " and the " poetic," call forth appreciation only qualified by the risk that they may tend towards the commonplace, as do the landscapes of the Ming and Ch'ing (Ts'ing) periods. But nothing of the sort is to be found at the outset, at least. The Kanōs are, indeed, preserved from this danger by their Japanese feeling for nature and close contact with the earth. Even when official patronage forced them to turn out the picturesque to order, they always remembered some little corner in the eastern seaboard provinces of the Tōkaidō, some bay, mountain road, or fishing-village — in fact, some real spot. We may admit that their works form a collection of traditional and classified scenes, but these scenes are none the less real. What is more, even the most hackneyed subjects bear the powerful stamp of the artist. Technical mastery and even virtuosity are no doubt always present, but always accompanied by a sensibility so genuine as also to have become hereditary and a matter of course. There is an obvious difference between this and Ming work, in which technical routine was no longer accompanied by real feeling. In fact, for all the erudition of Ming work, its academic skill cannot succeed in hiding its weakness. In Kanō Motonobu, on the contrary, we find richness of temperament, copiousness of design,[2] a seeing eye, and gaiety of spirit (cf. Fig. 76). Happy the country in which even classicism could still preserve such vigour! [3]

[1] Ibid., Pl. 145.

[2] Cf. the waterfall in the Akamoto collection, Tōkyō, in Grosse, op. cit., Pl. 141.

[3] See *Selected Relics* . . . , IX, 22, the two famous landscapes on a pair of screens by Motonobu in Prince Mori's collection.

THE MOMOYAMA PERIOD. NOBUNAGA, HIDEYOSHI, AND IEYASU [1]

ODA NOBUNAGA (1534–82) BELONGED TO ONE OF THE MOST ILLUSTRIOUS families of Japan. The house of Oda, which owned the region of Nagoya, in the province of Owari, was descended from that of Taira, which had played a historic part in the epic wars of the Middle Ages. Its estates, however, were not very extensive; but in the anarchical Japan of the sixteenth century a determined leader might aspire to anything, and where will was concerned, nobody was better endowed than this nobleman of ancient lineage, cold and sceptical, despising men and yet able to carry them away. His estates had the good fortune to be situated upon the Tōkaidō road, half-way between the Kantō and the Gokinai, the two poles between which the life of Japan gravitated. Moreover, while still quite a young man, Nobunaga had had to defend his heritage against the attacks of his neighbours, so he knew that without military strength a great name was worthless. He therefore formed one of the best feudal armies of the day and placed at its head a few adventurers of striking ability, such as Hideyoshi, who, from being a mere peasant, had risen to the position of leader of a band. Side by side with these upstarts, another daimyō of ancient lineage, Tokugawa Ieyasu, had entered his service. All those who attached themselves to the rising fortunes of Nobunaga, whether peasants or aristocrats, were to share with him the glory of making a new Japan.

Nobunaga proceeded slowly to amass Japanese territory, bit by bit, in a series of feudal wars. By the time his enemies began to perceive his object, it was too late; three quarters of his work was already done. Between 1560 and 1564 he wrested from the neighbouring daimyōs the provinces of Suruga, Tōtōmi, and Mino. It was now that he received an appeal from the Emperor and Ashikaga Yoshiaki, the

[1] The period of Nobunaga and Hideyoshi is also known in the history of art as the Shokuhō period (1573–1615).

heir to the shōgunate, who were both holding their own with difficulty against the appalling anarchy that reigned in Kyōto. At their request he made a triumphal entry into the capital in 1568, and between 1568 and 1570 he pacified the whole region. But Yoshiaki, the feeble shōgun, could not be content with the secondary role to which he was relegated, and had hardly been restored to his position by Nobunaga before he started plotting against his protector, who thereupon deposed him and in 1573 declared the Ashikaga family to be deprived of the shōgunate. Nobunaga now took the power directly into his own hands, with the modest title of *go-dainagon* (vice-grand-counsellor), conferred upon him by the Emperor. The great feudal houses made another attempt to resist, and the three most powerful daimyōs of Hondo, Takeda Shingen, who held the region of Fuji-san, Uesugi Kenshin, daimyō of Echigo, and Mōri Terumoto, then master of Sanindō and Sanyōdō, took up arms against him. But Takeda Shingen was held in check by Tokugawa Ieyasu and slain on the battle-field in 1573, while his son Katsuyori was crushed once and for all in 1582 by Nobunaga and Ieyasu. Uesugi Kenshin conveniently disappeared in 1578, upon which his son hastened to submit; and lastly, in 1582, at the very moment of Nobunaga's death, Mōri Terumoto was forced into submission by Hideyoshi. At the same time as he defeated the secular feudal nobility, this Japanese Richelieu overthrew the Buddhist Orders, which formed so many states within the State. This was by no means the easiest part of his task. The Tendai Order, entrenched in its impregnable monastery on the Hieizan, to the north-east of Kyōto, and the Honganji Order, with its fortified monastery of Ōsaka, commanded the capital. Accustomed for centuries past to have their word treated as law at court, they trusted to their religious prestige, which was still enormous among the common people. But such a man as Nobunaga could not tolerate the haughtiness of these warrior monks, more powerful than most of the secular princes, and their fulminations left him unmoved. Dreading neither excommunication nor hell, this inflexible great noble invested the monastery of Ōsaka, the most powerful fortress of Japan, which was, moreover, protected by a superstitious terror. After a ten years' siege, lasting

FIGURE 147
Hokusai. The washerwomen.
— *Vever collection. Photo, Pivot*

FIGURE 148
Hokusai. Abé no Nakamaro dreaming of his fatherland. From the *Mangwa.*
— *Vever collection. Photo, Pivot*

from 1570 to 1580, the fortress was taken. In the mean while, in 1571, Nobunaga had put the bonzes of Hieizan to the sword and destroyed their temples. On the other hand, not having the same grounds for complaint against the Catholic missionaries as he had against the Buddhist orders, he treated them with favour, and it was under his government that the evangelization of Japan made the greatest strides.[1]

Nobunaga was assassinated at Kyōto on June 22, 1582 by one of his officers, Akechi Mitsuhide. But another of the dictator's generals, Toyotomi Hideyoshi, the condottiere of plebeian origin mentioned above, rallied the faithful troops, and in 1582, at the battle of Yamazaki, crushed the traitor Mitsuhide, who was slain while trying to escape.

The murderer having been punished, a council of war was held by the generals of the army, which recognized Sambōshi, the grandson of Nobunaga, an infant a few months old, as head of the State, while the power really remained in the hands of Nobunaga's two chief lieutenants, Hideyoshi and Shibata Katsuie, though it was not long before they came to blows over it. Six months had not gone by before Hideyoshi was challenged by Katsuie and crushed him at the battle of Shizu-gatake, in the province of Ōmi, forcing him to commit suicide in 1583. The other commanders submitted to the victor with as good a grace as they might. Tokugawa Ieyasu, the only one who could possibly have withstood him, became his brother-in-law and ally in 1584. The new master of Japan obtained sanction for his power by causing the title of *kampaku* (mayor of the palace) to be conferred upon him, shortly afterwards changing it for that of *taikō* (or honorary prime minister), the name under which he is known to history (1592).[2]

The first article in Hideyoshi's program was the political unification of the archipelago. In 1585 he sent an expedition to Shikoku to

[1] See H. Nagaoka: *History of the Relations between Japan and Europe in the Sixteenth and Seventeenth Centuries* (1905); Nagayama Tokihide: *Collection of Historical Materials connected with the Roman Catholic Religion in Japan* (Tōkyō, 1927).

[2] See W. Dening: *The Life of Toyotomi Hideyoshi* (1930).

prevent the Chōsokabe family, who were daimyōs of Tosa, from oppressing the other daimyōs of the island; and in 1587 he further sent an army into the island of Kyūshū as a check upon the Shimazu family, daimyōs of Satsuma, who were attempting to subdue the neighbouring nobles. From that time onward the great southern island ceased to form a separate territory in the Empire of the Rising Sun, and this was one of Hideyoshi's most important achievements. All the same, he was careful not to humble Satsuma too far, for it was the corner-stone of Japanese maritime greatness. In the interval between these two wars he had personally conducted a campaign in the west and north of Hondo, crushing the Uesugi family and the other nobles of that region. In 1590 he completed this work by turning the Hōjō clan out of Odawara and handing over the region of Kantō, over which they had hitherto held sway, to his ally Tokugawa Ieyasu. For the first time since the early Middle Ages the archipelago was really unified.

In his origin and in the early stages of his career Hideyoshi resembled the founder of the Sforza family — the ploughman who, tired of being oppressed and pillaged by armed forces, left his plough and his hovel one day and took to the woods, becoming in turn a brigand chief, a condottiere, a general, and a sovereign prince who dined at the table of kings. Hideyoshi, too, had been by turns a simple peasant, a bandit chief, and a condottiere. But his fortune was even more dazzling. Japanese writers go so far as to compare him to Bonaparte. The accession of Hideyoshi, like that of Bonaparte, marked the beginning of a new order of things. It was the first time in Japanese history that a plebeian, a man risen from nothing, had been known to attain to a position of supreme power. The triumph of this adventurer, clumsily built and ugly to the point of vulgarity, marked a real revolution. Japanese society must have indeed been stirred to its depths during the great civil wars of the sixteenth century for its primitive elements to be thus brought to the surface.

Hideyoshi must, moreover, have possessed genius of a superlative order to have thus imposed himself from the first upon the most exclusive aristocracy in the world. The reason why he did so is that, though, when risen to power, the dictator retained the tastes and manners of a common man, he brought with him a wide view of affairs of which no statesman of his day was capable. Emperors, shōguns, daimyōs, and samurai all regarded Japanese politics in the

FIGURE 149
Hokusai. The bridge of Yahagi.
— *Vever collection. Photo, Pivot*

light of their caste prejudices and in accordance with age-old habits which they could not shake off. The political isolation of Japan and the particularist policy of her three great divisions were dogmas which had been binding even upon Nobunaga himself. But in such questions this son of a peasant of Owari was a stranger to the mental habits of the governing castes and listened to nothing but his own personal genius. Like Bonaparte, he ventured to launch his country upon ways which it had never entered before. He forced into the same unitary mould both north and south, both Sendai and Kyūshū. In accepting Christianity, which brought the insular population of Japan into contact with the West, he threw the country open to it, not cautiously, as Nobunaga had done, but officially and without restraint. He boldly abandoned the benefits of Japan's insular position, which had protected the country against invasion, and it was he who invaded the continent. Having broken the isolation of his country, which

FIGURE 150
Hokusai. The bridge with the eight turns.
— *Vever collection. Photo, Pivot*

had lasted for a thousand years, he desired for her the empire of Asia — a dream as boundless as that of Napoleon, but one which it was perhaps not impossible to realize in the Far East in the sixteenth century.

Hideyoshi's great idea, which will make his name immortal in history, was, in fact, the war with China and the Korean expedition.

For a long time past, the Japanese had regarded Korea as a natural appendage to their empire, their stepping-stone to the continent. Since the mythical expedition of the empress Jingō Kōgō their adventurers had descended twenty times over upon the coasts of the great peninsula which was their neighbour. Nor had they any lack of historical justification for intervention in Korea or of diplomatic grievances. In 1590 the King of Korea ordered the destruction of the Japanese trading establishments in Fusan. Hideyoshi seized the pretext of this latest insult to call upon the Koreans to accept the suzerainty of Japan. Counting upon the support of China, the Koreans declined to do so. Hideyoshi had been waiting for this; for he meant to strike at China through Korea. In grandiloquent language he announced the program of Japanese expansion in the Far East, as it was afterwards to be carried out at the beginning of the twentieth century: " I will gather together a mighty army," he said; " I will invade the land of the Great Ming, and the viper of my sword shall fill the sky of the Four Hundred Provinces! Let Korea be my vanguard! "

Enormous and over-populated, China at that time affected the same contempt as it was afterwards to do in 1894 for little Japan, " that shell which aspired to contain the ocean, that bee which presumed to sting the great tortoise of China through its shell." But the Japanese were unmoved by this mockery. The Ming dynasty, which had reigned over China for the last two centuries, was already utterly decadent. The crowned condottiere who ruled over the Empire of the Rising Sun was perfectly well aware of the state of affairs. He knew himself to be at the head of an army hardened by six centuries of civil war. For the first time in history all the samurai of Japan were united beneath the same flag — his own. He knew the worth of his fellow-countrymen; he knew the power of the *bushidō*, the code of chivalrous valour, when reinforced by the law of the *bakufu,* the discipline of the shōguns. With such means as these at his disposal Hideyoshi could not but be tempted to carry out the conquest of Korea and even to march through Korea to the invasion of the Chinese Empire. Historians have wondered whether a Japanese invasion of China could possibly have had any chance of success at that date; but the proof that the conquest of China presented no insuperable difficulty is that a few years later the Manchus effected it, certainly with far less resources at their disposal than those possessed by Hideyoshi. It would not have been so very astonishing if, after so many Turkish, Tungusian, or Mongol dynasties, the Middle Empire had had its Japanese dynasty.

In April 1592 Hideyoshi therefore dispatched an expeditionary force of a hundred and thirty thousand men to Korea, led by a group of illustrious generals, such as Konishi Yukinaga and Katō Kiyomasa. On landing at Fusan, the Japanese army seized Seoul, the Korean capital, and pushed on as far as Phyŏng-an. But in 1593 the arrival of an imposing Chinese force obliged it to retire on Fusan. Peace negotiations having broken down, Hideyoshi sent a fresh expedition of a hundred thousand men into Korea, which during 1597 and 1598 carried on the war against the Chino-Korean forces in the south of the peninsula, in the region of Fusan and Urusan. In the course of this struggle Katō Kiyomasa and his companions in arms distinguished themselves by feats of legendary bravery and endurance, and had it not been for the death of Hideyoshi, which led to the recall of the expeditionary force in 1598, the conquest of southern Korea would ultimately have been successfully completed.

From the religious point of view, Hideyoshi at first showed himself as favourable to Christianity as Nobunaga had been. In 1580 he several times granted an audience to Father Coelho, vice-provincial of the Jesuits. Two of his best generals, Konishi Yukinaga, who died in 1600, and Kuroda Yoshitaka, had been baptized into the Christian Church. The relations between the great man and the missionaries seemed to be excellent, when the menace of the Spanish conquistadores instilled suspicion into his mind, and he began to wonder whether from Macao and Manila, where they had established their rule, they were not preparing for an attack on Japan, of which the missionaries were the forerunners. This led to a change of attitude on the part of Hideyoshi, which went so far as to make him issue orders in 1597 for the persecution of Christians.[1]

Once Hideyoshi was gone, the same problem presented itself as on the death of Nobunaga. Like the latter, the *taikō* left a child as his

FIGURE 151
Hokusai. The "blue landscape."
— *Louvre. Photo, Louvre*

heir, his son Hideyori. And once again the late Emperor's generals were to contend for power among themselves.

The most energetic of these was Tokugawa Ieyasu, who, thanks to his understanding with Hideyoshi, had become master of the old

[1] See *Kyōto Imperial University, Report upon Archæological Researches*, Vol. VII (1923): articles by Professors I. Shimmura, K. Hamada, and S. Umehara, on "Christian Relics at Takatsuki, Settsu"; "Tombstones of Christians of Keichō Era found in Kyōto"; "Coat of Arms with Christian Monogram"; "Pictures of Portuguese Merchants"; etc.

military province of the Kantō, the land *par excellence* of the shōguns, where he established his residence at Yedo (or Edo, now Tōkyō).

Hideyoshi, who had regarded him as an ally rather than a vassal, had associated him closely with his policy, so that Ieyasu was the real heir to the dictator's ideas. Though disposing of fewer resources than Hideyoshi and possessing less fire and inventive genius, though

FIGURE 152
Hokusai. The fisherman.
— *Louvre. Photo, Louvre*

at the same time more method and talent for organization, he set out to carry on the same work, for which very reason the other aspirants to the dictatorship instinctively drew together into a coalition against him. Most of the heads of the great Japanese houses, as well as most of Hideyoshi's other lieutenants, such as Uesugi Kagekatsu, Mōri Terumoto, Yoshida Kazushige, and Konishi Yukinaga, banded themselves together with a view to preventing the establishment of the monarchy as Hideyoshi had planned and as Ieyasu was now attempting to establish it definitively for his own benefit.

Faced with this danger, Ieyasu resolved to open up the way to Kyōto at all costs. He realized that the first thing he must do was to seize the imperial capital, even at the risk of losing his own fief. Accordingly, leaving the defence of the Kantō in the hands of his friend the prince of Sendai, he took the bulk of his forces and marched down the Tōkaidō, the great historic route of invasion leading from Yedo to Lake Biwa and the imperial provinces. The princes of the coalition marched out to meet him, with the object of blocking his way to Kyōto. The encounter took place on October 21, 1600 in the gorge of Sekigahara, in Ōmi, to the north-east of Lake Biwa, on a field already stained with the blood of many battles. In the middle of the action one of the Mōri princes went over to the Tokugawa side. This defection and the tenacity of the old bands from the Kantō gave the victory to Ieyasu.[1] Several of the heads of the coalition fell into his hands, among them the Christian daimyō Konishi Yukinaga, whom he caused to be executed. One of Ieyasu's lieutenants, Katō Kiyomasa, rounded off the results of this victory by crossing to the island of Kyūshū and forcing it to recognize the authority of his chief, for which he received as his reward a considerable fief on that island.[2]

The period of the three dictators of Japan in the sixteenth century is generally known as the Momoyama period, from the name of a stronghold which Hideyoshi built himself in 1593 at Fushimi in Yamashiro, though, strictly speaking, this expression applies only to the years between 1593 and 1600.[3] In art it saw the development

[1] The "Battle of Sekigahara," by Tannyū Kanō, owned by the Shintō Temple, Tōshōgū, Nikkō, reproduced in *Selected Relics . . .*, XVII, 26.

[2] See Murdoch and Yamagata: *History of Japan*, II ("The Century of Early Foreign Intercourse: 1542–1651") (second edition, London, 1925).

[3] We may note that the personal influence of Hideyoshi on the art and culture of his time made itself felt very deeply, especially in the arrangement of the tea ceremony,

of the two great national schools of the Tosas and the Kanōs. This was the age of Tosa Mitsuyoshi (1539–1613) and his son Tosa Mitsunori (1583–1638). The Tosa school was characterized by a minute treatment, enhanced with gold and rich colour, which soon developed into what has been called " miniature painting on a large scale " and may be compared with illumination; but it none the less produced very fine works, which, though extremely studied, had all the breadth of the Kanō school. We reproduce here a few equestrian portraits from the Vever collection (Fig. 82) or the Louvre (Fig. 83–84). Such works are directly connected with the traditions of the *Heiji Monogatari* roll of the thirteenth century mentioned above (Fig. 42 and p. 172). Thus the epic tradition of Japan was faithfully preserved by the old national school of the Tosas.

Among the Kanōs, Yukinobu (1513–76) has left powerful studies of birds of prey, such as the eagle in the Boston Museum.[1] Kanō Eitoku (1543–90) was charged by Hideyoshi with decorating the walls of his palace of Momoyama and of the Nishi Honganji at Kyōto. As Fenollosa observes, in executing this command he was led to modify the Kanō manner, adding to the wash drawings of his predecessors with the slightest touch of colour the rich hues (Fig. 85) and gold backgrounds[2] hitherto belonging only to the Tosa school. He was thus able to rival the Tosas in depicting festive scenes, as is shown by the beautiful screen from his hand in the Boston Museum representing the court of China[3] (cf. Fig. 79).[4] Thanks to these novel subjects, the Kanōs were led to devote themselves largely to richly

---

which became a regular æsthetic cult in Japan, and in the art of the garden. Cf. Berliner: *Theekult in Japan* (1930), and Yeisaku Toyama: "Japanese Gardens in the Momoyama Age," in *Kokka*, No. 427 (June 1926) and the following numbers.

[1] Fenollosa, II, p. 102.

[2] See the pine-tree on a gold background (Tōkyō, Kujō) reproduced by Kümmel: *L'Art de l'Extrême-Orient*, Pl. 141, and in *Selected Relics . . .*, XII, 25.

[3] Fenollosa, II, p. 110.

[4] See also, in the style of the classical landscape, the famous eight scenes in Hsiao and Hsiang, by Eitoku Kanō, in the Kuroda collection, *Selected Relics . . .*, VIII, 27.

dressed figures as well as to landscape, a taste which was to lead the way to the school of popular art known as the *Ukiyo-e.*

This process of evolution seems to have been general, for Kanō Sanraku (1558 or 1559–1635) followed a similar course.[1] As Professor Elisséev points out, by using on a large scale the Chinese process which consisted in dusting colour over glue, Sanraku brought the manner of the Kanōs gradually nearer to that of the Tosas. Thus the Kanō school, too, became a form of decorative art.

This love of colour for its own sake, and especially of gold backgrounds, warns us that the age of drawing in wash with Chinese ink, which had been the glory of the school of Sesshū and of that of the early Kanōs, was over for good. The reason is that new influences had been brought from the Chinese mainland — though once again there is a certain chronological discrepancy, such as we have seen before. Under the Ashikaga shōguns, from the fourteenth to the sixteenth centuries, Japan had been inspired by Sung art, which went back to the eleventh, twelfth, and thirteenth centuries, and to this source of inspiration it owed its taste for monochrome painting. From the Momoyama period onwards, at a time when the Ming dynasty was about to disappear in China itself, the artists of that school at last made their influence felt in Japan. The Ming canon of art, as we saw in Volume III of this work, was characterized by a sensuous dilettantism which delighted in beautiful materials and colour for their own sake. This attitude of mind, when transported overseas, created new modes of artistic expression in the Japan of the Momoyama and Tokugawa periods. Artists in lacquer were now to take their place side by side with painters, or, rather, every great painter was to be at the same

[1] We may mention some horsemen hunting, a wall-painting by Kanō Sanraku formerly in Hideyoshi's Momoyama Palace, now in the Nishi Honganji Temple, Kyōto, reproduced in *Selected Relics* . . . , II, 35, in which we may trace a possible Persian influence. Also the delightful monkeys in Mr. Seiroku Noma's collection, *Kokka*, No. 460 (March 1929), Pl. 3.

FIGURE 153
Hokusai. The wave.
— *Vever collection. Photo, Giraudon*

time a master of lacquer-work. This was true, even before the days of Kōrin, of Kōetsu (1557–1637), a sumptuous decorator in every medium, whether we consider, in the sphere of painting, his portrait of the priest Kisen, in the Odin collection (Fig. 86), or, in the sphere of lacquer-work, the stags in the Vever collection (Fig. 87).[1]

FIGURE 154
Hokusai. Fuji in fine summer weather.
— *Vever collection. Photo, Laniepce*

THE TOKUGAWA SHŌGUNATE (1603–1868)[2]

THE VICTORY OF SEKIGAHARA (OCTOBER 21, 1600) HAD SECURED FOR the house of Ieyasu, or Tokugawa dynasty, an unchallenged predominance over the Japanese archipelago. The victor made a triumphal entry into Kyōto, where the reigning Emperor received him with

[1] See also the screens by Kōetsu in the Boston Museum and the Freer Museum, Washington, reproduced by Fenollosa, Vol. II, pp. 124, 130.

[2] Japanese historians of art divide the Tokugawa period into two parts: firstly the Yedo period from 1615 to 1736; and secondly the Yedo period from 1736 to 1868.

signal honours. After causing his personal rivals to be executed he proceeded to a general redistribution of fiefs for the benefit of his partisans. In 1603 he obtained sanction for his accession to power by receiving the title of shōgun from the Emperor. In 1605, in order to consolidate his dynasty during his lifetime, he nominally abdi-

FIGURE 155
Hokusai. Storm on Fuji.
— *Louvre. Photo, Giraudon*

cated in favour of his son Hidetada, but he continued to direct the affairs of state till his death, in 1616. For a long time he tolerated Hideyoshi's son, the feeble Hideyori, whom he had left in possession of the castle of Ōsaka; but when the young man showed some signs of independence, the shōgun took Ōsaka by storm, and in 1615 the son of Hideyoshi perished in the burning ruins of his castle.

Dissimilar as were the characters and methods of Nobunaga, Hideyoshi, and Ieyasu, history groups them together, for the great Renaissance nobleman, the plebeian condottiere, and the founder of absolute monarchy all collaborated in a common task—the first by reducing the feudal chaos of Hondo to order, the second by bringing the southern islands under the same authority as the central island, and the third by imposing upon the land thus restored to unity the strict order of a lasting and centralized administration, so that between them all they brought a modern state into being on the foundations of mediæval Japan.

A few remarks should be made about the Tokugawa shōguns. On the one hand, the restoration of the shōgunate for their benefit was no more than the recognition of a sort of geographical necessity. Throughout the whole history of Japan whoever was master of the Kantō, the region of Kamakura or Yedo, had possessed a prescriptive right to be the military head of the archipelago. Hence the accession to power of the Tokugawas came as a confirmation of the ancient military predominance of the northern provinces over the rest of Japan; for the northern clans were to remain masters of the land till the Meiji revolution. On the other hand, like all the other dictators who had fought their way to power before him, the new shōgun maintained the imperial dynasty, which continued to reign at Kyōto, side by side with himself, and even affected a devout respect for it. But for many centuries past, the functions of the emperor had been merely of a spiritual nature. The Japanese emperors of the seventeenth century were now no more than the supreme pontiffs of the Shintō religion, relegated to far greater insignificance and even less concerned in temporal matters than the Roman pontiffs of the same period. Half priests, half idols, confined to purely honorary functions, they made no difficulty about sanctioning the monarchy of the Tokugawas.

Japanese writers have compared Ieyasu to Louis XIV, and the Tokugawas to the Bourbons. Just as Louis XIV had completed and definitively confirmed the work of Richelieu and Mazarin, so Ieyasu consolidated the conquests of Nobunaga and Hideyoshi into a stable régime. Like the *Roi Soleil,* he was the founder of an absolute monarchy which would tolerate neither rebellion nor dissent. This monarchy he equipped with a complete system of civil and military institutions, recast on the basis of the old *bakufu,* with regular finances, a permanent army, a formidable police, and a magnificent court. The *bakufu,* the military government created by the Minamotos in the Middle Ages, had never been destroyed. But it had been thrown out of gear by civil war and the feudal rivalries of the nobles and reduced to impotence. Ieyasu revived it by once more giving it a hereditary head — in the shape of himself — a standard — that bearing the three leaves of the Tokugawas — and a court — his own court at Yedo (Edo). Unlike Nobunaga and Hideyoshi, Ieyasu did not move his capital to the south, to Kyōto or Ōsaka. He abandoned Kyōto, the city of extinct gods and past greatness, to the Emperor descended from the Sun, who roamed desolate among museums and ruins as the pope was to do in eighteenth-century Rome. For his own part, he had his own capital in the ancient hereditary domains of his house, at Yedo, among the ancient shōgunal and military lands of the Kantō. The city of Yedo attracted all the political life of the archipelago and was at once the Paris and the Versailles of the Tokugawas.

Like the monarchy of Louis XIV, that of the Tokugawas in some respects marked a reaction against the ideal of the Renaissance. Under the Tokugawas the Japanese society of the Renaissance, so unstable and fond of innovation that the son of a peasant had succeeded in becoming dictator, was divided up into fixed and rigidly delimited classes, carefully reduced to a hierarchy, and separated by a strict etiquette. A suspicious police — the terrible police of the *bakufu* — kept watch over the public and private life of the citizens and all that they wrote or did. All energies were disciplined, canalized, and repressed. The magnificent, warlike, fiercely restless nobles of the sixteenth century gave place to courtiers with formal manners, as docilely submissive to their master as those of Versailles or the Escorial. Ieyasu and his successors forced the nobles to dismantle their castles, disband their armies, and renounce all personal share in politics. The proudest of the daimyōs had to take up their residence at Yedo, at the court of the shōgun, where they passed their life amid festivities and ceremonies which ruined them. This taming of the terrible nobility of Nippon was carried out as astutely as that of the nobility of France under the absolutist régime. The free individuality and fiery spontaneity of the Renaissance were replaced by classicism and regulations. The whole of Ieyasu's work was marked by a genius for organization. It had none of the attractive aspects possessed by the work of a Hideyoshi. But Hideyoshi had been nothing but a crowned condottiere, a magnificent adventurer with neither a past nor a future; whereas Ieyasu was the ancestor of a long dynasty of shōguns, who were as well obeyed as the French Bourbons themselves, and even more dreaded.

In foreign as in internal policy Ieyasu's reign marked a reaction against the period of the Renaissance. The Japan of the Renaissance had been anxious to emerge from its isolation with feverish haste. Her sailors and merchants had descended upon every coast of the Far East, appearing in China, Formosa, the Philippines, Indo-China, and India. Her armies had attempted the conquest of Korea and challenged the Chinese Empire. Her official or semi-official envoys had sought by every possible means to establish relations with Europe, whose ideas and customs excited a lively curiosity in the archipelago at that time. Christianity had been welcomed with open arms, and the whole population of some of the daimyōs' domains had received baptism. The rise to power of the Tokugawas brought with it a complete change in the attitude of Japan towards Europe. They closed their country, in the strictest sense of the word, to all foreigners, whether navigators or missionaries. Ieyasu, who, like

FIGURE 156
Tokoyuni. Woman at her toilet.
— Vever collection. Photo, Laniepce

Nobunaga and Hideyoshi, had at first shown a lively curiosity about the affairs of Europe, did all he could in later days to restore Japan to her age-long isolation. His successors Hidetada (1605–23) and Iemitsu (1623–51) still further emphasized this policy.[1] Only with difficulty could they be persuaded to let the Dutch come and trade at a strictly defined point in Kyūshū, the islet of Deshima (Nagasaki).[2]

The painting of the early years of the Tokugawa period cannot be distinguished from that of the Momoyama age. It was a splendid, decorative school, rich in all that had been learnt by previous schools, and lavishing its hereditary resources on amazing *tours de force* and feats of virtuosity.

Among the Kanō school Kanō Sansetsu (1589–1651) is an example of this absolute mastery. We reproduce here (Fig. 91) one of his best landscapes from the Odin collection. In such works as these we see how in Japan the philosophy of nature expressed in Sung drawings in wash was translated into impressionist works, miniature in size, but big with picturesquely suggestive power, though perhaps the elegance and piquancy of the touch is hardly provocative of meditation. Such works represent episodes rather than a cosmic agony. Any school, it is true, might well be proud of episodes of such quality — all the more so since one artist of very great talent, Tannyū (1602–74), revived the mastery of the earlier Kanōs. Among his landscapes we need only mention the one in the Vever collection reproduced here (Fig. 92), or his studies of " moonlight on the snow," in the Odin collection,[3] and of " pouring rain." [4] In all these works, which are simply masterpieces, the artist shows an amazing clever-

[1] Murdoch and Longford: *History of Japan*, III ("The Tokugawa Epoch, 1652–1668") (London, 1928).

[2] For the influence of the Dutch on Japanese painting, see the book by Professor Kuroda Genji: *Occidental Influences in the Japanese Picture* (*Seiyo no eikyo wo uketaru ni nihongwa*) (Tōkyō: Chugwai-shuppan Publishing House, 1924), a notice of which by Professor Elisséev appears in *Revue des arts asiatiques*, V, I (1929), p. 59.

[3] *Ars Asiatica*, Vol. XIV, Pl. 36. Cf. the landscapes in the Prince Inao Matsukata's collection; see *Kokka*, No. 439 (June 1927), Pl. 3 and 4.

[4] Grosse, op. cit., Pl. 147.

ness — though here, again, it is still so obviously effortless and inborn as to be the expression of a personal sensibility — in his easy handling of the classic modes of producing the picturesque common to the Chino-Japanese school: effects of mist, snow, or moonlight; boats moored near a weed-grown shore;[1] fishermen's huts with "bird-like" roofs lost among the trees, branches so veiled in mist as to be no more than a blurred mass, vague mountains of which nothing emerges from the haze but the grey outline of their summits, while the foot of them is bathed in the whitish vapours rising from the valleys.[2] All of this still constitutes art of a very high order, with a sureness of drawing and a balanced composition which defy any suggestion of weakening — whereas in China during the same age but little still remained.

FIGURE 157
Kunisada. Horse.
— *Vever collection. Photo, Pivot*

The same may be said of Kanō Naonobu (1607–50), two of whose drawings in wash from the Henri Rivière collection we reproduce here (Fig. 93–94).[3] We may note how here these miniature scenes are

[1] *Selected Relics . . .* , XVI, 2.

[2] "Tannyū Kanō," says Professor Seiichi Taki, "was a versatile artist, with an excellent skill in portraying in light, simple touches, as witnessed in his landscape pictures in China ink. The method often employed in depicting the clouds and fogs by means of China ink touches is the so-called *Po-mo* method (literally, lineless method). This method was most deftly used with a special partiality by Sesshū Kanō. But it should be remembered that Sesshū's was a purely Chinese style, while Tannyū made pictures with his own characteristic Japanese conception. In this respect the latter has a just claim to merit as having succeeded in assimilating the Chinese with the Japanese elements." *Kokka*, No. 439 (June 1927).

[3] Naonobu was the younger brother of Kanō Tannyū. For his style see the broad

developing into conventional sketches in the style of a school: a few patches of ink, a few zigzag roofs, a few parallel streaks, and a vague, lumpy form outlined in the sky stand for water with willow-trees and a village round it, driving showers of rain, the atmosphere filled with vapours exhaled by the earth, and a line of mountains closing the view.[1]

But painting in the Tokugawa period did not consist exclusively of landscapes in wash; it was also represented by some great decorative painters. Kōetsu had led the way, and Sōtatsu, too, whose period of production may be dated between 1624 and 1643, loved gold backgrounds and transparent colour. But colourist though he was, he remained a subtle draughtsman, magical in his handling of movement and of impressions of space produced by giddy heights, as in his monkey leaning over an abyss (Fig. 95) and his wild geese dropping from the sky against the background of a full moon (Fig. 96).[2]

Thus we come to the brilliant Genroku period (1688–1703) and its most famous artist, Ogata Kōrin (1665–1716), an all-round genius both in painting and in lacquer-work, trained in the schools both of Kanō and of Tosa. Kōrin has the bold design and vigorous line of the former, and the sense of decorative values of the latter, as shown by the backgrounds like an illumination, the love of fine blues, blacks, and golds. As a draughtsman he breathed fresh life into the style of the Kanōs by a youthful spontaneity which is really the sign of an amazing art; as, for instance, when he represents a group of pine-trees springing upwards with a spontaneous and unbroken movement

landscape in the Shimazu Tadashige collection reproduced in *Kokka*, No. 423 (February 1926), Pl. 7.

1 For the beginnings of the "pictorial style" in the Kanōs (in Kanō Naganobu, who died in 1654), see the study by Professor Seiichi Taki in the *Kokka*, No. 423 (February 1926) ("Party viewing cherry-blossom," in the Rokurō Hara collection).

2 Sōtatsu also painted powerful battle-scenes, with cavalry charges in the style of the Tosa school. See Seiichi Taki: "Sōtatsu's Pictures of the Battle between the Minamoto and Taira Forces, Painted on the Paper Screens in the Possession of the Marquis Mayeda," in *Kokka*, No. 461 (April 1929).

and dominating the landscape (Fig. 97), or shows us, in a simple sketch in grisaille, a herd of deer silhouetted against the moonlight (Fig. 101).[1] As a lacquer-painter and colourist he renewed the manner of the Tosas by his astonishing patience in inlaid effects and in contrasting the values, tones, and vibrations of colour (Fig. 98). And, when he pleased, this artist with the careful minuteness of an artisan and an illuminator could display a genius of unequalled vehemence. Even Hokusai's well-known "Wave" is less fine than those of Kōrin on the screen in the Boston Museum, with the unbridled rage of the tempest dashing against the rocks and submerging them.[2]

The art of animal-painting, of which, among so many other titles to fame, Kōrin is one of the representatives, was to be carried on into the second half of the eighteenth century and the beginning of the nineteeth by Mori Sosen (1747–1821), whose works, in spite of the chronological discrepancy, we may group with those of the great artist in lacquer. We may mention his deer in the Vever collection (Fig. 102), or the monkeys in the Rivière and Vever collections (Fig. 103 and 104)[3] — for Sosen earned the name of the "*sennin* (familiar spirit) of monkeys"; in the quivering life of the creature's fur he can convey the whole instinct of a species.

One last great landscape- and animal-painter may be mentioned, Maruyama Ōkyo (1733–95). By the force of his personality Ōkyo once more breathed a soul into landscape, lending it reverie, peace, and mystery, for all the cleverness of his technique. Witness his Fuji among the clouds (Fig. 106), or his moonlight on the river (Fig.

[1] Cf. also the deer and roe in the Odin collection, *Ars Asiatica*, XIV, Pl. XLV.

[2] Kümmel: *L'Art de l'Extrême-Orient*, Pl. 146–147, and Fenollosa, Vol. II, p. 138. For the same quality of violence see "Gods of the thunder and the storm," a folding screen by Kōrin in the Tokugawa collection, in *Selected Relics . . .* , IX, 27. For Kōrin's work as a whole see the splendid album: *Selected Masterpieces by Kōrin and Kenzān* (Tōkyō, 1906), published by the Kokka Publishing Company; Seiichi Tajima: *Masterpieces selected from the Kōrin School* (Tōkyō, 1914); also Yone Noguchi: *Kōrin* (1922).

[3] See also Fenollosa, Vol. II, p. 172. *Selected Relics . . .* , XVII, 37 (deer in autumn); III, 38 (monkeys); and, in another style, the great landscape — with monkeys, of course — in the Daté collection, *Selected Relics . . .* , IX, 31.

107).[1] Even after him there were still noble landscape-painters in Japan up to the eve of the Meiji revolution, such as Buson (1716–83),[2] Buzen (1734–1806), and Bunchō (1763–1842), who succeeded in rendering, with no less power and delicacy than their predecessors, poignant impressions of night and mist, of paths and hamlets at the water's edge (Fig. 108), or trails of vapour half-way up a mountain side (Fig. 109).[3] But for a long time past public taste had turned away from these academic subjects towards the popular school of Ukiyo-e.

Here again we may trace the influence of China. A great part of Ming and Ch'ing painting is taken up with portraits of young girls or courtesans in full ceremonial dress or amorous undress (cf. Volume III, Fig. 261–263 and Fig. 110 and 111 of the present volume). Japan under the Tokugawas saw the development of a similar art, which was encouraged by the easy life of Yedo. Painting properly so called delighted in scenes of everyday life or the intimate life of women, whom it observed in their innumerable domestic occupations or glorified in their elegance (Fig. 112–115). But this new type of art found expression above all in the print.[4]

The artists who produced the popular prints so much despised by modern æsthetes had none the less learnt to draw in the best of schools.[5] This form of art could claim the sanction of such a name

[1] *Selected Relics . . .* , IV, 32. We may note that Ōkyo too was affected by European influences. Cf. Elisséev's notice of Kuroda's book in *Revue des arts asiatiques*, V, I, 59 (1929). See the extraordinary "Thunder-storm" by Ōkyo, already so much in the European style, now in the Enman-in Temple, Mi-i-dera, Ōmi, reproduced in *Selected Relics . . .* , IX, 30, c; and Ōkyo's snow effects reproduced in *Kokka*, No. 303 (August 1915); Kuroda Genji: *Occidental Influences in the Japanese Picture* (Tōkyō, 1924).

[2] See *Kokka*, No. 471 (February 1930).

[3] See the Fuji, a kakemono by Bunchō Tani, belonging to Mr. Takeo Hasegawa, reproduced in *Kokka*, No. 457 (December 1928), Pl. I.

[4] In connexion with the subject of Japanese prints, may I once more point out what a loss Orientalism has suffered in the person of René Trinquet, that wonderfully able art-critic who lost his life in the Great War in 1918.

[5] An interesting subject, which until recently had not been sufficiently studied, is that of the relations between the Japanese print and the popular Chinese print. A good study

Figure 158

Kuniyoshi. The monk Nichiren in the snow.
— *Vever collection. Photo, Laniepce*

as that of Matabei Iwasa (1568–1650), a free lance of Japanese painting who, after passing through the academic schools of Tosa and Kanō, turned in the end to that of the Ukiyo-e.[1] As a matter of fact, he was the master of Ishikawa Moronobu, who died in 1694 and was the founder of the popular art of wood-engraving. Moronobu made drawings and engravings of the daily occupations of women, or their walks beneath the blossoming trees. He followed them into their home life and left a permanent record of their gestures at every hour of the day. And since he knew that the people whom he loved needed dreams and romance, he delighted in creating epic visions such as his dazzling cavalcades of Amazons (Fig. 116).[2]

Kaigetsudō, or, rather, the Kaigetsudōs, whose school flourished from about 1707 to 1714, preferred large portraits of separate courtesans in sumptuous attire to Moronobu's groups (Fig. 117), and this source of inspiration was to dominate the popular prints for a century to come. Scenes from the life of the courtesans of the Yoshiwara, or "Green Houses"—the name popularly given to the courtesans' quarter—were to become more and more numerous, and Torii Kiyonobu (1664–1729) was to add portraits of famous actors.

Up to this time the prints had been in black and white only, with

---

of this point is to be found in Professor Shidzuya Fujikake's "Relation between the Japanese Ukiyo-e Colour-prints and the Chinese Colour-prints," in *Kokka*, No. 459 (February 1929).

[1] See "Portrait of Matabei Iwasa and Records concerning him," in *Kokka*, XXVI, No. 303–4 (August–September 1915). We may note, however, that Professor Seiichi Taki, in a remarkable study, denies that, as is generally asserted, Matabei was the originator of the "vulgar" school or Ukiyo-e. As the eminent professor points out, not only did Matabei always remain imbued with the academic spirit of the Tosa school, but he remained faithful to aristocratic subjects and historic and classic themes, as is shown, for example, by his screen of the *Heiji Monogatari* in Prince Mori Motoaki's collection. Most of the paintings in the popular style which are attributed to him are false. See Seiichi Taki: "The Characteristics of Matabei Iwasa's drawings," in *Kokka*, No. 450 (May 1928).

[2] See J. Kurth: *Die Primitiven des Japanholzschnitts* (1922); id., *Masterpieces of Japanese Woodcuts from Moronobu to Hiroshige* (1924); F. Rumpf: *Primitive Japanese Woodcuts;* Vignier and Inada: *Harunobu, Koriusai and Shunshō, estampes japonaises exposées au Musée des Arts décoratifs en janvier, 1910*, with preface by R. Koechlin (1910).

at most a timid essay at colouring by hand. But towards 1742 the discovery of the process of printing from several blocks charged with different colours gave rise to a more living art, the first master of which was Masanobu, who died about 1761. With Masanobu colour-printing showed itself already master, not only of its technique, but also of its whole repertoire of subjects: actors, popular heroes, legendary scenes, and, above all, the occupations of the women in the " Green Houses."

FIGURE 158 b
Hiroshige. Fish.
— *Vever collection*

The life of elegance which they represent is obviously not innocent of a certain crude luxury; but we may none the less take a pleasure in all these figures of the courtesans of Yedo, with their decorative poses, full of a fallacious ingenuousness and a discreetly erotic suggestion. In this connexion we may mention Toyonobu (1711–85), and his three geishas personifying the winds of spring, summer, and autumn, with light but sumptuous fluttering robes, disclosing their long legs, whose seeming thinness is but a delicate gracility[1] (cf. Fig. 118).

[1] P. A. Lemoisne: *L'Estampe japonaise*, Pl. 8, p. 37.

There is the same charm in the bathing girls of Kiyomitsu (1735–85), plump and delicate, with the kimono slipping from their rounded shoulders,[1] or in those of Kiyohiro (who died in 1776), who seem more modest—though perhaps merely for the reason that their immodesty is more naïve.[2]

Polychrome colour-printing triumphed completely with Harunobu, who was born about 1730 and died in 1770—a very great artist and the earliest of the great poetic interpreters of Japanese womanhood.[3] Though dainty almost to the point of over-refinement, his talent none the less possesses great charm and sweetness. The Vever collection possesses excellent states of his prints—for instance, the one showing women looking out at the snow (Fig. 119), with its delicate feeling, or that of women washing their hair, with its nude figures, at once full and gracile (Fig. 120); and, above all, the one reproduced as Fig. 121 — a study in black, grey, white, and pink of a couple in the snow, with its light flakes loading the trees and deadening their footsteps on the ground; the ground is white beneath a grey sky, and the figures, hooded and elegantly sentimental, lend the whole scene a delightful feeling of intimacy.

Koriusai, a pupil of Harunobu's, who was at the height of his artistic activity between about 1770 and 1780, added a strong talent for animal-drawing to his mastery as a colourist. The sumptuous robes of his courtesans (Fig. 122), and his cocks with brilliant plumage, or falcons attacking pheasants (Fig. 123), alike reveal a remarkable sense of decorative effect.

Katsugawa Shunshō (1726–92) has painted powerful portraits of actors and wrestlers, in which his vigour makes him a forerunner of Sharaku. Shunshō had as his pupil Shunchō.

Kichizaemon Shunchō (*c.* 1780–1800) has left figures of women

[1] W. von Seidlitz, *Der japanische Farbenholzschnitt*, Fig. 26 (trans. Lemoisne, Fig. 16, p. 50).

[2] Ibid., Fig. 28 (trans. Lemoisne, Fig. 18, p. 58).

[3] J. Kurth: *Suzuki Harunobu* (1923).

with harmonious lines and a calm and noble expression, smoking at the water's edge (Fig. 124), enjoying the pleasures of boating, or talking on some poetical terrace in a spring garden.[1] These are not

FIGURE 159
Hiroshige. Among the reeds. — *Vever collection. Photo, Pivot*

FIGURE 160
Hiroshige. Eagle on a pine-tree. — *Vever collection. Photo, Pivot*

FIGURE 160 b
Hiroshige. Wild geese against the moon. — *Vever collection. Photo, Pivot*

the plump young girls of Masanobu or Toyonobu, but real women, with some affinity to our Western canons of female beauty, and bodies

[1] As P. A. Lemoisne says, Shunchō was perhaps a little too much inspired by Kiyonaga; yet he has a sort of harshness of line which must be the heritage of his master Shunshō.

that already show a tendency to elongation (Fig. 124). The best of Shunchō's works approximate closely to those of Kiyonaga (Fig. 125).

Bunchō (Ippitsusai, who probably died about 1796) worked with Shunshō and Shunchō and has left us figures inspired by the same themes, but softer and more feminine.

The Japanese colour-print reached its highest level with Torii Kiyonaga (1742–1813 or 1815), in whose sense of beauty nothing survives that is conventional, trifling, or childish; on the contrary, it acquires a new breadth and ordered arrangement.[1] No other master of popular Japanese art has so much affinity with European canons of art. Without sacrificing any of the charm of Nippon, he restored the normal proportions of the body. Curiously enough, in an artist of that " vulgar school " which cultured Japanese, whether art-critics or amateurs, show themselves unwilling to appreciate without considerable reservations, his figures have a tranquil dignity reminding one of Greek art. This sane and harmonious realism extends to the setting as well; the calm atmosphere of the surroundings is a complement to the moral serenity of the figures, so that Kiyonaga's women rise above the dainty charm of other masters and achieve a classic quality akin to the canons of Renaissance Italy (Fig. 127, 134, etc.). Witness the young mother preparing for her toilet while another woman plays with her baby, from the " series of broadsheets " (Fig. 128). Another affinity between Kiyonaga and the Italians lies in the fact that, like them, he understands the art of composition on a large scale, of scenes with an ordered classic arrangement. In this connexion we need only mention the celebrated scene on the terrace of a tea-house looking out over the bay of Shinagawa, with the delightful attitudes of the women in the foreground, and, in the background, a wide outlook over a

[1] See Vignier and Inada: *Kiyonaga, Bunchō, Sharaku, Estampes japonaises exposées au Musée des Arts décoratifs en janvier, 1911*, with preface by R. Koechlin (Paris, 1911).

shore swept by the seawind and bathed in the quivering light which plays over marine horizons (Fig. 132). Or, again, we have another terrace looking over the sea, with a charming study of the back view of a woman leaning over the balustrade (Fig. 130, 131). No less remarkable for the grouping of its figures is the "Landing on the Quay of the Sumida," from which we reproduce the fragment often incorrectly called "The Farewell" (Fig. 129).

FIGURE 161
Hiroshige. Moonlight over the bay of Takanawa.
— *Vever collection. Photo, Pivot*

But in Kiyonaga we have to take into account not only this classic conception of beauty and feeling for *ensemble*, but also the qualities proper to his own country and age. However classic his spirit may seem to us, no other artist has so well understood the secret of the charm of Nippon. Without seeking after any of the subtle or dainty effects which enchant us in the later masters, he achieves poetry of a suave and pervasive charm. His fascination is inexhaustible — as, for instance, in his print of "Young Girls Fixing Poems to the Blossoming Trees in Spring," in which everything is bathed in a pale-golden light with which the shades of the objects represented, ranging from pale yellow to deep red, form a delicate harmony. The choice of the shades of colour would alone suffice to make this scene immortal, even without the poetic charm of the garden which forms its setting, the grace of the attitudes, and the subdued richness of the fabrics. It shows no trace of over-refinement or of clever artifices due solely to technical skill. The sumptuousness of the decorative effect is kept within discreet bounds; no detail monopolizes attention to the detriment of the whole—in fact, the very soul of the painter has passed into his work. Another print that is a real poem is that of "Young Women Crossing the Sumida in the Ferry-boat," an excellent state of which is to be found in the Vever collection; or, again, the various scenes of "Boating on the Sumida," or "Girls on the Seashore," in which we do not know what to admire most—the suavity of the colour, the youthfulness of the attitudes, or the luminous atmosphere in which the landscape is bathed. Or what are we to say of his joyous festivals in temples, in which he created a *genre* copied by all his successors; or of many other episodes of feminine life, in which we see the same woman, with her noble lines, placed in a setting full of charm and conceived in accordance with a canon of beauty which is truly universal?

It is not surprising, then, that Kiyonaga should be so favourably judged in Europe, for no other of the great Japanese engravers approximated so closely to our Western canons of art. "The lines," writes Fenollosa, "are more harmonious than Botticelli, more suave and flowing than Greek painting, and indeed suggesting . . . even Greek sculpture."[1] Or again, to quote M. Louis Aubert, "The air of gaiety, youth, and grace in Kiyonaga's prints, and the serenity maintained by his heroines, awaken memories of the life of antiquity: women at their toilet, scenes of banqueting or the dance, love-scenes,

[1] Op. cit., II, 195.

youths and courtesans such as those whom the Athenian painters traced in black lines on the white backgrounds of their lecythi "[1] (cf. Fig. 135). The fact that an obstinate social and literary prejudice forbids Japanese critics of the present day to admire the masters of the Ukiyo-e without reservation is immaterial. It would be an odd piece of unoriginal snobbery on our part to consider ourselves bound to concur in this ostracism.

Sharaku at least stands to some extent outside this prejudice, for the reason that, throughout his whole career — which is, moreover, very little known, though his best work may be placed about 1789 and 1800 — he devoted himself to painting the most famous actors of his day — always a very popular theme in Japan. Moreover, we may recognize the power and amazing psychological violence expressed in the faces of Sharaku's actors, in which the popular print unconsciously goes back to the great tradition of the portraits of the Zen ascetics (Fig. 136 and 59–61).[2]

With Utamaro (1754–1806) a new manner makes its appearance.[3] Kiyonaga, while devoting himself in the first place to the feminine form, had chiefly admired beauty of line and rhythmical beauty of pose in woman; but Utamaro painted the Japanese woman for her own sake, from the point of view not only of an artist, but of a lover. An intimate of the " Green Houses," of which he became the licensed painter, he lived at a time when the courtesans of Nippon were at the height of their influence, forming, so to speak, a sort of priesthood of art in the society of Yedo. It was such courtesans as these, themselves more or less cultured and, at any rate, the inspirers of the greatest writers, upon whom Utamaro attended as adorer, confidant, and friend at every stage of their existence, whether in the artificial en-

[1] L. Aubert: *Les Maîtres de l'estampe japonaise*, p. 129.

[2] See J. Kurth: *Sharaku* (1922).

[3] See J. Kurth: *Utamaro* (1907); Yone Noguchi: *Utamaro* (1925); Vignier and Inada: *Utamaro, Estampes japonaises exposées au Musée des Arts décoratifs en janvier, 1912*, with preface by Raymond Koechlin (Paris, 1912).

chantment of their outward life or in the charm of their intimacy (Fig. 137–139). In this respect certain of his portraits of great courtesans are of priceless value as social documents, as well as works of dazzling sumptuousness and decorative magnificence. And similarly the sets of prints devoted by Utamaro to the same theme — such as the " Courtesans and Geishas compared to Flowers," the " Twelve Hours at the Yoshiwara," the " Events of the Year in the Green Houses," or the erotic series such as the " pillow-poems," or " fallen flowers " — give him a place as accredited exponent of the amorous mysteries as understood in Japan.

Like Kiyonaga, Utamaro loved to paint the Japanese courtesan in the triumphant setting of great festivals or pleasure parties; but the latter was equipped for the reproduction of such scenes with a more direct faculty of observation, a more popular vigour, and, in spite of the increasing deformation of the physical types which was becoming a convention, a greater realism in *ensemble* compositions. Kiyonaga and Shunchō were more reserved, and painted, as a rule, only groups. But Utamaro had an eye for the crowd and, as a friend of the people, regarded it with an amused and sympathetic glance. There is, however, no vulgarity in his work, even in his scenes of popular life. His crowds move in the same setting as his groups — the enchanted setting of a court of love or a Venetian festival. For Utamaro is an exquisite colourist, almost decadent in his refinement. To recognize his virtuosity in this respect, we need only recall such prints as those of which the Vever collection possesses good states: for instance, his " Young Girls Gathering Mulberry-leaves," his " Women Strolling under the Blossoming Cherry-trees," his " Festival on the Sumida by Night, near the Ryōgoku Bridge." In the last-named print women and children are sauntering indolently along the shore of the river, silhouetted against the dark water, which is bounded in the distance by a procession of innumerable junks. But the masterpiece of Utamaro as a colourist is, perhaps, the print of

"Women on the Great Bridge of the Sumida, on a Summer Evening," a fine state of which is to be found in the Musée des Arts Décoratifs, Paris — an amusing crowd dressed in violet, black, yellow, and green, with a touch of red — a crowd of mousmés and geishas on holiday, in an enchanted setting.

Utamaro's voluptuous and caressing brush at first attempted more than to portray Japanese womanhood in accordance with the tradi-

FIGURE 162
Hiroshige. Looking down on the bay.
— *Vever collection. Photo, Pivot*

FIGURE 163
Hiroshige. The descent of the eagle.
— *Vever collection. Photo, Pivot*

tional type made fashionable by the school of Kiyonaga. But soon he took this idol of his life and art and transformed her into an unreal being, fashioned entirely according to his caprice, half flower, half butterfly, like a figure in a dream.[1] The form of his heroines

[1] See "A beauty dressing in summer," by Utamaro, reproduced in the album *Thirty Masterpieces of Modern Japanese Pictorial Art, Tokugawa Period*, edited by Kanroku Kubota (Tōkyō, *Shimbi Shoin*, 1925).

sways and bends into a great flower-like curve; the face becomes conventionally elongated, and is lent an added touch of strangeness by the double line indicating the half-closed eyes and the two tiny petal-like lips. This disproportionate and almost hieratic elongation of both face and body cannot fail to produce an impression of aristocratic elegance, to which the Japanese are even more keenly sensitive than we are. None the less, whatever may be said to the contrary, this second manner of Utamaro's, in which he shows himself an æsthete and a symbolist — though also, perhaps, an artist in a hurry — marks a real decadence, especially when compared with the sane and balanced art of Kiyonaga.

Like Utamaro, his contemporary Eishi (Yeishi) (1764–1829) painted almost exclusively the Japanese courtesan. He, too, regarded her somewhat in the light of a legendary princess, whose measured and at times stiff grace fascinates us by its reserve. The Vever collection possesses certain prints of courtesans by Eishi, with a dark, neutral-tinted background, which possess the naïve and supple distinction of Botticelli's Bella Simonetta, with the addition of a wealth of soft-hued fabrics which is a feast to the eye (Fig. 143). His qualities as a colourist are likewise to be found in his print of a " Seated young woman, holding a goblet of *saké,* with the attributes of fortune " (tortoises): the jet-black hair, in which are stuck some gold pins, sets off the pale, sweet oval of her face; the robe, of a subdued tone of beige, harmonizes with the cream background and forms a perfect symphony of colour with the brownish-red flowers. In spite of the distance which separates the two countries, it has something of the spirit of the French eighteenth century. And, lastly, in his " Tea-houses on the banks of the Sumida " Eishi shows a skill in the treatment of groups worthy of Kiyonaga himself. With Eishi should be mentioned his two pupils Eisho (Yeisho), who has left us a very touching head of a woman (Fig. 144), and Eiri (Yeiri), one of whose silhouettes, full of youth, freshness and lightness, I am allowed to reproduce here by Monsieur Vever (Fig. 145).

We now come to Hokusai (1760–1849), the head of the realistic school, "the old man mad with drawing," who is considered in Europe, though not in Japan, to be one of the masters of art of all ages or countries.[1] We may at once admit all his faults. He cares nothing for the traditional calligraphic style or elegance of costume. He is undeniably lacking in distinction of mind, and his colour, too, is vulgar — faults which cause him to be regarded by Japanese art-critics as no better than a designer of picture postcards or cheap chromolithographs. But when all is said and done, he remains a designer of incomparable power and skill. His variety and productiveness are positively prodigious: the monographs on the subject enumerate no less than a hundred and fifty-nine works from his hand, produced during more than sixty-two years of uninterrupted work.

Unlike his predecessors, Hokusai did not confine himself exclusively to painting women and actors, but was the first to introduce the "realistic landscape," peopled by animated crowds alive with a varied, stirring, ever changing movement. He thus sets out to interpret the whole of Japanese life and every side of nature as seen in Japan, with a touch full of sly humour, which, whatever the purists may pretend, is never devoid of charm: boating-scenes on water rippling among reeds and water-lilies, and boatmen with brisk, elegant gestures in the foreground, or washerwomen kneeling on the brink of a river, the vigorous movements of whose humble calling is clothed with grace by a rising moon which casts a haze over the whole scene, dims the rosy tones, and lends the greens a faded hue (Fig. 147); or the Japanese poet Nakamaro cast by a storm on the coast of China and dreaming of his own country before a sea flooded with brightness, in which floats a wooded island bathed with light by the rising moon (Fig. 148). Then we have inimitable scenes of squalls of wind, such as that in the seventh volume of the *Mangwa*, slashed by slanting lines of rain, or that in the twelfth volume of the *Mangwa*, with its

[1] Yone Noguchi: *Hokusai* (1925); Vignier, Jean Lebel, and Inada: *Yeishi, Choki, Hokusai, estampes japonaises exposées au Musée des Arts Décoratifs en janvier 1913*, with preface by Raymond Koechlin (Paris, 1913); H. Focillon: *Hokousai* (Paris, 1914).

whirl of dead leaves; all of these contain bent, distracted figures, in which Hokusai seizes the abrupt gesture, the comical distress, or the absurd angle of a wind-blown garment, in scenes of everyday life turned to caricature by the gestures of surprise.

For he possesses the secret of gesture — whether of the man in the street or of the man pursuing a humble calling, the artisan in his workshop, the shopkeeper in his store, the fisherman putting on a fresh hook or drawing it out of the fish's mouth, the cooper raising his mallet — as in the print of Fuji seen from Fujimigahara in Awari — the fisherman pulling in his nets (Fig. 152), the sawyer in his saw-pit, the blacksmith hammering the glowing metal, the baker's apprentice spoiling the rice-cake, or, lastly, the lazy writer stretching his arms before the page that he has begun, by a round window through which, rising above a fir-wood skirted by a long string of birds in flight, Fuji raises its summit above the mists into the bright light.

Hokusai's fame in Europe rests above all on his "Thirty-six Views of Fuji," round which he has grouped every aspect of Japanese life and the Japanese country-side. Here we have a glimpse of Fuji from near Kamagawa, framed by a breaking wave with its curling crest, with boats rising and falling on the tossing water. The wave is alive with a mysterious and almost divine life, like some monstrous and irresistible power, which makes a sport of the life of man. Strangely decked with white foam-flowers scattered on the wind, it seems to melt into a cloud of little birds (Fig. 153). Or, again, we have Fuji in high summer, seen against a sky barred with clouds which trail their long lines of vaporous mist (Fig. 154); or Fuji seen across the island of Tsukuda, the happy island with its houses lost in a tangle of greenery; the calm, smiling sea, of a blue melting towards the horizon into a white slightly touched with gold by the gleams of the setting sun, gently washes a wooded shore which forms the nearest plane of Fuji itself, while round the island the heavily laden boats churn the

Figure 164

Hiroshige. Landscape by moonlight.
— *Vever collection. Photo, Giraudon*

water into choppy waves. Or we have a glimpse of Fuji in a similar landscape, the " blue landscape " of Fig. 151; or of Fuji beneath the snow, which falls in great flakes, flecking the dark sky with its myriads of white dots; or, conversely, of a passing convoy leaving the dark traces of footsteps on the snowy ground; or of Fuji seen through the cobwebby meshes of a fisherman's net, through a spider's web itself, or through a thick veil of reeds blurring the outline of a river-bank, while lumber-rafts float past, and in the foreground two fishermen are sitting on piles, one of them carefully baiting his hook, and the other casting his line with a light, sure movement, while a child, lounging on the light boom, leans over the water, and a bird glides over the surface of the water looking for fish — a scene of silence and of reverie. Or, again, we have yet another Fuji, seen from the top of a hill near by, through a grove of bamboos, with long, grooved stems and drooping branches. Or the red Fuji, seen against a sky streaked with "*chih*"-shaped clouds, with its powerful decorative effect; a few streaks of snow still linger on the summit, while at the base the dull red gradually fades into the dull green of a pine forest. And, lastly, we have Fuji in a storm, reproduced as Fig. 155.

After the Fuji series we have the equally popular one of the bridges. Everybody knows, for instance, the " Bridge with the eight bends " or " Bridge of the irises " (Fig. 150). Such works as these are far removed, it is true, from the delicate, vaporous landscapes of a Sōami or an Ōkyo, with their vague, dreamlike quality, for their view of things is sometimes conventional and sometimes crude; at times they represent mists and clouds " like the fingers of a glove "; at times they are almost photographically exact panoramas of real scenes (Fig. 149). But there is no reason why this should make us decry these anecdotal scenes, depicted with such an amusing touch, and with an exotic flavour which we find so diverting. Hokusai's waterfalls, like the bridges, have an exquisitely Japanese quality and a feeling for nature which belongs to all ages. We may single out at random the cascade of Yoro, with its foaming waters turning from blue to white and breaking in spray like dust among the green trees whose foot is veiled in the vapours rising from the waterfall, while on the left the river subsides into tranquillity and flows on its way, and on the right the foreground is indicated by a hut with a few spectators; or, again, the "Waterfall of Kirifuri," seen through the undergrowth of a charming wood; the "Waterfall of Amida in Kiro," which is the most popular of all; the cascade of Rōben; and, lastly, "the poet Rihaku meditating before a cascade" — one of the master's noblest works.

We cannot take leave of Hokusai without mentioning the boating-scene reproduced as Fig. 146, in which the young girl is poling the boat along with a graceful, sweeping stroke, which points to a feeling for feminine grace not unworthy of Shunchō, Kiyonaga, or Utamaro in this master of power and movement.

Very contradictory opinions of Hokusai have been expressed in Europe. In the Goncourt brothers' day, when the age of Sesshū was as yet unknown, he stood as the sole representative of Japan. It was in vain for the Japanese to smile at the spectacle of Europe mistaking what they regarded as cheap, inartistic work for the great art of their country, and picking out as the most representative of their engravers an artist "lacking in distinction," whose skill in drawing could not hide his deficiencies as a colourist. It was almost as if Teniers had been chosen as typical of the art of Flanders instead of Rubens or Van Dyck. Nowadays we have perhaps gone too far in the reaction against our early admiration. The veto of Japanese æsthetes cannot be binding upon us, and surely we may emancipate ourselves from fashions in art, whether these consist in undervaluing or in over-estimating a great artist. Let us frankly admit that, whatever view may be held of his position in Japanese or in universal art, Hokusai remains one of the most powerful designers and delineators of animated scenes of all time.

There is another name directly associated with that of Hokusai — that of Eisen (1790–1848).

Another school, which, though of secondary importance, is by no means to be despised, is that of the Utagawas, founded by Toyoharu (1733–1814) and Toyohiro (1773–1828). We need mention only the latter's " Evening bells at Veno (Uyeno)," in which the ground is already bathed in twilight, while long bands of rosy vapour, treated like " the fingers of a glove," float in a pale sky and veil the tops of the pine-trees, beneath which groups of people standing round the temple are listening to the bells of the Buddhist church; in spite of the conventional design, the landscape is steeped in an ethereal peace. Toyokuni (1769–1825), who belonged to the same group, is a second Utamaro, who, instead of that artist's excessively elongated feminine types, depicts women with more rounded contours, in the manner of Hokusai, as, for instance, in his charming young woman at her toilet (Fig. 156). The Vever collection also contains admirable states of his very fine triptych " Courtesans and maidservants rolling a snow-ball," and another print representing two young women with kimonos slipping from their plump shoulders, almost revealing one of the breasts — one of the most voluptuous visions of the Ukiyo-e school.

Kunisada (1786–1865), who began by collaborating with Toyo-kuni, often draws with a vigour worthy of Hokusai, as in the sketch of a horse reproduced as Fig. 157. Kuniyoshi (1797–1861), a fellow-pupil of Kunisada's, has left us picturesque landscapes, such as that of the monk Nichiren going off to meditate among the snow (Fig. 158): the ground is covered with snow, still light and feathery, and rosy in the glow of dawn, which is breaking low down on the grey sky; a rosy tinge steals over the sea on the horizon; in the foreground, to the left, a mountain rises precipitously from the edge of the sea, and at its foot, close by the waterside, huddles a fishing-village, asleep beneath the snow; a steeply sloping path can be seen ascending the mountain side, up which the monk Nichiren is climbing; stooping in his ascent, Nichiren has reached the level of a snow-covered tree; snow is still falling, flecking the grey and black sky and the deep blue sea, and the monk's footsteps leave black traces in the pink and

FIGURE 165
Seiho. Landscape.
— *Odin collection. Photo, Laniepce*

grey snow. The whole scene breathes a human melancholy rather than a religious emotion.

A far greater figure is Hiroshige (1792–1858) — as great, indeed, as Hokusai, with whom he is often compared.[1] M. André Lemoisne has well indicated the difference which separates them. "Hokusai had breathed fresh life into landscape-painting, but he was no colourist. Besides, while interpreting it in a more realistic spirit, he

[1] See Jiro Harada: *Hiroshige* (1929).

had always seen it through the medium of his romantic imagination, so that the fiery vigour of his design overleaps the bounds of his landscapes and introduces into them, as it were, a certain lyrical spirit which is bound to work a transformation in them. What distinguishes Hiroshige and sets him on a higher level than Hokusai in this *genre* is his love of nature and his sincerity, which lend him an affinity with a Corot or a Daubigny among European painters — not to speak of his simplicity and the poetry which he knows how to draw from his subject in itself, without transforming it in any way; and, above all, his power of suggesting atmosphere. We no longer find in him precipitous rocks fantastically piled one upon another, or the violent, tormented aspect of nature seen by Hokusai, crudely outlined against a hard sky; but wide views of sinuous foam-fringed coasts, whose elusive, undulating lines melt into the horizon with a mastery which is quite novel; or blossoming trees reflected in a brook, or a smiling valley in which nestle a few yellow-roofed houses, or grey dunes, intersected by blue streamlets — a new and idyllic Japan." [1]

It would, however, be a mistake to see in Hiroshige no more than a lover of the picturesque. As a matter of fact, he, too, was prodigiously romantic, living as vehemently as Hokusai himself, and perhaps even more consistently. It is, indeed, this consistent quality of his inspiration which makes his work liable to be disparaged by superficial minds. The anecdotic side which played so great a part in Hokusai now disappears or is, at any rate, lost in the general impression. Hiroshige's figures are so much in keeping with their setting that the two form but a single whole — so much so that the figures seem to be merely one element in the setting, just as in Wagner's orchestration the human voice has no more importance than that of a single instrument.

Many of Hiroshige's landscapes are popular in Europe: his bridges of the Sumida, or bridges in the open country, whether seen

[1] P. A. Lemoisne: *L'Estampe japonaise* (Paris: Laurens), p. 138.

in the rain, in bright sunshine, at dawn, or at twilight; his view of Kiribatake or of the road to the sanctuary of Akiha, etc. One of the most famous is a moonlit landscape which might have been composed by a reader of Shakspere or Victor Hugo: a road fringed by secular trees runs beside a river, glimpses of which can be seen through tall water-plants; the moonlight forms pools of light of unexpectedly geometrical shapes on the surface of the water; the sky is a little lighter in the middle, giving a phantom-like appearance to the sombre masses of the giant trunks; on the road travellers leading horses follow the incline and cross the open spaces bathed in light, only to plunge once more into the shadow. It is a romantic landscape, suggesting ideas of water-sprites, wood-gnomes, and magic spells (Fig. 164).

The scenes most frequently rendered by Hiroshige are impressions of the earth and sea as seen from above, in a bird's-eye view. This may be seen in Fig. 160–163, in which, borne on the wings of some flock of wild geese or bird of prey, we plunge down from the heavens towards the wide bays and rice-fields stretched out like a panorama far below our feet. We have an impression of falling giddily downwards, of flight, space, and immensity.

This is, indeed, one of the favourite subjects of Hiroshige, who returned to it incessantly in all its variations: wild geese in full flight, silhouetted against the orb of the moon above scudding clouds; another flight of wild geese on a moonlight night over the bay of Takanawa (Fig. 161); or wild geese over the marshes of Hanada. In another print we find an eagle settling on a snow-covered pine-tree on a frosty night sparkling with stars; the pine-needles, covered with frost-crystals, and the plumage of the bird of prey are treated with a sense of decorative effect equal and even superior to that of Hokusai.

With Hiroshige the list of the great masters of old Japan comes to an end, while even his technique reveals a knowledge of European perspective learnt by the Ukiyo-e school from the Dutch traders at the ports.

The greatest Japanese sculptor of modern days was a simple joiner — or, rather, a master carpenter — Hidari Jingorō (1594–1634). This artisan of genius, who built and decorated the temple of Ieyasu at Nikkō and decorated the Nishi Honganji at Kyōto, as well as the great pierced friezes of the castle of Nagoya, was indeed the Hokusai of sculpture. Beneath his mighty hand a whole world of fabulous existence wakes to life in wood and runs over every surface of the building, from the doors and the friezes of the walls to the beams of the ceiling. First of all we have a luxuriant vegetation, brilliantly decorative in its effect. Giant chrysanthemums, blossoming peach-trees, and plants of every sort twine and tangle, or fall into vast interwoven patterns of a more formal sort. Next a whole world of beasts and people, emerging from this floral profusion, seems to come to life in turn and spring forth from the panel to live a life of its own. We have here the breadth of fresco and the finish of miniature translated into terms of wood-carving.

The tiny *netsukes*, or bosses of wood or ivory, share in the same delicate yet powerful life. None but the old masters of Nuremberg have hollowed out the wood with such loving care. They are like so many fragments detached from the world of swarming life created by Jingorō; and an intense animation and amazing power of action are concentrated within their tiny limits. Some of them are studies of animals — snails or grasshoppers, mice or rabbits, so perfectly beautiful in their sober, vigorous realism that the artists who carved them rank among the leading animal-sculptors of all time. But this realistic art is also essentially comic in spirit, full of wit, satire, and caricature. It catches to the life, in a fleeting moment, a picturesque feature, a comical foreshortening, a grimace, or an absurdity, the distorting effects of passion, age, or a man's profession. Most of the figures on the *netsukes* in our collections might have walked out of a print of Hokusai's; for the *netsuke* followed a course of evolution parallel with that of the print. It first appeared as a form suitable for artistic treatment in the Genroku period and reached its height in the middle of the eighteenth century in the hands of a dynasty of famous carvers — that of the Miwas. We may add that the greatest Japanese artists, such as Kōrin or Ritsuō, did not disdain to carve *netsukes*.[1]

In the art of metal-chasing, the armour of the Hideyoshi period is already more elegant than that of the Middle Ages, but that of the Tokugawa period in particular can vie with any work of the Moslem East. The sabre-guards of the seventeenth century are the very finest of their kind. In this world of samurai, living for the *bushidō* alone, the beauty of this, the gentleman's weapon, was of extreme importance; so that sabre-guards became to Japan rather what ceramics were to China — a pretext, or subject-matter, on which design and work in relief were carried to the highest pitch of virtuosity. Many a simple sabre-guard of the seventeenth or eighteenth century bears a charming picture in miniature, a poem in little, which tempts us to reverie. Indeed, the history of landscape, flower-painting, and animal art is incomplete unless we exhibit side by side with the paintings the objects in chased metal produced by workers in iron; but for this subject it must suffice to refer the reader to the fine studies of Dr. Poncetton.[2]

Finally, in the seventeenth century ceramics, too, shook itself free from its imitation of Sino-Korean decoration, in the work of Ninsei of Kyōto, the true creator of the national ceramic art. The pottery produced in Kyōto, Satsuma, Owari, and Bizen carried this art to its highest point.[3]

[1] See A. Brockhaus: *Netsuke, Versuch einer Geschichte der japanischer Schitzkunst* (1909).

[2] See F. Poncetton: *Les Gardes de sabre japonaises*, portfolio of 50 plates illustrating 182 pieces (Paris, 1924); Shinkichi Hara: *Die Meister der japanischen Schwertzierathen, Überblick ihrer Geschichte, Verzeichnis der Meister mit Daten über ihr Leben, etc.* (Hamburg, 1902).

[3] For all that I have been able merely to sketch in outline in this section, and especially for Jingorō, I refer my readers to M. Migeon's charming and erudite volume *Au Japon: promenades aux sanctuaires de l'art*, 2nd edition (Paris: Geuthner, 1929).

While this exalted society was flourishing in Japan, the ancient civilizations of the continent were falling into ruin, or had already done so, and India, China, and Persia were in course of forgetting their most noble systems. At the far extremity of Asia insular Japan alone had preserved the precious essence of the old Eastern civilizations. The great Tokugawa shōguns had been wise enough to keep their country by force in a salutary state of seclusion, which was one day to render possible the Meiji revival. Faced with the decadence of the East and the mercantilism of the world in general, Japan adopted the only possible attitude — an aristocratic isolation, jealously and absolutely enforced. Thus alone in the whole of Asia she was able to escape denationalization, as had happened once before, in the days of the Mongol menace. The chief merit of the shōgunate of Yedo was that it preserved all the treasures of Nippon intact till happier days. Faced with the jostle and stir of the rest of the world, the land of Amaterasu immured itself sternly and thus preserved its art, its gods, and its soul.

If we wish to grasp the secret of the history of Nippon, the Japanese recommend us to make a pilgrimage to the sanctuary of Ieyasu at Nikkō.[1] Iemitsu, the shōgun who closed Japan, built this tomb for his ancestor in 1617. Having walked up a long avenue of cryptomerias and passed the red lacquer bridge and the granite *torii,* the pilgrim enters the forest of pine-trees which has grown up to old age with the shrine. Having passed through the temple, in which are accumulated the marvels of seventeenth-century art, he ascends by a narrow path through the wood to a tomb of a grandiose simplicity. There, amid the silence of the giant cedars and the secular pine-trees, rests the creator of Japanese unity. The great shōgun wished to sleep his last sleep amid the sanctity and mystery of the inviolate mountain. Japan slumbered like him for two centuries in the seclusion of art, poetry, and expectation. When she emerged, voluntarily and with

[1] See R. C. Hope: *The Temples and Shrines of Nikkō* (1894).

the trusty sword of the samurai in her hand, the potentates of Asia had disappeared one after the other; the various cultures of the continent — Persian, Indian, and Chinese — had completed the cycle of their evolution. Only Japan preserved her faculty of creation and self-renewal in both art and politics. Alone in the deserted East she still held herself upright.[1]

The genius of a Seiho — to quote but one name among the artists of today — still bears witness to the splendid continuity of her traditions (Fig. 165).[2]

[1] Okakura Kakuzo: *Ideals of the East, with special reference to the art of Japan* (1921).

[2] For the Japanese schools of the present day, I refer the reader in particular to Professor Elisséev's fine work *La Peinture contemporaine au Japon* (Paris: de Boccard, 1923), with 81 plates; Professor Y. Yashiro: *Japanische Malerei der Gegenwart* (1931); and the collection of the *Year-book of Japanese Art* (Tōkyō: National Committee on Intellectual Co-operation of the League of Nations, Association of Japan). Also Hirafuku Hyasukui: *Nihon yōgwa no shokō* (*Beginnings of Occidental Painting in Japan*) (Tōkyō, 1930).

CHAPTER II

Bengal, Nepal, Tibet

SIGNIFICANCE OF TIBETAN CULTURE AS GUARDIAN OF THE TRADITIONS OF BENGAL

THE INTEREST OF JAPANESE CIVILIZATION LIES IN SHOWING US how a country essentially personal, active, and aggressive in character, like a second Greece situated at the far end of Asia, was bound to react to the influx of Chino-Indian culture brought to it as the accompaniment of Buddhism. This spectacle of one of the most intelligent peoples of the earth receiving Greco-Buddhist, Indian, and Chinese art simultaneously, rapidly extracting from them the highest significance of which they were capable, and, having, as it were, in this process divined and reconstituted for its own benefit Hellenic, Hindu, and Taoist culture, assimilating and surpassing its models and using them as the stepping-stone towards the realization of its own genius in uninterrupted sequence with all that had come to it from foreign sources, forms a remarkably instructive human experiment, one of the most intensely interesting in the whole of history, in that it was carried out freely and without outside interference over a period of twelve centuries.

But another human experiment was to take place under precisely opposite conditions. The same revelation of the Buddhist arts was to be granted to a people as conservative and metaphysical as Japan was practical and tireless in innovation — the people of Tibet. Like Japan, and almost at the same period — about the seventh century of our era — Tibet received the teaching of the Indian and Chinese schools simultaneously, though through very different channels. We shall now see what she made of them.

FIGURE 166
Mahārājalīla Mañjuśrī.
— *Indian Museum*

FIGURE 167
Mahāpratisarā.
— *Dacca Museum*

For centuries these varying lessons were to be faithfully and scrupulously recapitulated by the artists of Tibet, who preserved them unchanged with pious care so that when, in the nineteenth century, their country began to be thrown open to our researches, we were to find there intact, buried in the monasteries, the traditions of the mediæval Buddhist art of the Ganges valley, the Pāla art of Bengal, Nepalese art, and, in quite a secondary place, specimens derived from the Chinese school.

It is obvious that this phenomenon provides us, as it were, with a most valuable commentary upon the history of Buddhist art. So far

FIGURE 168
The green Tārā. Late Pāla school.
— *Musée Guimet. Photo, Pivot*

the forms of it whose development we have traced have been chiefly those influenced by Hellenic models or the strictly Gupta schools.[1] But our examination has not so far included the continuation of Gupta

[1] See Vol. II of the present work.

FIGURE 169
The white Tārā. Tibetan statuette.
— *Musée Guimet. Brazier and Dublain bequest*

art in that of Bengal under the Pāla (750–1060) and Sena (1060–1202) dynasties. The time has now come to fill this gap, and it is most satisfactory to find that the Bengali sculpture and painting of the Pāla and Sena periods — not to speak of the art of Nepal, which is derived from these — played an overwhelming part in the development of Tibetan iconography; and, what is more, have been discovered in their entirety in the monasteries of Tibet in the present day. Just as the treasure-houses of the Shōsōin and the temples of Nara have preserved for us the masterpieces of Chinese art in the Wei, Sui, and T'ang periods, so the banners and statues of Tibet have restored to us the age-old models of the ancient Gangetic schools.

FIGURE 170
The green Tārā. Tibetan statuette. — *Musée Guimet. Bacot donation*

Thus Indian art completes its cycle of evolution, as follows: in Volume II of the present work we have shown how Buddhist India saw the formation of two great schools of art, the first of which, that of Gandhāra, was Indian in religion only, being really Greek in workmanship; while the second was a genuinely Indian school which appeared as early as the Maurya and Śuṅga periods and blossomed in the Ganges valley into the classic Gupta style. The influence of these two schools spread through half Asia: first, Greco-Buddhist and, later, Gupta art followed in the train of the Buddhist missionaries across the whole of what is now Chinese Turkestan, as far as the

China of the Weis and T'angs and the Japan of Nara or Heian. On the other hand the strictly Indian classic style known as Gupta inspired all the schools of the south from the Deccan to Java and Cambodia, the school of Mayurbhañj, in particular, forming a transi-

FIGURE 171
Ḍakinī. Mazot collection.
— *Photo, Musée Guimet*

FIGURE 173
Vajradhara and *śakti*. Nepalo-Tibetan bronze.
— *Musée Guimet*

tional stage between the Gupta and the Pāla art of Bengal and the schools of Orissa and the Dravidian lands. But it still remains to follow Indian art on the third route by which it became diffused through the world: that is, the one leading northwards from the eastern basin of the Ganges, across the terai of Nepal to the plateau of Tibet. It is generally known now that the art of Khotan, Kuchā, Tun-huang, Yun-kang, Lung-mēn, and Nara is derived partly from Gandhāra and partly from Sārnāth. Equally important is the relationship existing between Tibetan art and the late Pāla art of Magadha, in which Nepal is again the link.

Though Tibet is now the stronghold of Buddhism, it did not receive this religion till comparatively late. Though the presence of Buddhist missionaries in the Far East is recorded as early as the first centuries

FIGURE 171 b
Ḍakīnī. Mazot collection.
— *Photo, Musée Guimet*

FIGURE 172
Ḍakīnī. Mazot collection.
— *Photo, Musée Guimet*

of our era, and, as we have shown, from the fifth century onward Kashgaria and Wei China were almost entirely Buddhist, Tibet was not converted till the middle of the seventh century, during the reign and on the initiative of King Srong-bcan-sgam-po, who reigned from about 630 to 650. This monarch sent one of his ministers to study the great Indian religion in Magadha — that is, the holy land of the Ganges, the region now known as Behar. In order to establish civiliza-

FIGURE 174
Tibetan bodhisattva.
— *Musée Guimet*

FIGURE 175
Tibetan bodhisattva.
— *Musée Guimet*

tion firmly in his country and link it up with the great cultures of the neighbouring countries, the same monarch married at a short interval a Chinese and a Nepalese princess. This double union was symbolic, for it was accompanied by a lasting religious influence coming from both quarters: the influence of T'ang Buddhism and of the Gangetic form. Tibetan art, in particular, was formed out of preponderantly Indian, Pāla, and Napalese elements, with a lesser contribution from China.

In the eighth century the celebrated Padma Sambhava, an Indian monk from Nālandā in Magadha, imported Tantrism into Tibet — that is, a form of Buddhism at once mystical and gross, full of sorcery and magic, and a symbolism based on terror and sensuality. The adepts of Tantrism placed their faith in the miraculous power of the hermetic books, or *tantra,* and magic diagrams, or *maṇḍala,* as well as in the supernatural intervention of bodhisattvas and *dhyāni* Buddhas or their feminine principles, or *śaktis.* In all essentials the influence which now invaded Tibetan Buddhism in a scarcely veiled form was none other than that of the Śivaite Hinduism which predominated at that time over the whole of India.[1] We have already noted the simultaneous infiltration of the same influences into the Japanese Buddhism of the Tendai and Shingon sects during the Heian period; and even in such a land of balanced moderation and humanist tendencies as Japan these influences produced an art with Śivaite affinities, full of such visions of terror as the Fudō of the Kōyasan (see above, p. 75). The action of these doctrines was naturally much stronger in a land whose culture was but new and where the innate tendencies of the race to sorcery and mysticism, as illustrated by the " *Bon* " sects, ensured them free scope. In spite of all the later reforms made under the régime of the lamas, Tibetan religion and art were never to be entirely rid of them.

[1] Cf. Vol. II, pp. 186–204. For the tantric mysticism common to Śivaism and the later phases of Buddhism, cf. Vol. II, Fig. 76, and Vol. IV, Fig. 173 and 194.

Even at this early period the Tibetan pantheon was not content with the usual bodhisattvas of the Indian classic age: Amitābha, Amitāyus, Vajradhara, Avalokitēśvara, Maitrēya, Mañjuśrī, and Vajrapāṇi, not to speak of the Buddhist goddess Tārā, with her two forms, the white and the green Tārā, the former seated in the Eastern fashion and having an eye in the centre of her brow (Fig. 169), the latter seated on a throne with her left foot hanging down (Fig. 170.) The Tibetan heaven was peopled with a host of strange or terrible divinities, the heritage of later Bengal and Nepal (cf. the detail of Fig. 192–194). Such are the goddess Mārīcī, represented with three heads, the middle one of which is calm, and the right-hand one distorted into a grimace, while the third one has a sow's face; Śrīdevī, or Lha-mo, riding on a mule with a bridle of poisonous serpents, and having a young man flayed alive as her saddle (cf. detail of Fig. 192); Hayagrīva, with a horse's head appearing among his hair; Yamāntaka, a terrible form of the bodhisattva Mañjuśrī, with nine heads — the central one of which is that of a bull — sixteen feet, and thirty-two hands brandishing every kind of weapon, as well as a man being impaled and an elephant's hide; Mahākāla, " the Great Black One " — that is, Śiva in the unexpected character of a protector of Buddhism; [1] Yama, the god of death, riding on a bull, having him-

FIGURE 175 b
Mañjuśrī. Gilt bronze. Tibetan, eighteenth century.
— *Musée Guimet. Bacot collection*

[1] M. Pelliot points out that Mahākāla as protector of Buddhism is known to Indian Buddhism as early as the seventh century.

self a bull's head, and carrying a baby's skeleton; the Dakīnī, a sort of Tantrist fairies, represented as nude dancing female figures

FIGURE 176
The Nativity of Buddha.
— *Musée Guimet. Bacot mission*

adorned with garlands of skulls (Fig. 171–172). Even the mild Avalokitēśvara (the Chinese Kuan-yin and the Japanese Kannon) assumes here a somewhat disturbing aspect, with his eleven pyramidal heads, nine of which are calm, while the tenth is Śivaite and menacing, with an eye in the centre of the brow, and the topmost represents his spiritual father Amitābha. We may add a host of " tutelary " divinities, the Yi-dam, who are really quite as terrible in appearance, and

FIGURE 177
The seven steps of Buddha.
— *Musée Guimet. Bacot mission*

the best-known of whom was Hevajra, with eight heads, sixteen arms, four legs, etc. Like many of these Tantrist divinities, Hevajra is represented as clasping his *śakti,* or deified female principle, closely to him — a union which in Tibetan theology always assumes a profoundly mystical symbolism (Fig. 173, 194).

Indeed, the prevailing motive of the Tantrist art of Tibet is this haunting twofold motive of terror and sexualism, as symbols of the

FIGURE 178
The Buddha cutting off his hair.
— *Musée Guimet. Bacot mission*

Divine and the Unknowable (Fig. 194). But though the magicians and necromantists of Tibet delighted in these constantly recurring themes, they did not by any means invent them. We have only to turn over the pages of a manual of Buddhist iconography to convince ourselves that most of the forms in question appeared in Bengal dur-

FIGURE 179
Offering of the platter of rice and of the four bowls.
— *Musée Guimet. Bacot mission*

ing the Pāla and Sena periods, from the eighth to the twelfth centuries — or later, in mediæval Nepal.[1]

This appendage to Indo-Buddhist art is too often ignored. Critics stop short at Gupta — that is, Indo-classic art — and fail to continue their researches into the Pāla and Sena art of Bengal; but these are

[1] The essential work to consult on this question is Miss Alice Getty's fine book: *The Gods of Northern Buddhism, their history, iconography and progressive evolution through the Northern Buddhist countries, with a general introduction on Buddhism* (2nd edition, London, 1929). Also G. Roerich: *Tibetan Paintings* (1925); J. Hackin: *Chefs d'œuvre de la sculpture indienne et tibetaine au Musée Guimet* (1931); Grünwedel: *Mythologie du Bouddhisme au Tibet et en Mongolie* (Paris, 1909).

none the less of great interest to us, for it is precisely in them that Tibetan art consists. If we look at the various Pāla statues of Dacca, Lucknow, and Nepal in Benoyytosh Bhattacharyya's *Indian Buddhist Iconography*,[1] we shall see that they are almost point for point identical with the Tibetan bronzes in the European collections. Even at Nālandā many-headed, many-armed figures of Yamāntaka may be found, adorned with necklaces of skulls and brandishing swords; [2] on the reliefs in the Indian Museum, South Kensington, and the Lucknow Museum, we find figures of Ashṭabhuja Mārīcī waving their eight arms, each with its different attribute, such as a bow, etc.; and though these are still inspired by the elegant Pāla convention, they already foreshadow the whole of Tantrist art.[3] In the Dacca Museum, again, there are some figures of Mahāpratisarā, or Buddhist goddesses, seated in the Indian fashion and brandishing swords, bows, etc., in their eight arms.[4] Tibetan art did not invent this style, it merely carried it further; or we may put it in this way: that Tibetan art, so far as it was subject to Tantrist influences, was born, not on the high plateaux of the Brahmaputra, but in Behar and Bengal, between the eighth and the thirteenth centuries of our era.

Tantrist influence was, of course, not the only one to find its way in this fashion from the Ganges up to the Tibetan plateau. Behind all the demonology, sorcery, magic, and symbolic images of religious terror and sexualism in which the later phases of Buddhism clothed themselves, there still remained Buddhism itself, as it had appeared in the Gupta and Harsha periods, during the fourth, fifth, sixth, and seventh centuries of our era — a religion of charity and tenderness, of gentleness and renunciation, as seen in the lives of the " Blessed One " and in the pure poetry of the *sūtras* and *jātakas* (birth-stories). This Buddhism, which, in spite of the Tantrist tendencies of the popu-

[1] Oxford University Press, 1924, with 283 illustrations.
[2] Benoyytosh Bhattacharyya, op. cit., Pl. XXVI b, p. 72.
[3] Ibid., Pl. XXX c and XXXI a.
[4] Ibid., Pl. XXXV b and c.

lar cults, was the only true form, had been brought to Tibet or revived there periodically by the missionaries. First there was the pundit Atīśa, who journeyed from Magadha to Tibet in 1040, spend-

FIGURE 180
Fragment of Fig. 178

FIGURE 181
Fragment of Fig. 178

ing some time in Java on the way — an interesting circumstance in view of the relations which we shall have to note between Pāla art, that of Java, and that of Tibet. While restoring monastic discipline,

FIGURE 182
The descent from the heaven of the Thirty-Three gods.
— *Musée Guimet. Bacot mission*

abstinence, and celibacy in the convents of Tibet, Atīśa brought with him a fresh influx of Pāla art. Later on, another great monk, also Tibetan in origin, the famous Tsong-kha-pa (1357–1419), introduced still more thoroughgoing reforms into the local form of Buddhism. He seems to have tried as far as possible to eliminate Śivaite ritual from the liturgy, and, like Atīśa, he re-established discipline and chastity in the monasteries. By reviving interest in the Indian Scriptures he set up quite a literary renaissance. He was himself nurtured in the sacred books, and, as Monsieur Hackin has pointed out, in his works we find the primitive Buddhist ideal of universal charity, uncontaminated by all the diabolism of the Middle Ages. The Church as reformed by him — the "Yellow Church" — decidedly got the better of the ancient sects known as the "red" sects, which were utterly given over to sorcery, and is still the chief ecclesiastical organization of Tibet today. The Dalai Lamas, who are the spiritual successors of Tsong-kha-pa, established a sort of Buddhist papacy at their centre in Lhasa, which even now continues to enjoy a sort of spiritual primacy over most of the Buddhists of central Asia (cf. Fig. 192 b, 193).[1] From the fifteenth to the nineteenth centuries the Yellow Church was to be found treating on equal terms with the China of the Ming or Ch'ing emperors. These uninterrupted relations explain, moreover, the Chinese influences — especially those of Ming art — which we shall find in Tibetan painting alongside of Indian influences.

TIBETAN ART

In adopting the above title for this section of the present work, we do not deny that we are conforming to custom rather than following our own personal conviction. For in sculpture, at least, we should prefer to speak of a wider school, of which Tibetan art is

[1] E. Kawaguchi: *Three Years in Tibet*, with a beautiful coloured view of Lhasa (1909).

FIGURE 183
Subhūti protecting the *nāgas* against the *garuḍas*.
— *Musée Guimet. Bacot mission*

merely a component part, and not an independent one at that: a school to which we would give the name of " Pāla-Tibetan " art.

In previous volumes of the present work (Vol. II, p. 124; Vol. III, pp. 179–82), we defined Pāla art as a "Gothicized form of Gupta art."[1] As we have indicated, this art had its origin in the characteristically melting softness and simplicity of the art of the Ganges region from the fourth to the sixth centuries. But little by little the Gupta

FIGURE 184
Fragment of the same picture as Fig. 183

treatment of the nude tended towards a more elongated elegance and poses of greater preciosity — a more pronounced sideward sway of the hips, more sophisticated finger-gestures (*mudrās*), and a most subtle combination — paradoxical though this may sound — of greater flexibility with a more hieratic character, together with a profusion of decorative motives and ornaments, a taste for complicated decorative themes and for back-pieces, backgrounds, and decorative settings

[1] On the Pāla and Sena arts in general, see J. C. French: *The Art of the Pāl Empire* (Oxford, 1928); Stella Kramrisch: "Pāla and Sena Sculptures," in *Rupam*, October 1929; Nalini Kanta Bhattasali, Curator of the Dacca Museum: *Iconography of Buddhist and Brahmanical Sculptures in the Dacca Museum* (Dacca Museum, 1929).

of pointed arches, flames, and points, the whole of which, as we have pointed out, to some extent goes to produce the impression of an

FIGURE 185
King Kulika Mañjuśrīkīrti.
— *Musée Guimet. Bacot mission*

Indian flamboyant style. In this process Gupta forms, so harmoniously constructed and softened as to be reduced almost to a " caress in lines," tended to be fined down into torsos of a cold elegance, to

FIGURE 185 b
Bhavaviveka converting a heretical ascetic.
— *Musée Guimet. Bacot mission*

contort themselves into angular gestures, or to soar upwards with a single impulse towards the mystic heavens of Mahāyāna Buddhism. Art became a form of symbolism. So strongly marked is the hieratic character which we have just pointed out that certain statues of this school might lead us to suppose that the light and naturalistic forms of the Gupta period were undergoing a process of Byzantinization. But we soon see that this tendency towards stiffness is only apparent, and that the hieratic quality of Pāla art not only preserves all the vigour of the Gupta school, but at times even adds a youthful freshness which, combined with the gracility of the forms and the preciosity of the attitudes, often produces an impression of rare elegance [1] (Fig. 166, 167, 168).[2]

In our opinion, what constitutes the charm and we may almost say the piquancy of Pāla and Tibetan art is precisely the sight of these fresh Indian nudes still surviving beneath all the hieratic and symbolic accretions of the Mahāyāna in its later phases. It is as though we had here a plastic convention like that of the Romanesque imprisoning within its rigid lines the palpitating life of the most pleasing Alexandrian nudes, and even at times giving free expression to it.

Now, all these remarks that we have just applied to the sculpture of Bengal in the Pāla and Sena periods are equally true of Nepalese and Tibetan statues, and there can be no better proof of how directly these are derived from the art of Bengal. Indeed, the persistence of these tropical nudes — though now in an ornate style, decked with flowers and garlands — on the high Tibetan plateaux, in a region where they are absolutely opposed to climatic conditions and native

[1] I refer the reader in particular to the delightful Padmapāṇī (Avalokitēśvara), seated on the lotus throne in the attitude of pastime (*lalitāsana*), a black schist figure nearly five feet in height from Behar or Bengal, dating from the late Pāla or Sena period, now in the Boston Museum, which is well reproduced in Coomaraswamy: *Portfolio of Indian Art*, Pl. XXIV. One type of bodhisattva found in the Tibetan paintings is directly derived from this type.

[2] See Nalini Kanta Bhattasali, op. cit., Pl. XIX (Bhṛikuṭī from Bhavānīpur) and XXIV (the Mahāpratisarā of our Fig. 167). With our Fig. 168 cf. ibid., Pl. XXI and XXII (two Tārās from Sompāḍā and Khailkair).

FIGURES 186 AND 187
The great sorcerers (Mahāsiddha).
— *Musée Guimet. Bacot mission*

habits of life, bears witness to the fact that Tibetan art is foreign to Tibet, but was imported and adopted once for all and preserved, so to speak, on ice among the glaciers. Nothing could be more touching than these voluptuous and intoxicating tropical flowers continuing, by a miracle of some bodhisattva, to blossom among the snows for ten centuries (Fig. 169, 170).[1] We may even note how, in spite of its Tantrist frenzy, or perhaps even because of this, a work such as the Ḍakīnī in the Mazot collection (Fig. 171–172) is derived from the tradition of the Dravidian nudes (Vol. II, Fig. 91–99).

Side by side with this Indian influence, which is by far the strongest one apparent in them, Nepalese and Tibetan sculpture none the less reveal affinities with other schools. In the first place, however unexpected such a statement may seem, the art of Bengal in the Pāla and Sena periods, from which Tibetan art is derived, was not without affinities with the Javanese art, first of Prambanan, and afterwards of Siṅghasāri. Among the Javanese bronzes of the Prambanan period (ninth century) presented to the Musée Guimet by Mr. J. J. Meijer, there is a plump, pot-bellied Kuvēra curiously reminiscent of the Jambhala in the Dacca Museum;[2] while the lean, elongated torso of a certain Avalokitēśvara illustrated in Volume II (Fig. 126) has a certain kinship with the Pāla school of Nepal; or, again, the Prajñāpāramitā in the Leiden Museum (Vol. II, Fig. 127), belonging to the Siṅghasāri school, of the thirteenth century, could easily find a counterpart, if not in æsthetic value, at least in the general type of subject, in some statues of the Gangetic group.[3] In so saying, we do not imply that Mahāyāna Buddhism in Tibet was directly influenced by that of Java, but we may recall how, in the middle of the eleventh century, the apostle Atīśa only reached Tibet after a visit to Java;

[1] In point of elegance the Tārā of Fig. 170 may be compared with the delightful Lokanātha of the Dacca Museum reproduced by Mr. Nalini Kanta Bhattasali, op. cit., Pl. VI, b.

[2] Benoyytosh Bhattacharyya, op. cit., Pl. XXXIV, d; Nalini Kanta Bhattasali, op. cit., Pl. XI, e.

[3] Benoyytosh Bhattacharyya, op. cit., Pl. XXXVI, c.

FIGURES 188 AND 189
The great sorcerers (Mahāsiddha).
— *Musée Guimet. Bacot mission*

FIGURE 190
The Sa-skya paṇḍita.
— *Musée Guimet. Bacot mission*

and we may emphasize the point that between the eleventh and twelfth centuries Java, Pāla and Sena Bengal, and the lands of Tibet and Nepal, which received their teaching from Bengal, must have had mutual intellectual relations, and consequently artistic ones too, of a far more active nature than has been supposed. The spiritual territory over which the monastic city of Nālandā held sway extended from Siṅghasāri to Lhasa.

Chinese influence was necessarily more direct. And here we find a curious coincidence. On reaching Tibet the tendencies of Chinese Buddhist sculpture, which had become stereotyped since the Wei and

FIGURE 191
Mañjuśrī and Yaśodhvaja.

Sui periods, contributed towards reinforcing those " Gothic " tendencies which were already to be found in Bengali art, whether Pāla, Sena, or Nepalese. The same tall slenderness of form, attenuated to the point of stiffness, the same angular quality in the ornaments and jewels, as we have already noted in the Chinese sculpture of the sixth century (cf. Vol. III, Fig. 157–161) are to be found in two Tibetan statuettes, evidently of a much later date, in the Musée Guimet (Fig. 174, 175).

Tibetan painting likewise offers the most happy combination of Indian and Chinese influences. Most of the banners which have come

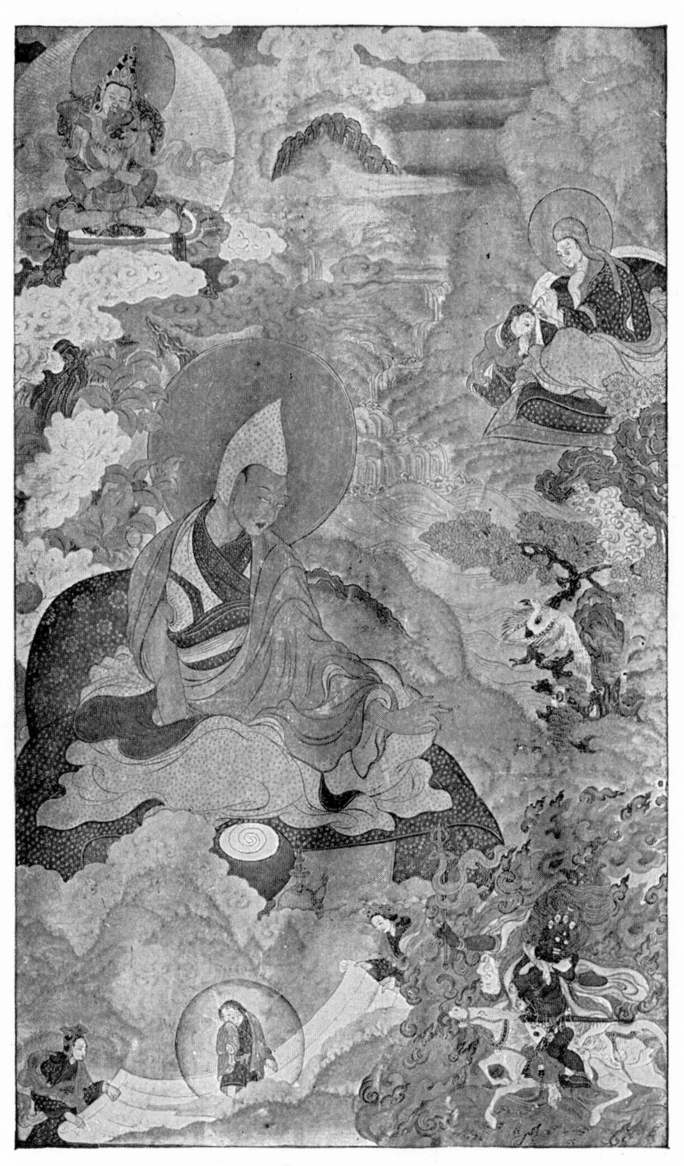

FIGURE 192
bSod-nams-phyogs-glang.
— *Musée Guimet. Bacot mission*

down to us date only from the eighteenth century, and some even from the nineteenth. But the " faithful repetition " characteristic of

FIGURE 192 b
Portrait of the Pan-chen blo-bzang ye-śes dpal-bzang (1663–1737).
— *Musée Guimet. Bacot mission*

the Tibetan image-makers is so scrupulous that here the question of chronology is of but small importance. There are scenes dating from the late eighteenth century which are no more than copies, pure and simple, of fifteenth-century models, and, through these, of some original from south of the Himalayas. The religious motive is a guarantee of origin; for in order to perform an act of piety the

FIGURE 193
Pontiff of the Yellow Church.
— *Musée Guimet. Bacot mission*

painter, who was also a lama, was bound to trace the design which he had before him, without adding any innovations of his own. He had no more right to modify any feature in the sacred scenes which he reproduced than to change a single line in his formulas of prayer or incantation; for the task of image-painting was considered in itself equivalent to a prayer.

Here, therefore, as in the sculpture, we shall find the lessons of Bengali painting untouched. The derivation from this source is so obvious that we are bound to accept it in spite of the disappearance of the intermediate links of connexion. Hardly anything remains of late Indo-Buddhist painting, after the days of Ajaṇṭā and Bāgh, but there are a few fragments extant which suffice to assure us of the continuity of the tradition. For the Pāla period we may cite in particular the illumination in the famous manuscript on palm-leaves of the *Ashtasāhasrikā Prajñāpāramitā* in the British Museum, dating from the beginning of the eleventh century, among which there is an elegant little bodhisattva, seated on a fabulous beast in the " pose of pastime," with the left hand outstretched, the right arm hanging down negligently and resting carelessly upon the right knee, with the right leg slightly raised. The delicate slenderness of the limbs and the youthful line of the bust give this image an affinity with the figures of lovers at Ajaṇṭā [1] — a watered-down and rather childish Ajaṇṭā, it is true, reduced to the level of illumination, but with nude forms of a still charming freshness.

FIGURE 194
Tantric scenes.
— *Musée Guimet. Bacot mission*

[1] See the reproduction in J. C. French: *The Art of the Pāl Empire* (Oxford University Press, 1928), Fig. XXIII, 1. There are also seven similar manuscripts in existence, one coming from Bengal (Cambridge MS. Add. 1464 and 1688), four from Nepal (Cambridge MS. Add. 1643; Calcutta Royal Asiatic Society MS. A15), one in the Vredenburg collection, and one in the Tagore collection, Calcutta.

FIGURE 195

Buddha of Lopburi. Transition between Lopburi and Siamese schools.
— *C. T. Loo collection*

The greatest treasure of this school of art consists of another manuscript of the same work found in Nepal, in a painted wooden case and with two palm-leaves, also painted, now in the Boston Museum, and dating from the reign of Gopāla, king of Bengal, about 1136. The paintings in the Boston Museum have been reproduced,

FIGURE 196
Siamese head.
— *Musée Guimet*

FIGURE 196b
Siamese head.
— *Musée Guimet*

partly in colour, by Mr. Ananda Coomaraswamy in his fine album: *Portfolio of Indian Art.*[1] I would call the reader's particular attention to two paintings of the highest importance: the two bands from the painted wooden case (Pl. XXXII), one of which represents the Assault of Mārā, the other a youthful Tārā with her attendants. It is essential to compare the uppermost of these scenes with the paintings

[1] Museum of Fine Arts, Boston, 1923, Pl. XXXII, XXXIII, XXXV.

of the same subject brought back from Tun-huang by the Pelliot mission, and those in the Tibetan temptation scenes brought back by the Bacot mission with a view to establishing the analogies and differences between them;[1] it is still more indispensable to compare the Tārā in the second row and the white Tārā in Pl. XXXV of the same portfolio with the gracious bodhisattvas of the Tibetan paintings.[2] We repeat once again that these supple, elegant, elongated, youthful Bengali nudes, with their unsymmetrical, drooping poses and their marked sideward sway of the hips, noticeable even in the seated posture, obviously represent the transitional stage between certain figures on the ceilings of Ajaṇṭā and a whole range of Tibetan figures. From these two seated types of Tārā illustrated in the Boston manuscript, in particular, are derived not only the Tibetan Tārās in Fig. 169 and those following it, but also the charming figures of Mañjuśrī seen in the detail of Fig. 191 and those following it. And if we are astonished at the virtuosity of the Tibetan animal-painters, we should remember, for example, the powerful yet supple form of the white elephant in the *Vessantara jātaka,* a Nepalese manuscript of the thirteenth century in the Tagore collection, illustrated in Mr. Coomaraswamy's fine manual.[3]

Tibetan painting, derived from these Pāla-Nepalese schools, was no more nor less than miniature-painting on a large scale, and was to preserve the freshness of colour and decorative richness of the hagiographical miniature, as well as its sincerity of inspiration and didactic precision. But, working on a larger scale than the Bengali or Nepalese illuminators whose works have come down to us, it mar-

[1] We may also point out that Sir Aurel Stein has brought back from Tun-huang to the British Museum a painting of a bodhisattva which is decidedly Nepalese, dating from about the ninth century. See the Japanese review *Kokka*, No. 437 (April 1927), Pl. I.

[2] Cf. also Coomaraswamy: *History of Indian and Indonesian Art*, Pl. XCIII, Fig. 280, 281.

[3] Coomaraswamy: *History of Indian and Indonesian Art*, Pl. XCIII, Fig. 279. Very good reproductions of Buddhist miniatures of Bengal in the eleventh century will also be found in Nalini Kanta Bhattasali, op. cit., Pl. I, II.

shalled its figures in enormous and often very well-balanced compositions. The distribution of the scenes and their respective importance were, moreover, still dictated by religious tradition. But even within its narrow limits the good Tibetan monks were to display a charming freshness of imagination.

FIGURE 197
Siamese head.
— *Musée Guimet*

FIGURE 200
Head from Lopburi.
— *Pila collection*

Let us consider, for instance, the delicious Nativity scene in the Bacot collection in the Musée Guimet (Fig. 176). Beneath the *aśoka*-tree, Queen Māyā, with nude bust and the elegant Indian sway of the hips, is giving birth to the Predestined One, a little gold icon which has sprung forth from her side and has been received by the gods Indra and Brahmā. We may observe the pious care with which the holy tree is treated, leaf by leaf, in the manner of Japanese lacquer-work, the flying streamers and many-coloured scarfs, and the curling trails of smoking perfumes, also many-coloured, which rise from the vases and perfume-burners. Over the tree, in the clouds, we see a two-fold vision: on the one hand a Chinese kiosk, purporting to be the heaven of the *Tushita,* or "Satisfied Ones," in which the bodhisattva Śākyamuni, at the moment of his descent to earth, is installing upon his throne his successor Maitrēya, the Buddhist Messiah; and on the other hand an archipelago of fleecy clouds, in the Chinese fashion, bearing the bodhisattva on his descent from heaven in the form of a white elephant, also treated in the Chinese manner and surrounded by an escort of deities. This beatific vision of some Tibetan Fra Angelico has a charm that can hardly be denied. Equally delightful is the scene of the Seven Steps from the lower part of the same banner, with the delicate nude form of the Sacro Bambino, the wonderful peacocks spreading their tails in his honour, and the elegant antelopes drinking from a pool in the foreground (Fig. 177). Though the peacocks have as much affinity with the Chinese decorative art of the Ming and Ch'ing periods as with that of the Moguls, the antelopes are surely derived from an Indian tradition extending from Ajaṇṭā to Mogul and Rajput art (cf. Vol. II, Fig. 241, 244, and p. 154). Thus uniformity of religious inspiration and the necessity of strict adherence to tradition in the illustration of the sacred books here succeed in harmoniously blending both Indian and Chinese decorative motives.

Still more charming is Fig. 178, representing the Buddha cutting off his hair in order to become a monk.[1] The Blessed One is a slender nude figure, chaste, soft, and still youthful, set off by the varying hues of the cloak, while the gesture with which he cuts off the locks of hair, which are then picked up or carried off to heaven by the gods in a scroll-like figure of many colours, is long, elegant, and delicate. The setting is a fresh, smiling glade, with brooklets descending in foaming cascades; farther away, in a peaceful spot under the trees,

[1] The Buddhist myths referred to in this and the following paragraph are briefly related in Vol. II, pp. 40, 42. 58.

the Buddha is abandoning himself to meditation with such fervour that he does not notice the importunities of which he is the object (Fig. 181); higher up, on the left, there are mountains in the Chinese style, inhabited by flocks of antelope, and with caves full of hermitages in which ascetics are meditating (Fig. 180). Below (Fig. 179),

FIGURE 198
Siamese head.
— *Pila collection*

FIGURE 199
Siamese head.
— *Musée Guimet*

after the scene of the cutting of the grass and the offering of the bowls, comes the farm of the pious Sujātā, with its buildings in the Chinese fashion, its trees, its fold full of beasts, and its charming little cows. If we may confess to a personal preference, we may say that we infinitely prefer the rustic freshness of these naïve little pictures to all the Ch'ing landscapes produced during the same age.

Next comes a perfectly enchanted scene. The sky opens, and, amid a dazzling array of clouds in the "*chih*" style and many-coloured spirals of trailing vapours, in a shower of wondrous flowers, high up among the clouds against a background of gushing waters and green meadows, we see the Buddha, who, having ascended to the palaces of the Thirty-Three gods to carry his gospel to his mother, is descending the stairway of heaven amid the rejoicings of spirits and apostles (Fig. 182).

Further on, this scene of enchantment takes on a more human character and a sweetness worthy of the religion of St. Francis (Fig. 183). The worthy painter shows us Subhūti, the disciple of the Buddha, reconciling the two hostile races of Indian mythology, the *nāgas* and *garuḍas,* mythical creatures, the former of which have an affinity with the water-serpent, and the latter with birds of prey. The apostle, with an expression of gentleness and compassion, is preaching on the brink of the ocean, a vast expanse of water producing an impression of submarine transparency. The tumult of the waves as they break into foam is rendered with remarkable animation and a charming sense of decorative effect worthy of the best Ming calligraphers. Equally elegant in design, but with a freshness and fascination which are quite Indian, are the King and Queen of the *nāgas,* with their cobras' heads issuing from between their shoulders, hastening up from the depths of the ocean to the feet of the apostle. The treatment of the *garuḍas* is full of a humour that is quite Chinese; they take the form of little monsters, half cat, half parrot, which are occupied in attacking the hated *nāgas* with an infinite display of turns, twists, and grimaces. Up above (Fig. 184) are a seated Buddha and a Subhūti in a pose of adoration — both of them figures with an intellectual quality worthy of the Sung painters of ascetics (cf. Vol. III, Fig. 224, 225, 228, 229).

Chinese influence asserts itself even more decidedly in Fig. 185, representing King Kulika Mañjuśrīkīrti. The splendid decorative effect of the pavilions, foliage, and flowers would suggest a late eighteenth-century copy of a Ming painting, but for the fact that the god embracing his *śakti,* in the upper left-hand corner, warns us that

FIGURE 201
Siamese head.
— *Haase collection*

we are still under the influence of the Tantrist practices of the Himalayan lands. The whole of Tibet is summed up in this juxtaposition of an ascetic mysticism with these frenetic carnal unions.

Fig. 185 b shows us the saint Bhavaviveka in a charming landscape of valleys, meadows, and streams, first converting a Brahman ascetic and then admitting him to the tonsure and to orders. Above him is a portrait, full of spirituality, of the philosopher Nāgārjuna.

Figures 186 to 189 represent the *mahāsiddha* — that is, the " great sorcerers " of the Tibetan sects — and are, in our eyes, among the most interesting. Without entering into a detailed exposition of their iconographical significance, for which I refer the reader to Monsieur Hackin's learned studies,[1] I will merely call attention to the quality of these delicate and delightful nudes, reposing in attitudes full of charm and abandonment in fresh meadows, among springs, brooks, groves, caves, rocks, or flowering hill-sides. We know the origin of these ascetic faces, with their subtle intellectual quality: they come from India the eternal, from Ajaṇṭā to the fakirs of the Mogul and Rajput schools described in Volume II of this work (p. 370). As an outward and visible sign of this origin, one of the sorcerers in Fig. 187, Bandhepa, is wearing the costume of a young Indian rajah, treated in the manner of the Mogul portraits (cf. Vol. II, Fig. 220–223). Similarly, the charming antelope cropping the sward trustfully in the presence of the saints in Figures 187 and 189 are certainly derived from the schools of India; there is something very Indo-Persian in the action of the antelope scratching its ear with its hind foot in Fig. 187. We may also mention the nude feminine forms in Fig. 188, with their pure, delicate grace — for instance, those of the sorceresses Mekhalā and Kanakhalā, and, above all, of the sorceress Manibhadrā, who is shown disporting herself in the air, wearing as her sole garment a long, floating scarf, but with her hair adorned with a wreath of flowers, and her hands and feet set off by bracelets, quite in the manner of an Indian *yakshiṇī,* while the freshness of the nude body has still a tropical savour, and when transported to the high heavens, among the lofty mountain peaks, has something the character of the

[1] *Guide-catalogue du Musée Guimet; les collections bouddhiques*, p. 102; and *Bulletin archéologique du Musée Guimet*, Pt. II: *Asie centrale et Tibet, Missions Pelliot et Bacot*, p. 36.

heavenly visions of the early Italian masters. It is impossible not to recognize in this exquisite body, with its flawless forms, a descendant of the *apsaras* or nymphs of Ajaṇṭā.

With their persistent lack of comprehension for some aspects of their own art, Oriental critics have not yet realized that in the works of the Tibetan illuminators the art of the East possesses a counterpart to the work of Van Eyck and Memling, Fra Angelico and Benozzo Gozzoli, with the addition of the " pagan spirit."

FIGURE 202
Wood-carving from Laos.
— *Photo, École française d'Extrême-Orient*

Next come the Fathers of the Tibetan Church. We reproduce here, as Fig. 190, the portrait of the lama Sa-skya paṇḍita (1182–1252), who had great influence over matters both religious and political in Tibet during the Mongol period. " The Sa-skya paṇḍita," writes Monsieur Hackin, " is seated upon a golden throne covered with a sumptuous yellow stuff; the lissomness of his young body, still further emphasized by the preciosity of the gesture, reveals an Indian inspiration which still preserves its mastery." Equally Indian, and more especially Pāla in its elegance, is the handsome and fascinating Mañjuśrī with a flaming sword in the upper part of the same banner, illustrated in Fig. 191; while, on the other hand, the Yaśodhvaja in the same figure shows the strictly Chinese type of ascetic spirituality familiar to us since the Sung period (cf. Vol. III, Fig. 228, 239; Vol. IV, Fig. 54, 55).

The banner illustrated in Fig. 192 is devoted to the monk bSod-nams-phyogs-glang (1439–1505), represented in the setting of which he was particularly fond: a landscape with steep, precipitous mountains, and peaks veiled in mists and cloud, with springs, foaming cascades, leaping torrents, trees with great birds leaning over the abyss, and, far below, giddy glimpses down on to the steppes on which the tiny antelope are grazing. In the foreground are celestial beings standing upon the clouds, holding the ends of a cloth across which a child with an aureole is passing — the prophetic vision which determined the saint's vocation. Higher up he is seen as a youth receiving the tonsure from his master; and at the top is represented the union, at once carnal and mystic, of a young bodhisattva and a supple Śrīdevi.

We also give the portraits of a few pontiffs of the Yellow Church, built up by Tsong-kha-pa and his disciples (Fig. 192 b and 193), portraits revealing an obvious Chinese influence of the Ming period; besides some Tantrist scenes in a spirit which is, on the other hand, quite Hindu (Fig. 194).[1]

In conclusion, we reproduce here a few Siamese statues, the photographs of which could not be included in Volume II of this work (pp. 339–43), where we stated that they would be postponed to this volume (Fig. 195–201).

[1] We think it may be of interest to close with a reference to the views of the learned Japanese Professor Seiichi Taki on the origins of Tibetan painting. Professor Taki divides the old Tibetan arts into two periods: namely, that preceding the Yüan dynasty in Chinese history, and the Yüan period. In his opinion, the Tibetan arts since the Yüan dynasty show a decadent tendency and are of inferior quality, while those belonging to pre-Yüan times are of a little better quality. The excellent specimens of the Tibetan arts belonging to pre-Yüan times consist in the pictures that have been discovered in Chinese Turkestan and the Kan-su provinces. On reviewing the materials for the study of Tibetan art, Professor Taki comes to the conclusion that the pictures of Buddha on the four banners brought back from Tun-huang by Sir Aurel Stein, the picture of Kannon from the same source brought back by the same eminent scholar, and the woodcut of Mandalas beside a picture of a high priest, discovered at Kara-Khoto in the province of Kan-su by M. Kozloff, constitute the most essential and valuable materials for our present purpose. Professor Taki is further of opinion that an investigation of these notable specimens reveals the fact that the characteristic trait of these pictures is "an ornate character, peculiar to Tibetan art, combined with a realistic treatment of objects" (*Kokka*, No. 439, June 1927).

We have thus completed our tour of Asia. It will remain to sum up our conclusions in a future work — that is, to clarify the conceptions of art of which we have obtained a glimpse in the course of these four volumes, classifying them and distinguishing the elements which remain proper to each group after eliminating all those which have been borrowed from neighbouring groups; and, lastly, to compare these æsthetic ideals with those of the Western world from the broadly human point of view. Perhaps it may then be possible to estimate more precisely what is the contribution of Asia to the common work of civilization.

Index

A
NOTE
ON THE
TYPE IN
WHICH THIS
BOOK IS SET

This book is composed on the Linotype in Bodoni, so-called after its designer, Giambattista Bodoni (1740–1813) a celebrated Italian scholar and printer. Bodoni planned his type especially for use on the more smoothly finished papers that came into vogue late in the eighteenth century and drew his letters with a mechanical regularity that is readily apparent on comparision with the less formal old style. Other characteristics that will be noted are the square serifs without fillet and the marked contrast between the light and heavy strokes.

SET UP, ELECTROTYPED, PRINTED AND BOUND BY THE PLIMPTON PRESS, NORWOOD, MASSACHUSETTS · PAPER MADE BY S. D. WARREN CO., BOSTON, MASSACHUSETTS